# THE EMBODIMENT OF LOVE

D1637346

*Other books by Peggy Mason*

TALES OF TWO WORLDS (ISBN 0 905512 01 4) 1972
NEW AGE COMPANION (ISBN 0905512 006) 1975

# SATHYA SAI BABA

---

# THE
# EMBODIMENT OF LOVE

Peggy Mason and Ron Laing

DISTRIBUTED BY
SATHYA SAI BOOK CENTER
OF AMERICA
306 W. FIRST ST
TUSTIN, CA 92680, USA

PILGRIM  BOOKS
TASBURGH   NORWICH   ENGLAND

Originally photoset for
Sawbridge Enterprises and published in 1982
Second impression 1984
This edition 1987


Other editions
In India by Payonidhi Printers, Bangalore
In Japan by Hodeki Watanabe
In Great Britain a 'Talking Book' edition
by the R.N.I.B.
In U.S.A. a braille edition by Sathya Sai
Book Center of America, Tustin, CA

British Library Cataloguing in Publication Data


Mason, Peggy
Sathya Sai Baba: the embodiment of love.
1. Sathya Sai Baba   2. Gurus—Biography
I. Title   II.   Laing, Ron
294.5'61   BL1175.S385
ISBN 0–19–946259–20–8


Printed in Great Britain
at the University Printing House, Oxford

To

'BABA'

Who fills our lives

# CONTENTS

# PREFACE

Dear Reader,
the following pages make no pretence of being a book—indeed,
we would not have the temerity, or the ability, to write one on a
subject of such cosmic scope. But we have been asked to gather
together under one cover the various articles in connection with
our experience of Bhagavan Sri Sathya Sai Baba, including our
pilgrimage to India in 1980 which proved the most inspiring and
overwhelming event of our lives, and which lives in our consciousness during every waking moment.

We would like to acknowledge our gratitude to the late Maurice
Barbanell who, as Editor of *Two Worlds* monthly magazine and
of the weekly newspaper *Psychic News,* printed the majority of
the following articles, and also to the Kingdom of Sathya Sai for
our contributions in Golden Age 1980.

So we invite you most lovingly to share with us the experience
and conclusions of two very ordinary individuals who sought and
found 'the pearl of great price'.

Peggy Mason
Ron Laing, M.A. (Cantab)

The Lodge,
10 Broadwater Down,
Tunbridge Wells,
Kent, TN2 5NG,
England.

**BOOK ONE**

by

**Peggy Mason**

*"Man extols God as omnipresent, omniscient and omnipotent—but he ignores His presence in himself! God is in the heart of every human being . . . All men are cells in the divine organism."*

Sri Sathya Sai Baba

# 1

# THE CALL

*"Take one step forward, I shall take a hundred towards you;*
*shed just one tear, I will wipe a hundred from your eyes."*

. . . Sri Sathya Sai Baba

I am nobody in particular; an individual drop of water among myriads of drops of water in as many streams, buffeted and bruised by rocks and boulders, at times caught in deep pools, and escaping again to trickle on towards the river which in due time will mingle and merge in the Boundless Ocean. I have no worldly or intellectual qualifications, no letters after my name, and though many years ago it was up in lights over London theatres, as the author of a play or two, those lights were dimmed in the black-out of World War II and its aftermath.

The most I can claim is that I have been privileged to be of some service during the past thirteen years by writing regularly for a magazine whose readers have come to regard me as adviser and friend, and have found my books helpful in their hunger for God and the true meaning of life, and living in the materialistic desert we have created in so much of the world. And even this opportunity took twenty years to materialise from the day I decided, in 1948, to stop writing mediocre filmscripts and novels. I went down on my knees to pray, with a sincere heart, that whatever talent had been given me could be used to enlighten and inspire. During those intervening twenty years I had much to learn, and to suffer, while sharp edges were hammered and chiselled away to mould a better shape, before the door which had seemed locked opened with scarcely a touch! (As it always does when the time is ripe.)

I hope I may be forgiven for making this a personal, and necessarily very brief, sketch of a pilgrimage spanning seventy years, and of how the often stony path eventually led HOME. It seems to me that this path sometimes goes in a circle, in the sense that while one imagines one is travelling somewhere during one's search for Truth, one is led back to the point of <u>inner knowing</u> with which one started out. But what previously existed inwardly becomes externalised, recognised, and accepted through the wisdom gained by experiencing, and by the painful path of self-awareness and, hopefully, by overcoming in the process of becoming.

I came into this incarnation (into which it seems that I have packed about five lives) <u>knowing</u> the existence of other dimensions, and feeling a stranger on an alien planet, constantly astonished at what my elders considered to be quite normal — such things as killing each other on a grand scale, by the millions (my childhood was during the First World War), and eating our friends the animals, and the extraordinary concept that life would probably end with the demise of the physical body. I was to realise later that even the Christian clergy, while declaring faith in 'life everlasting', were totally uncertain that their faith was justified in <u>fact,</u> and always evaded questions on the subject. Indeed, the funniest thing occurred when, at seventeen, I was invited to teach the village Sunday School children (which both they and I enjoyed), only to be dismissed when it was discovered that I was telling them the glorious truth of the continuation of life!

In the family and social background into which I was born, assuredly for good reasons, I was therefore called "the peculiar one" by my parents, whom I rarely saw, as the children were relegated to nannies. What can one think of a child of seven who weeps at the sight of trees being cut down because God is being hurt? I felt that God must be in the tiniest flower, the smallest insect, in the stones under one's feet, as well as in the vastness of the starry heavens. I was a natural pantheist, though I did not know the word at the time. And like all children who have felt crushed or unloved I grew up with an in-built sense of inadequacy, afraid to be truly myself — to liberate the bird beating against the cage — in case I should alienate those I loved or whose love I craved. I felt I would never be able to mix with grown-ups on an equal footing, and though I entered fully into life and all its activities, I never really felt part of it, but rather the observer, except when I was excelling at some purely physical pursuit. I could talk to animals, or to my special trees with my arms round them, when I was lonely, but not to people.

When I was very young I found a friend in the Beloved Jesus. He was very close to me, very real, and not at all as the Church had fabricated Him during centuries of bitter dissension, sects and schisms and the mind boggling theology invented by priests and prelates who had not scrupled to burn and butcher their fellow humans in the name of the Prince of Peace. Malcolm Muggeridge, the former editor of *Punch*, once summed it up so well when, speaking to a group of Indian pundits, he remarked jokingly, "God could never pass an exam. in Theology!" So in due course I left the Church, because I felt He had been betrayed yet again – and is still being betrayed over and over by the multiplicity of narrow, separative sects which not only deny one another but deny the Message of Universal Love, the Fatherhood of God and the Brotherhood of Man which He came to demonstrate and suffer for by the total crossing out of the 'I', the complete surrender of the lower nature, to merge with the Will of the Father. It always strikes me as a travesty of pristine Christianity, as taught by Jesus, that when a person goes into a hospital in England and has to register his religion, he is not allowed to put "Christian"! It has to be one of numberless denominations.

Through the years of a very active and varied life I studied a range of metaphysical subjects. I started with philosophy. But I found it stopped at intellectual enquiry. Philosophers, it seemed to me, are like people who prefer sitting on the edge of the pool rather than plunging in to swim. They prefer speculations to conclusions. Perhaps they prefer to stay on the edge fearing that they might fall beyond the intellect, to which they cling like a safety belt, into an abyss. Yet if they took that plunge they might find they had water-wings! So I left the philosophers to their books and endless discussions and journeyed on, searching to find in outward expression the corroboration of what I inwardly knew within myself all the time . . .

I delved deep into Theosophy, *yoga*, both the phenomena and the higher teachings of Spiritualism (which included having a most remarkably gifted psychic living with us for several years), and comparative religion – and I came to love the Lord Krishna through the *Bhagavad Gita*. Because, too, I had lived so much of my life in close proximity to animals, I espoused the cause of animal welfare, to lessen the intolerable abuse of our younger brethren for which mankind is incurring heavy *karma* for the future. The 'answer' was always the same and what I already knew it had to be: "There is only ONE religion, the Religion of Love; ONE God who is omniscient, omnipresent; ONE Life, of which all and everything is a part, drops in the Universal Ocean." And this I endeavoured to inculcate in all my writing.

My soul yearned to identify with that Ocean, to become immersed in It, even if it took aeons for this little stream of which I was a part to trickle along its stony course to reach It. I yearned for the whole suffering, groaning, wayward world of humanity to be embraced in that Ocean, and the burden of this yearning, and compassion for the hideous consequences of sheer ignorance often became unbearable, and in anguish I would weep for the world. How long, O Lord, how long . . . ?

But the Ocean was aware of the cry of the little stream which had just managed to negotiate an emotional boulder which seemed very formidable. The little miracles, the seeming coincidences started to happen, as they do when the Voiceless Voice of the Ocean calls. To recover from the bruises I visited Australia as Guest of Honour at a national Spiritualist conference, and to give some talks. An Australian friend lent me a magazine from New Zealand called *Heralds of the New Age*, and from it I learned for the first time of the existence in the world of a Being called SRI SATHYA SAI BABA. It was like being impregnated by an electric shock. I immediately subscribed to this magazine and lent it to friends when I returned to England, for it always contained references to this Beloved Being. I had to find out more.

Then I came across a smiling photograph in a newspaper in which there was a review of Dr Samuel Sandweiss's book, *Sai Baba . . . The Holy Man and the Psychiatrist*. I was impelled to cut out this photograph, which I stuck on a card and put on a piece of furniture opposite my bed. The eyes looked straight at me. As I was contemplating this newspaper photograph whilst in bed one night, an extraordinary thing happened which made my heart thump with a sudden shock. The photograph definitely jumped to one side and back, while the whole area lit up in shimmering, irridescent light! I was stupefied, because I am not normally clairvoyant, and as I looked round at other furniture in the room it was obvious that this phenomenon was only centred round the photograph. "Oh Baba!" I think I said and, while I recovered from the shock, the light gradually faded.

Now, at this time, early in 1978, I had become progressively crippled by increasing pain in the calf of my left leg, to such an extent that I could not walk more than a few yards without stopping for the acute pain to subside enough to walk another twenty yards, and the foot was always white, even after immersing it for long periods in the hottest water. My doctor sent me to a specialist who diagnosed a blocked main artery between knee and thigh. He told me it would get progressively worse, and was keen for me to have an operation through the abdomen to the spine. But he warned me that it was a very tricky operation, with only a fifty-fifty chance of success, and if it did not prove successful the artery would be so impaired that the leg would eventually have to be amputated. He asked me to think about it and let him know what I decided at a further appointment. (As I hobbled out of his consulting room I had already decided to keep my leg as long as possible.)

That night, after some prayer and meditation, I spoke to my Friend the Photograph. I simply said, "Oh Baba, I wish you could do something about my leg . . . " and went to sleep. About two days later, a stranger telephoned me. "You won't know who I am," he said, "but I'm a friend of an Indian lady called Swami Ganesha Ananda. This was the name given her by her teacher, Sivananda, many years ago. She is impressed by your writings and very much wants to meet you. I could bring her over as she only lives fifteen miles away." I was prompted to agree, for I had the strangest feeling that this was connected in some way with Baba. I made an appointment for later the same week.

In the meantime, Dr Sandweiss's book had arrived and was on my table when this lady was brought to my home, though I had not had time to start reading it. As she entered the room she glanced at the picture on the cover and smiled. "Do you know Sai Baba?" I asked, knowing full well the answer. "Oh yes!" she said. "Have you been to see him in India?" "Oh yes!" she said again, smiling. It transpired that her family had been ardent devotees of Sai Baba of Shirdi (Sathya Sai Baba's former body from which he passed in 1918 saying he would return in eight years) and that she, too, being elderly, could recount many miraculous things that had occurred when she was young and used to call on the Shirdi Body.

I never mentioned my leg, but at the end of a delightful afternoon she suddenly said, "I have a pain in my left leg. Is it yours?" I said that indeed it was. "May I give it healing?" she asked, and added, "I only do this when I am prompted to do so." She knelt down and laid her hands on it for less than two minutes. "You won't get any more pain," she said matter-of-factly. And from that moment I never have! The blood flowed normally to the foot and has continued to do so. I cancelled the appointment with the astonished surgeon. This was one demonstration of the thousand ways in which the Divine works, the thousands of methods which are utilised. My simple plea was answered in this way. It seemed unbelievable.

With what avidity I started to read the book! After only the first ten pages I was in a ferment of excitement. How many times, weeping for the world, I had cried out, 'How long, O Lord, how long . . . ?' Now hope, certainty, burgeoned forth within me. The Lord was here! This had to be the World Teacher, the *Avatar* for the New Age for whom the world was waiting. This was no wishful thinking, no clutching at straws, or *gurus*, or false or suspect prophets. This was Truth — Sathya. I have never met Sam Sandweiss, but I would like him to know that his book is pure magic for the Western seeker. Baba's Love and Majesty, his Power and Gentleness, his Divinity and his adorable Humanity, shine from its pages and bring tears to the eyes however many times it is read.

In one of the issues of *Heralds of the New Age* magazine an address was given of a Sai Centre in England. I had no idea there were others. So I wrote to this Centre in Wellingborough, asking for further books and information. A correspondence resulted which was full of love from the Secretary, Pravin Patel, and then one day a big envelope arrived, filled with a fragrance which was not of this world. This loving devotee had sent me a plastic bag containing a large amount of divine *vibhuti*, the sacred ash materialised by Sri Sathya Sai Baba.

The effect of receiving this was instantaneous. Something in me broke, and I wept and wept for half an hour. It was as if the dam gates had been lifted, and the trickling stream was suddenly swept along in full flood. And with it came a sense of release from years and years of trying to 'keep my end up' through thick and thin. There seemed no need any more. I saw myself as I really was. I accepted myself, made peace with myself, became myself. Strangely, too, my sense of inadequacy dissolved in the acceptance of my littleness and limitations. In spite of all the years of turbulent events and experiences in my life I realised that in my heart I was essentially that little girl of seven who cried because God was being hurt. And what was wrong with that if that was what I was? All pretence vanished. Baba says: "To get to the core of God at His greatest one must first get into the core of oneself at one's least, for no one can know God who has not known himself." The humble worm has its vital part to play in aerating the soil of the field for the growing crop, and God is also in the worm.

During this time, for reasons which are irrelevant here, my husband was elsewhere. When we were together again I pestered him unmercifully to read the Sandweiss book, and his reaction was the same as mine. We made our first journey to the Wellingborough Sai Centre and were overwhelmed by the love and hospitality they showered on us, and the fervour of their *bhajan* singing. We were shown films of Baba and I could not take my eyes off this unique, graceful, fluid Form. A large group of devotees, including many children, were off to India in a week's time. Their excitement was intense. I had now written an article about Sathya Sai Baba and the healing of my leg, just in time for them to take a copy of the magazine with them to India. Furthermore, they took our breath away by saying they would take a letter from each of us, and give them, with the article, into Swami's hands.

When it was time to leave the devotees, and after I had gone up to the shrine room to kneel before the lifesize picture of Swami, the tears started to run down my face and I felt a fool. "Is it because you would like to come to India with us?" they asked. "No," was all I could say. "It's just Baba . . . "

With what excitement we awaited their return from India! Swami had taken the letters, and the article, and sent a little message: "Tell Peggy to write Sathya Sai Baba in future, not just Sai Baba . . . " He had been so kind, so loving – and the message meant that I could write many more articles. In the following months, too, it meant that the hundreds of enquiries from readers became thousands. Yet we had never met Swami! Rumours that he might pay a visit to England did not materialise.

Time passes quickly, and I was now seventy. There was only one thing to do – go to India.

# 2

# MEETING LOVE INCARNATE

*"It is the heart that reaches the goal. Follow the heart, for a pure heart seeks beyond the intellect – it gets inspired."*

. . . Sri Sathya Sai Baba

How, on this earth, can one describe adequately a journey to the summerland of heaven? The culmination of seventy years of searching? The blessings which filled our cup to overflowing? The discovery that all we had read and studied, and in some measure experienced over the previous two or three years paled into insignificance when face to face with the Reality?

"It is not enough to see a stone and say, 'The mountain is a million times the size of this'. You have to see the actual mountain, at least from a distance." These words of Sathya Sai Baba sum it up graphically.

Our invaluable friend, Sri Vemu Mukunda, a former nuclear physicist, now an international musician (whose strange story is told in Chapter 18 of Howard Murphet's book, *Sai Baba Avatar*), had written to Sathya Sai Baba whilst on a concert tour in the United States to ask if Peggy and Ron Mason (my husband uses the pen-name of Laing from his mother's family) could come to India in January. The reply received through a friend close to Swami was, "Very happy, very happy." And when Vemu went to India in December he took a letter from each of us.

On the occasions when Shri Indulal Shah, Swami's convenor of conferences, visited England in October 1978 and again in June 1979, I was asked to give him copies of further articles. (Incidentally, a few days after Shri Indulal Shah returned to India on the latter occasion, Baba appeared to me in a dream and said, "Swami thanks you very much for the articles.") So I took with me to India articles I had written since then, in *Two Worlds* and *Spiritual Healer* magazines, *The Christian Parapsychologist Journal*, and others printed in New Zealand and South Africa. I also took a copy of W. Hunter Mackintosh's excellent and deeply penetrating review in *Psychic News* of Howard Murphet's second book, *Sai Baba Avatar*, because, as I said later to Swami, "This Scotsman has a much greater understanding." I also included a copy of my address at the Birthday Celebration in Wellingborough the previous November.

We postponed our departure for a week, for I had the strong feeling that dear old Catherine, the remarkable medium whose several years of living with us in our home I have written so much about in my books, *Tales of Two Worlds* and *New Age Companion*, was about to be released, at eighty-one, from her useless body paralysed by a stroke. Her last words to me were, "Hallo, darling", on Christmas morning. After that it was unkind to rouse her. She was peacefully released on New Year's morning and we could not have wished her a happier New Year. We were so glad for her. The cremation service was performed on January 7th (the very day we had originally planned to leave). All necessary affairs being dealt with, we were free to go on the 13th of January (1980) with a clear mind — and with the hope that Catherine, too, might be permitted, from the spirit spheres, to share some of the radiance we were about to experience.

India seemed a very long way away at 5:45 a.m. on a dark, cold winter's morning. We had scarcely slept for excitement and some natural apprehension. Our son Gavin drove us to Heathrow Airport and our Air India jumbo landed in Bombay just after midnight, local time. We queued for ninety minutes at one barrier after another of good humoured but leisurely bureaucracy before we could get our luggage, change money, and go round to the internal flights section.

As our flight to Bangalore did not leave till 9 a.m. we sat in the airport's uncomfortable plastic chairs for the rest of the night. However, an 'English breakfast', when the restaurant finally opened at dawn, made us feel human again.  Carrying our overcoats in a temperature of 80 degrees, and scarcely having slept for two nights, we landed at Bangalore at 10:30 a.m. pretty exhausted.

Our good friend Vemu could not meet us as he was rehearsing for a big concert in Bangalore with Maynard Ferguson who, though Scots-Canadian, is the jazz trumpeter of America, and a staunch devotee of Sathya Sai Baba.  But we were rescued by Vemu's brother and Mrs Flo Ferguson who took us to the modest Gautam Hotel which Vemu had selected at our request.

It was a mad drive among hooting cars, hooting auto-rickshaws, scooters, bicycles, bullock carts, pony carts, narrowly missing by a whisker an assortment of placid, self-contained animals going about their business totally unruffled − water buffalo, cows, white bullocks, ponies, donkeys, dogs, and a few goats. After a few days of this kind of traffic we gave up clinging on and just had faith that if Swami wanted to see us we would survive!

Bangalore, 3500 feet above sea level, is spacious, beautiful, fascinating and friendly, abounding in shady parks, masses of brilliant bougainvillea which flowers all the year round, and always the blue sky, magnificent colours, and the terracotta earth. It is a city of contrasts: here, stately buildings and villas set in leafy gardens; there, straw covered huts and maimed beggars, many of whom 'work' for begging syndicates which the authorities are trying hard to stamp out.

We fell in love with Bangalore, and our 'home' in the hotel − a large double room with bathroom, covered balcony, armchairs, telephone, a table where we ate our snacks and boiled tea and coffee with the aid of our mini-immersor (we could not eat the hot Indian food in the hotel which did not cater for Westerners), and all for the modest cost of £1.50 a day each.

Having recovered during the day and slept well on the springless beds, Vemu called for us next morning, full of vital energy. It appeared that Baba was at Puttaparthi, at his *ashram* Prasanthi Nilayam, 110 miles away.  Would we have to pack up and go there?  Or, might he be coming to Brindavan, the *ashram* at White-field, some 15 miles outside Bangalore? Or, was he going to Madras as rumoured?  Until his movements could be ascertained, Vemu suggested that we should drive out to see Brindavan − and it took our breath away!

Facing us as we entered the gates, within high compound walls which enclosed a vast expanse of hard, level sand (bliss to walk barefoot on with my normally troublesome feet) was the most gorgeous building in our favourite colours of deep pink and soft blues, its domes sculptured in pink, blue and white against a deep blue sky. It is the hostel for the thousand young men who attend the even more astonishing and enormous Sri Sathya Sai Arts, Science and Commerce College just down the road. Other buildings, including the bookshop and information centre, are at one end.

At the opposite end a beautiful archway with pale blue wrought iron gates leads into Swami's tree filled garden and modest residence. Behind it again are little pink cottages and living quarters, and the original farmyard and cowshed. The enchanting story of the removal of Swami's large herd of cows to their beautiful new home in the land behind the College must be told elsewhere.

Situated in the compound, under a huge spreading banyan tree, with a circular roof fitted around fourteen great branches, is the Tree *Mandir*, a circular area marked out rather like a clock. Here, people sit, men on one side, women on the other, for morning and evening *darshan* — when Swami emerges to walk among the crowd down the avenues provided by the pattern. On Thursdays melodious *bhajans*, sacred songs, are sung all day to the soft accompaniment of hand cymbals and a hand drum. Everywhere, on every building and gateway (even on the pale blue cowshed doors, as we discovered later), is the Sathya Sai emblem of the combined world religions. The silence and peace are all-pervading. Whether Swami is there or not, one is aware that one is on holy ground.

We lunched with the Fergusons at the splendid Ashoka Hotel. I shall always bless Flo Ferguson for lending me the most lovely *saris*, which are always worn at the *ashram*. Later that day, rather to our horror, Vemu announced, "I've sent a telegram to Swami in your names. 'Shall we come to Puttaparthi?' He will get it at four o'clock. If there's no reply it will mean he is coming to Brindavan."

Inwardly I felt this really rather cheeky, because who were we, two old codgers from Tunbridge Wells, to ask Swami if we should come to Puttaparthi? We did not know that Swami had asked to be informed. Several days previously he had asked, "Are they here? Are they here?" when Vemu had mentioned us to him, for we had put off our journey by a week.

No reply came. All evening I rang up Brindavan, but the number was always engaged. Finally, at 10:30 p.m., I got through and was told, "Yes, Swami has come." Our hearts leapt with joy. It could not have worked out better. Hastily I rang up Vemu Mukunda and the Fergusons, and we arranged to meet at eight o'clock in the morning to go out to Brindavan by car. We got up at 6 a.m., which comes naturally in India, for one is woken by the loud, strident calls of the birds at dawn, and everyone in the hotel appears to turn on their radios!

We did not join the seated crowd under the Tree *Mandir* but were taken to wait a little nearer to Swami's private gates, by the end of the hostel building. After a time hundreds of white-coated students streamed out of Swami's quarters. We scrutinised each passing face. Never had we seen such splendid young men, clean, quiet, natural, dedicated, and every face looking spiritually energised and inspired. These, and thousands like them in Swami's colleges (women's colleges too), rising all over the country, are the future leaders of India in various sections of society, whether political, commercial, academic, of all the professions, which he has chosen, for he knows the past, present and future of each one. Indeed, of us all.

Then, activity at the open gate, and a great stir from the Tree *Mandir* as everyone shifted position, like flowers turning to the sun. The small, slender figure in the brilliant red robe and the dark crown of hair came into view, accompanied by several men in white suits to whom he was talking. He walks slowly, naturally, so smoothly and gracefully, as if there is all the time in the world.

He was coming straight towards us, with deep scrutiny, and then the most wonderful smile lit up his face. I felt a tinge of panic. It was too soon! I wasn't ready; I was too disoriented, there was too much happening too quickly. There had been too much chatter in the car. I was simply not sufficiently prepared at that instant for the meeting I had dreamed of, and imagined, for so long. In fact, I felt it wasn't really happening . . . Could I really be in India, with Swami walking towards us?

Suddenly, when still some distance from us, a blank expression wiped the smile from his face, as if he had suddenly been called urgently from afar, (which was perhaps the case, for he stopped, his expressive, upturned hand weaving a pattern in the air, making movements with his fingers). He once said, in reply to a question about these movements, "You see me smiling, or moving my fingers. Sometimes it even looks as if I am writing in the air. People are curious to know why. I am then in communication with people you do not see. I am engaged in tasks you cannot understand. I write replies to questions asked by someone far away. I help thousands of people every moment. But I do not publicise all this. A father does not publicise the help he is rendering his children."

Whatever the reason for his stopping, and then turning to the left, facing the Tree *Mandir*, the awful thought crossed my mind that he had taken one long look at us, perhaps seen our auras, and turned away! Meantime Vemu had approached near to him, and apparently Swami indicated, "Not now. Tomorrow." He proceeded slowly to the crowd, speaking to one, taking a proffered letter from another, materialising *vibhuti* for someone in need, his eyes taking in all, and his thousand minds aware of every emanation.

Then, watching from the distance, we saw him get into a car that had drawn up and he was driven out of the gates in the direction of the College.

So it was to be tomorrow! That evening we attended a superb concert in Bangalore given by Maynard Ferguson and Vemu Mukunda, a combination of Eastern and Western music – Maynard with his fantastic trumpet and group, and Vemu with his beautiful *vina* and backing musicians. But our thoughts were centred on the following morning. We set off early for Brindavan, taking up the same position because Swami had said he would see us.

Once more that graceful red robed figure emerged through the gates flanked by white-coated students, and this time he came straight towards our little group. Going immediately to Ron, he said very softly and sweetly, with a beautiful smile, "Would you like some *vibhuti*?" What a question! Circling his hand twice, very quickly, he poured the sacred ash first into Ron's upturned palm and then into mine, saying, "Eat it, eat it." The extraordinary thing is that even if he produces enough *vibhuti* for several people at one time, not a vestige falls to the ground as he drops it into one's hand. It just seems to flow from his fingers.

I think he asked Maynard and Vemu about their concert, while Flo went down and quickly touched his feet. I longed to do the same, but I felt I should have permission. He was suddenly standing close in front of me, glancing toward the crowd awaiting *darshan*, but not moving, just waiting. Overcome by his presence, and something which seemed to flow out of him and surround one, I felt tongue-tied and terrified that he would leave without a word; so I finally said, "Swami, may I have your approval of my writings?" And I showed him the large envelope I had with me. For a moment I thought he was going to take it, but instead he said very gently, "Go in . . . "

This meant we should go up to his private garden and wait, while he moved away to give *darshan* to the crowd under the tree. Feeling overcome by the blessing of those two words, and with Ron still holding some of the precious fragrant *vibhuti* in his hand, we made our way through the gates which so many thousands, millions even, long to enter. We were directed to sit either side of the patio outside the side porch of the house. There we were, in Swami's garden, Flo and I and a few Indian women on the left, and Ron, Maynard and Vemu on the right.

As we sat waiting for Swami to return, the whole scene reminded me of a particular out-of-the-body visit I had been privileged to be taken on – one of so many – to a place of teaching in the summerland of heaven. Here were the pink and blue buildings, set off by tall juniper like trees, flowers and shrubs, with an exquisite design of different coloured bougainvillea petals outside Swami's door which emitted an intoxicating perfume.

Beyond, in the wooded garden, dappled with sunlight, completely silent except for some rooks around huge trees covered in large red blossoms, I glimpsed little spotted deer, white and black and white rabbits hopping about, white fan-tailed doves, and two or three little grey monkeys playing. A striped squirrel like creature slowly crossed the patio by our feet.

The silence, and stillness, the rich colours, the warm sunlight, the scent of flowers, the brilliant blue sky and the little pink and blue house amid the tall trees, bearing the painted emblem of the combined religions, were simply not of this world. And there was old Ron, sitting awkwardly on the ground with his gammy leg, from a strained tendon, his cricket hat on his head, one knobbly sock inside out (men are permitted to keep socks on), finally eating his *vibhuti*, with tears in his eyes.

After a time Swami's shining figure appeared. We lined up as he stopped to speak a word to each one in his soft voice. When he came to Ron he asked, "Where is your wife?" He replied, "There, Swami." "Bring her and come." And he led the way across the petals into the house, and closed the door behind us.

There are sacred moments in our lives which cannot, perhaps should not, be described in words or in print. Every human being longs, some acutely, some less so perhaps, to discover that sublime love which can be found only in a Being who is aware of one's innermost self, all of it; who knows one's long past, one's present, even one's future; who knows all the frailties, faults, successes, failures, aspirations and yearnings; a Being from whom no secret is hid. A Being who has said: "Bring me the depths of your mind, no matter how grotesque, how cruelly ravaged by doubts or disappointments. I know how to treat them. I will not reject you. I am your Mother."

At long last, being in the presence of such a stupendous, divine love is overwhelming in its impact. What one had dreamed, or imagined in advance, is as nothing compared with the reality. Just as no photograph or film can give even an inkling of the thousand facets and expressions, the movements, the tenderness, or the fantastic aura of this *Avatar* of all *Avatars*.

When Dr Frank G. Baranowski, the Kirlian photography expert who has been able to see auras all his life, saw Sathya Sai Baba step into the garden early one morning he looked to see where fluorescent pink lights had been switched on. Then he realised, with a gasp, that the pink light which had suddenly flooded the garden all around, emanated from Swami himself, and moved with him.

The expression of tenderness, compassion and understanding in the unique, so lovable face, and in the dark luminous eyes which see into one's soul — and into which one can gaze without the slightest trace of self-consciousness but in utter trust and surrender — enveloped us in an ocean of love as he looked down so tenderly at our tearful faces and said softly, "*I* know . . . *I* know . . . " How well I understood what Dr Sandweiss meant when he wrote, "What was conveyed in that brief moment? <u>The world!</u>"

## 3

# GIFTS OF GRACE

*"My affection and love for you is that of a thousand mothers."*

... Sri Sathya Sai Baba

To the vast majority, especially Westerners, the idea of kneeling down and touching with hands, forehead or lips the feet of another human being is somewhat alien. Even my husband, Ron, before we went to India, said one day, "I don't know about all this kissing of feet. I feel I 'know' Swami so well in my heart that I could go up to him and simply say, "Hallo, Swami – I'm Ron'." I smiled to myself and thought: you just wait! Sathya Sai Baba only appears to be a human being because he has taken a human form.

Because we are merely human beings we can express our deepest feelings only through bodily actions. We cry, we laugh, we sing, we punch in anger, we caress in love – and when the inner urge is overwhelming, we go down on our knees.

Swami knows this deep need in those who flock to him, and allows it in certain circumstances – for our sakes. He in no sense requires it. In fact, if he is talking to a group of men in the *ashram* grounds, and the women in the party all go down on the ground to touch his feet, he appears totally unconscious of it. No normal human being could be so unaware of self as Swami is, without a trace of ego, whether alone in private interview or in front of a crowd of a quarter of a million people.

I remembered the words of a professor of psychology, president of a university, with doctorates in philosophy and literature, and a brilliant academic record. He said, "When I first saw this elusive man walking . . . I thought, he is not of the earth, but has come to the earth to bless it . . . I was a stranger and did not know how to behave . . . If they took the dust from his feet into their mouths, I would do the same." And what manner of Being is it that makes a hard-headed lawyer from South Africa write in his diary, "At last – Baba smiled at me at *darshan* this morning!"

So there we were, alone with the *Avatar*, in that small bare room. And there, of course, was Ron on his knees, tears running down his face, saying, "Swami, I can't believe it . . . "

I, too, realised at last my ardent ambition to kneel down and kiss his bare foot – the skin so smooth and fragrant. I wished the moment could last forever, but Swami said gently, "Get up, get up", and stretched out his small hand. I could not resist kissing that, too.

His other arm was round Ron's shoulders as he knelt, and he looked deep into his eyes for several seconds. Then he said to me, "This is a good man." "I know, Swami!" Then he smilingly added, putting his head on one side, "Sometimes you have differences of ideas, sometimes a little short temper, but you have a good man here." I am happy to say that at other private interviews I was also to receive encouraging remarks.

I bent my head in front of him, as near as I dared, to hide my wet cheeks, and he put his hand on my head in blessing. Oh, how the child of seven longed to hide her head on his shoulder, but I felt that could not be. I must have appeared very dumb! With his left arm round Ron and his right hand on me, it was as if he was enfolding us both like a mother hen enfolds her chicks with her wings, but with such an ocean of love emanating from him that merely to be within that unique, all-pervading aura left one speechless.

Yet he has such a wonderful way of turning tears into smiles, and bringing one down to earth in his divine-human way. For after he had answered a very personal question of Ron's he turned to me with the gentle smile of a concerned mother. "You are not always very well in here," he said, tapping his tummy. "Wind! And sometimes one gets a bad tummy in India!" I couldn't help smiling because it was true, and the way he said 'tummy' was enchanting. He speaks English with such a soft, correct intonation, and has been known to chastise Indians for not speaking English properly. Yet he has never learned all the languages he uses when he wishes to do so.

Fleetingly, the thought crossed my mind: have I come all the way to India to the *Avatar* of all *Avatars* to be told I suffer from wind? But he knew this human intimacy would put me at ease. It was a mother speaking to a child she loved. "Swami," I said, "I sometimes feel you are in our home." He thought, and replied, "I am in your <u>heart</u>. But I came twice in a dream. But you wonder if it's just imagination."

The maddening thing is that I can only remember one – and the words in that dream were very clear. I wrote them down at the time. But I don't always remember dreams as clearly as I once did. It did not seem the moment to ask about the other time – or perhaps I was just too dumb to do so!

Then he did <u>exactly</u> what I had prayed, the night before, that he would do. (In such wonderful little ways he lets you know he knows.) He took hold of the chain round my neck, with the pendant on it, which a friend from Australia had kindly sent me after she had visited Baba a year previously. It was only a cheap one bought from a stall, but I treasured it because it had Baba's head on it. He handled the chain and, with a smile, examined the pendant for a long time, turning it this way and that in his hand.

"I've worn it for a year," I said. I was determined not to let the desire escape that he would replace it! I had not come to India to get objects from him, but to lay my love at his feet. I just wanted him to handle it and thus consecrate it. This was exactly what I had prayed for, no more. Of course he knew this. After thoroughly handling it, he let it go. My unasked for reward was to come later.

I had been asked to give Swami a letter from Hema Bharti, the lovely daughter of Gulab Bharti, a leading light of the Wellingborough Sai Centre. So I fished it out of my bag and gave it to him, explaining that they wanted to know if they could bring a group to India in July. He spoke most sweetly of Hema, and asked me to give her his love. Swami is always anxious for as many Westerners as possible to go with these groups from the various Sai Centres, of which there are some twenty-five or thirty in Britain.

Ron asked if he could show Swami an article he had written on the similarities between Sathya Sai Baba and the Christ, and whether this was permissible. Swami took the article and, seeing the name on it, said enquiringly and thoughtfully, "Ron Laing?" Ron told him it was his writing name.

We wondered if he was recollecting the name of Ron's great grandfather, Samuel Laing, who was in Gladstone's cabinet, and was sent to India under the governorship of Lord Dalhousie to set up the fare system of the Indian Railways some hundred and twenty years ago.

It is strange that both our families have had strong connections with India in the distant past. My own direct ancestor was Governor of Bengal, and his son was in Warren Hastings' Council in Calcutta — two paintings of the latter by Sir Joshua Reynolds are dated 1781. We now learn that when someone mentioned our 'colonial background' to Swami after we had left, Swami replied that he knew all about our backgrounds.

Swami read out the first few lines in an undertone and, in reply to Ron's question, said, "Yes, that's all right. I'll get Kasturi to go through it." (Professor Kasturi has been among his closest devotees for thirty-three years, edits the monthly magazine, has edited all the volumes of Swami's life — but, more of this adorable saintly old man of eighty-three later, for we were privileged to spend two and a half hours listening to his fascinating stories in our hotel room a few days later.)

Ron took back his article, and I produced my own photocopied published articles about him since those Shri Indulal Shah had taken the previous June. Swami took them one by one, slowly, looking at them all. I had also included Hunter Mackintosh's review in *Psychic News* of Howard Murphet's *Sai Baba Avatar* which was headed "Has God Incarnated as Indian Mystic?" I said, "This reviewer has great understanding." (Subsequently, Kasturi reprinted the review in the *ashram* magazine, *Sanathana Sarathi*.)

Then, to our joy, Swami asked, so sweetly, "Are you staying a little time?" "Of course, of course!" I said. "Come back the day after tomorrow, and I give one hour, to discuss all these things. I'll get Kasturi . . . "

The words, when read, might appear casual, but Swami talks to you as if you are the only person in the world. He does so with tender concern, intimacy, and emphasis, looking into your eyes, and with that beautiful, understanding smile. He gives everything.

With a last smile to us both, he turned towards an inner room through a curtain. He seemed to float away rather than walk, with that gentle movement which is indescribable. I have to keep on using the word 'gentle' in connection with Baba. He is the embodiment of love. If, on occasion, he appears stern in any way it is only the appearance, only out of love, if correction is needed, or in order to induce people to examine themselves, to 'enquire within', for their own sake.

I have no idea how long or how short that first interview was, for time stands still in his presence. One is transported to another dimension. When he bestows personal attention one experiences so much more than any actual words – from his expressions, movements, voice, those amazing eyes which can look into the depths of your soul, melt with love, or twinkle in merriment, and being within that radiant rose-pink aura, the memory of which can never dim once it has been experienced.

The fact is that no one can attempt to analyse or explain anything about Sai. As he once gave out: "I am beyond the reach of the most intensive inquiry and the most meticulous measurement. Only those who have recognised my love and experienced that love can assert that they have glimpsed my reality."

We came out over the mat of flowers to take our places again either side of the patio, overwhelmed not only by this precious interview but by the promise of another one. We both needed our handkerchiefs, which is usual when anyone meets Baba for the first time. Both men and women are choked. Everyone understands this, and one's neighbour remains silent until addressed.

After a little time we discovered the patio was empty. Someone said, "Baba has gone." No one else had been called in.

Swami's work never ceases. It is said that he sees as many as two hundred people a day in various connections, in interviews, and this probably discounts the College students. Our very dear friend Vemu Mukunda was returning later to give a lecture at the College, so we returned to Bangalore where he would collect us the next morning at eight o'clock.

I passed a strange and wonderful night. My whole being, when I woke, seemed galvanised into greater intensity and life. My normally too low temperature rose one and a half degrees. (Is that the meaning of the phrase "a fever of excitement"?)

When we arrived at Brindavan next morning, expecting no meeting today, we were told we were again to go and wait in Swami's garden – our friends Maynard and Flo Ferguson, Ron, Vemu and myself.

This time I took some photographs while we waited, and later managed two of Swami in the patio. He came out, his red robe seeming to blaze with light in the sun against the dark green shade of the trees. He smiled at Flo and me, and went out to give *darshan* to the crowd under the great banyan tree. And when he returned he told us all to go in.

A chair had been placed in the room. About six Iranian women were already sitting on the floor. They were refugees from Iran and did not know if they would ever return. I felt I was dreaming when I found myself squatting beside Swami's chair, touching it with my bare feet.

Before we sat down Swami materialised *vibhuti*, the sacred ash, into our hands, which we ate. When he sat down in the chair, looking round at the little circle to see that all were comfortable (again reminding me of a mother hen collecting her chicks), he turned to Flo and asked with a mischievous smile, "And how's Sir?" She was sitting beside me. At first she was non-plussed – till she suddenly realised he must <u>know</u> the private joke between her and Vemu!

When she wears a trouser-suit in the Ashoka Hotel, Vemu addresses her as "Sir"! How could Swami know? But then Baba can be anywhere and in all places. Turning to me he asked how I was feeling. I replied, "Rather feverish after seeing you yesterday, Swami." He smiled.

"What's divine?" he suddenly shot at me. I could only think of saying "God". So he replied with one of his sayings which I should have remembered had I not been caught unawares: "Duty without love is deplorable. Duty with love is desirable. <u>Love without duty is divine.</u>" He went on to speak of physics, chemistry and science, adding, "First comes knowledge, then skill, then balance, then wisdom – and <u>then</u> you go within."

After a little discourse he spoke of matters personal to all those concerned which I naturally cannot mention. In due course Ron asked if there was going to be a nuclear holocaust, especially in view of present difficult situations in the world. "No," said Swami. There would be a lot of play and threats and so on. But it would not come to a blow-up.

"But what about the planet, Swami?" I asked. I said someone had said that he had heard from someone else that Swami had said that 30% or 70% or 40% or 60% of the population would go.

Swami replied that he had never mentioned these figures. (This is how wrong information percolates.) But he did say, in answer to my question, "There will be <u>physical repercussions because of growing selfishness, minor adjustments to the planet, and a certain clear-out.</u>" This presumably means a certain amount of clearing away.

As I had recently written an article in *Two Worlds* on the subject of the very many prophecies of doom and disaster received from so many quarters, I mentioned this. I added that some people I knew had even felt that they had been called upon to found 'survival colonies' in high mountains and certain other places. At this Swami laughed and said this was not necessary at all.

I think I should add here a question I asked at another interview about UFO's. I mentioned the great increase in both landings and actual contacts with beings from space in what we call flying saucers. I asked if they were trying to help the earth, and to bring the idea of brotherhood, and a wider understanding of other dimensions. Swami replied that this was so, and added, "And they have much work to do."

At one point I asked how I could best be of service. "By serving others," was the immediate reply. "And by writing?" I asked. "Oh, certainly by writing." Then he turned to me and became very emphatic. "You write very well because you write from the heart. Writing with the head only means very little − it must be from the heart. You write very well. You have a good heart."

It can be imagined how thrilled I was at this encouragement of my efforts, and spoken with such emphasis. Then he turned to Ron and told him his article was good. This was another demonstration of Baba's 'inside knowledge', because Ron had not left the article he had shown briefly the day before. Swami had read only the first few lines and Ron had taken it with him. But Swami does not need to read.

"You must write an article for *The Golden Age*," he told Ron, and turning to me again, added, "And you must write one, too." We discovered later that this was a magnificent production of over 200 pages filled with contributions from the most eminent people, including scholars, judges, ministers, generals, air-vice marshals, former Presidents of India, scientists, professors, and numerous such devotees of Swami, published on his birthday by the Kingdom of Sathya Sai, an association of former students of Swami's colleges. In the 1979 volume there were fifty-four contributions, one for each year of Swami's present life, with a long contribution from Swami himself. Needless to say, we felt this a most daunting assignment.

(After we had returned home we received an official invitation from the Kingdom of Sathya Sai, and our contributions appeared in the 1980 volume.)

Swami is so full of love, and also of the kindest humour. "You get depressed sometimes," he suddenly said to me. "I sometimes get depressed with myself, Swami, when I have a monkey mind." He laughed hugely and opened his eyes wide as he retorted, "Monkey mind? Mad monkey! Sometimes all confusion." We all laughed, but it is so true, when I am beset with six things to do at once, and all of them urgent.

Now Swami did what I am sure he had planned to do the day before . . . He took hold of my chain and pendant again, and asked, "Wouldn't you like a real one? This is imitation." And before I could say a word, he circled his hand in the air and produced a charming silvery disc, with his head on one side, and the AUM sign on the other. What a joy! It was of course what I had secretly longed for, but would not ask.

A little later he asked Ron what he wanted. Ron answered, "To love more − and something from you, Swami." Immediately

Swami circled his hand again, and produced a gorgeous oval ring made of Swami's five metals, with a coloured portrait of his head on enamel. He leaned forward and pushed it firmly on to the fourth finger of Ron's left hand. It fitted perfectly, and was exactly what Ron had day-dreamed about in the aeroplane on the flight to India — even the correct finger. Ron's eyes are not too good. He fumbled for his spectacles to examine it closely, and Swami joked, "Can't you see my hair?"

But a further and most unexpected blessing was yet to come which completely overwhelmed me. During a general conversation Swami turned to me again, in that sudden way he has, when you least expect it. "Do you do *sadhana* (spiritual practice or endeavour)?" "Yes, Swami." "When?" "At night, Swami."

To my wonderment he circled his hand five times in the air. As everyone gasped, out fell a long, beautiful 108-bead *japamala* — prayer beads. Its total length, were it undone, is 48 inches and it can be worn doubled round the neck and still be ample.

It just streamed down from his fingers like a cascade of crystal light. With an almost casual gesture he spread it out with both hands and threw it over my head on to my shoulders without touching a single hair. "Oh Swami!" was all I could say, hardly believing that I had been blessed with two gifts from him at one interview. (And always there was *vibhuti*.)

This is what he has said about such gifts: "Do not crave from me trivial material objects: but crave for Me, and you would be rewarded. Not that you should not receive whatever objects I give as signs of grace out of the fulness of love.

"I shall tell you why I give these rings, talismans, rosaries, etc. It is to mark the bond between me and those to whom they are given. When calamity befalls them, the article comes to me in a flash and returns in a flash, taking from me the remedial grace of protection. That grace is available to all who call on me in any Name or Form, not merely to those who wear these gifts. Love is the bond that wins grace."

These gifts cannot be either lost or stolen, for they instantly return to him. Indeed, there have been cases where Swami has returned a ring or a *japamala* to someone who thought they were lost. On one occasion a man was with Swami on the sands of the River Chitravati at Puttaparthi and Swami materialised a *japamala* for him. "But Swami," said the man, "why do I need two? You gave me one just like this and it is in a silver box at home." "You are mistaken," replied Swami. "Your home was broken into last night and the silver box was taken. This is your *japamala*!" And when the man returned home he found that it was so.

When Baba brought the interview to an end by standing up in the centre of that small room, everyone clustered round him to take the opportunity of touching or kissing his feet. As I stood up again I found myself standing on his right side, looking at the profile of his face which is so much more 'clean cut' than appears in photographs. I was reluctant to move away until I had to. A cloud of gay *saris* seemed to be dropping to the floor around him, making it impossible for him to move, and I marvelled at his infinite patience and love, day after day, year after year, always giving, healing, blessing, correcting, teaching, explaining spiritual truth, transforming, bestowing bliss.

I thought of the thousands in all walks of life — intellectuals, scholars, scientists, judges, generals, industrialists, ministers, teachers, *gurus* and *swamis*, priests of all religions, everyone from politicians to peasants — and millions of little people like me, from all over the world who, after experiencing Baba, find themselves impelled to sink to their knees as the only way human beings have of expressing a unique and inexpressible reaction never before encountered.

I was filled with compassion, and murmured, involuntarily, "Poor Swami . . . " Whether he heard or not I do not know, but in a few moments he turned his head and without changing his expression looked straight into my eyes for fully five seconds, while I looked back into his, wordless. I suppose I could have said something totally inadequate, like "Thank you, Swami, thank you", for had he not just blessed me with the materialisation of a locket and a *japamala*? But such facile words seem totally out of place in Baba's presence.

For he was looking at my naked soul — the soul that aspires yet has such a long journey ahead. For five long seconds those deep, wonderful, all-seeing eyes held mine. And then he slowly turned back his head, looking round to the open door through which people were beginning to leave. The very slowness of his turning took away any feeling of rejection. The interview had been concluded. Later, I thought: what a thing to say — 'poor Swami!' Had he heard those murmured words? Was it impudent to feel compassion for Divinity? Even for God? Compassion for the Infinite Love which embraces, sustains, and gives all to people like us?

As Vemu took his leave Swami told him, "Bring them tomorrow at 9:30 . . . "

# 4

# THE RESURRECTION OF JESUS

*"The good fortune that has brought you face to face with Me is something for which you must thank your merit won through previous lives."*

. . . Sri Sathya Sai Baba

So there we were again, for the third morning in succession, sitting outside Baba's porch in that tranquil leafy garden. The silence which literally bathes the *ashram* at Brindavan is balm to the soul. The raucous bombardment of pop music, television and radio seemed to exist in some other mad world of constant noise and unrest. Here it was difficult even to visualise our own little home so far away, yet I could still hardly believe that at long last I was really in India, with the beloved Sathya Sai . . .

This morning, he smiled at Flo and me as he passed to speak to an elderly lady in a chair in a shady corner of the patio, before going out to give *darshan.* He must have selected two for interviews, for soon a grey-haired Australian appeared and sat down beside Ron, Maynard and Vemu, followed by a young man from Texas.

25

When Baba returned he motioned us all to follow him in. Today there were some Indian women and two Malaysians present. Swami talked to them in their own language, materialising a ring for one of the Indian women. Later, he also materialised a ring for Flo Ferguson and, at the Australian's request, when asked what he wanted, something for the woman he hoped to marry. He was overcome with delight. As usual, before we all sat down, he circled his hand and produced *vibhuti* for us to eat — this time for the women only.

Professor Kasturi, who has been with Baba since Baba was twenty-two, says that Swami's entire physical frame seems suffused with this fragrant sacred ash. When leaving the body to go to help his devotees, *vibhuti* emanated from his face, mouth, thumbs, toes or forehead. But Kasturi told us that nowadays Baba does not suddenly fall down, or slump, when a call comes. It would be impossible with so many millions of devotees.

He is able to 'go' or 'be' anywhere with his limitless mind, while carrying on his normal activity. I personally know of instances here in England where Baba has "visited informally", as he puts it. One person asked, "Are you in your etheric body?" Baba replied, "Feel my arm." It was solid. Then he moved towards the door and disappeared.

It was a long interview, for all were taken into the inner room, either singly or in twos and threes. Flo and Maynard were returning to the United States in a day or two. They are old devotees, and Swami had promised Flo a *sari*. When they had gone into the next room through the heavy curtain, Swami fetched a folded *sari* from the corner and went in with it tucked under his arm, like a loving mother with a beautiful present for her daughter.

When one uses the word 'mother' in connection with Baba, it must never be thought it implies the slightest degree of effeminacy, far from it. But the purely spiritual qualities of the All-Father-Mother are combined, the *Shiva-Shakti* aspect. It is typified by his most moving words: "I ask only that you turn to Me when your mind drags you into grief or pride or envy. Bring me the depths of your mind, no matter how grotesque, how cruelly ravaged by doubts or disappointments. I know how to treat them. I will not reject you. I am your Mother."

I knew we would be left till last, for we both had written questions on small pads which he must have noticed. He probably knew the questions, too. When a South African had an interview and was too overcome to speak, Swami helped him out by saying, "You have four questions in your pocket." He told him what each question was, giving the answers to all of them, one after the other.

When our turn came Swami looked at Ron and said, "Come." As the husband is addressed first in India, Ron asked, "Peggy, too?" "Of course!" replied Swami, adding, "Go in there and fight!" which is a joke he has with husbands and wives. Perhaps he knew that Ron and I each feel it difficult to 'get a word in'! To avoid this, we had carefully divided our questions in advance. Even so, I did wonder how much time would be left for me if Ron started first.

It is strange in life how matters of the deepest and most far-reaching significance are often mixed up, in our human condition, with the most ludicrous, not to say embarrassing, events; always a mixture of the ridiculous and the sublime. We went into a smallish square room with wall sofas. In the middle was a fairly large, round table with a thick glass top. Swami had not yet entered, when suddenly those outside heard a loud report like a pistol shot, followed by a dreadful clatter. We learned later that Baba put on a comical look of surprise. He had told us to go in and fight, and this explosion immediately followed!

Ron, feeling he wanted to kneel on the floor, and having difficulty with his leg, had leant too heavily with his hand on the edge of the glass table which, to our absolute horror and consternation, broke clean across. A large half-moon section of heavy glass clattered down onto the table legs beneath.

Swami entered, glanced at the damage, and while poor Ron was abjectly begging forgiveness for the awful thing he had done, said gently, "Don't worry about it. Just put it on the sofa." So between us we picked up the heavy section of glass and laid it carefully on the sofa, leaving just enough room for us to sit down beside it. I was thinking it just _had_ to be old Ron, out of the millions, to break the _Avatar_'s table.

I must add here that next day, when we sent a message requesting permission to replace the glass, the reply was so typical: "Tell them that when you break something in your own home you don't necessarily have to replace it."

Baba sat facing us, very close, his elbows on his knees, his face with those wonderful eyes about twelve inches from ours. Such was his loving attitude of concentrated attention that in a moment the incident was totally forgotten. He was completely "at our service". ("I am the servant of all," he has said. "I have no rights. I am yours. You are mine. I am in each one of you; the Resident in every heart, whether you accept or reject. I am in the atheist, but he will only know it when he has got over his illness.")

Naturally, I cannot report private matters, except to give one small example of Baba's 'all knowing'. Ron wanted to ask about a deep problem, a chain of events which had been the cause of much suffering and distress to us both, and which he felt had a _karmic_ origin.

He felt he had to explain, so began, "Swami, this is very personal. Seven years ago . . . " But before he could continue with his saga Swami quietly interjected, "Seven and a half years ago." He already knew, in fact more accurately than we did. For when we later counted up, we found that the problem had entered our lives exactly seven years, six months and four days before the actual date of this interview. It is impossible to describe the wonder of talking to a being who knows all.

After Ron had asked questions about this matter, we asked questions about a variety of subjects — the task of visitors from outer space and Unidentified Flying Objects, which I have already mentioned; about healing, and asking for his help if we mentally called on him; about mediumship, as we wanted to clarify a report I had once read that he did not approve of what mediums did. (But who can approve of what some mediums do?) So we asked:

"Is mediumship, to communicate with those in the next sphere of life, provided the medium is honest and a pure instrument, wrong?"

"No, not at all," Swami replied quite categorically. Indeed, as we had expected. And of course Swami was well aware that for a period of several years we had had a particularly gifted psychic and medium actually living with us in our own home, or rather in the cottage of our house across a small courtyard, and that much of our very wonderful and uplifting experiences during that time were contained in my books.

We also spoke about what Swami referred to as "the very bad *karma*" incurred by mankind's abuse of the animal kingdom. When I mentioned science in this connection, Swami raised his eyes, turned his head away, and said, "Ah . . . science!" with such pain in his voice. "It is essential to spread knowledge of the oneness of all life. God is in every creature."

Now, because it is written that the triple incarnation of this *Avatar*, "the *Kalki Avatar* on the white horse" of ancient scriptures, as Sai Baba of Shirdi, then Sathya Sai Baba, and again as Prema Sia Baba, represents the *Shiva, Shiva-Shakti* and *Shakti* aspects of Divinity, we wondered if the next descent as Prema Sai, to come very quickly after the present form is vacated at the age of ninety-six, would be female.

Baba replied, "No, male. In Mysore — Karnataka." (Since 1972, the State of Mysore is called Karnataka.) The Incarnation will be in a place between the cities of Bangalore and Mysore. Both the name of the place, and that of the parents — perhaps not yet born — have been given by Baba, but I do not recall them, at least not accurately.

What will the form of Prema Sai be like? We already know! Dr John Hislop of the United States recounts in *The Golden Age*, 1980 volume, how one morning, in the presence of a group of his College boys, Swami asked Hislop to give him the heavy gold ring which he had materialised for him only the day before. Enclosing it in his palm, Hislop writes that "he blew the creative breath three times through the thumb and forefinger, opened his hand, and there was Prema Sai!"

The ring had changed from solid gold into silver colour and Hislop describes it as "a brownish stone, highly glazed, sculptured in profile, the bridge and length of the nose visible and a suggestion of the arch of the left eye, a noble head with shoulder-length hair, moustache and beard, the head resting on or emerging from a lotus flower. His countenance was tranquil, peaceful, majestic."

Swami told him, "He is only now in the process of birth (an Ideata), so I cannot show more of Him. This is the first time He is shown to the world."

The amazing thing is that during the period since the ring was created, it is changing! Hislop writes: "Now the entire nose is there and visible, whereas at first the entire nose was not visible – or better to say the nose merged into the edge of the stone and did not appear fully visible. But now there is a space between the nose and the edge of the stone. Moreover, a portion of the left eye can be seen and also a portion of the left cheek. We can hardly wait to see it a few years from now. What will it be in ten years? In twenty?" (I cannot help the feeling that the form of Prema Sai will somewhat resemble the traditional concept of Jesus.)

There was one question I particularly wanted to ask Swami. I had thought about it a great deal, and the answer – if he wished to answer – would be of great importance to me, and obviously to many who were not hidebound by orthodoxy built up over the centuries. We should never be afraid of Truth, but always pursue it, wherever it may lead.

In April 1979, I had written an article in *Two Worlds* entitled "Did Jesus Die on the Cross?" I had become fascinated by a book called *Jesus Died in Kashmir* by A. Faber-Kaiser, and other books on the same subject; also by the fact that some Indians and Pakistanis are puzzled by one's look of surprise when they say with such great pride: "The beloved Jesus died at Srinagar in Kashmir. Pilgrimages are made, and many prayers answered in times of trouble. To us he is the *Avatar* of Love." I had also been surprised by the fact that so many Christian readers of my article had written to me expressing interest and joy, and even saying that they had always felt 'in their bones' that he had not actually died.

The weight of evidence, garnered from the Shroud of Turin, that

Jesus suffered a state of catalepsy, or 'clinical death' in modern medical parlance, after just three hours on the Cross (death by crucifixion could take upto four days) is so strong that on June 30th 1960 Pope John XXIII issued a most revealing proclamation, printed on July 2nd in the Vatican newspaper, *l'Osservatore Romano*, entitled 'The Complete Salvation of Jesus Christ's Body'.

In this, the Pope told Roman Catholic bishops, who accepted and spread the news, that the complete 'salvation' of the human race was effected through the blood of Jesus, and that death was not essential to this end. (Incidentally, the word 'salvation' does not mean what most people assume, that is, saved. It means a 'return' to the path of evolution leading ultimately to the Godhead.)

Why did the Pope issue such a proclamation? Why was it necessary to state, in 1960 A.D., that death was not essential to this doctrine of the Church? It was because the Vatican was convinced, after years of most meticulous tests and analyses, using the most advanced techniques, that modern science had proved a) that the Shroud of Turin is authentic, and b) that it proves that Jesus was still alive when his unconscious body was laid on it.

Even today, with our modern medical skills, people have been certified dead and have later recovered in the mortuary. The prolonged death trance of *yogis* is well known. And how many people have been pronounced 'clinically dead' and have later revived, as described in Dr Raymond Moody's book, *Life After Life*?

In 1969, the Vatican commissioned a further detailed scientific investigation which lasted seven years and confirmed the previous findings.

There are twenty-eight blood stains on the Shroud, from crucifixion, scourging, the lance, lacerations, and the crown of thorns. These continued to bleed. Even the wounds from the crown of thorns started to bleed after it was removed. This is not possible unless the heart is still beating, albeit faintly. When the heart stops, the blood ceases to circulate, retracting in the veins, and the capillary blood vessels below the skin surface drain, producing the pallor of death.

The tests also showed that the lance pierced the right side of the chest between the fifth and sixth ribs, emerging on the upper left side at an angle of 29 degrees. This means that the lance passed close to the heart, but did not damage it. The "blood and water" which John tells us flowed from the lance wound could not have come from the heart. And since blood did flow, this shows that the heart was continuing to beat, however faintly.

One suspects that it was never the wish of Pilate himself that Jesus should have to die. Indeed, there was scarcely time, in view of the Jewish Sabbath starting at sunset on the same day. The two thieves were still alive and had to be killed. Death by crucifixion was a long affair, sometimes lasting three or four days, and was due to a combination of hunger, thirst, exhaustion, loss of blood, and birds of prey. Very occasionally, after a day and a half, the punishment was considered sufficient and malefactors were taken down. If their wounds could be successfully healed they recovered and went on living.

When Joseph of Arimathea, a wealthy member of the Sanhedrin and a devotee of Jesus, asked Pilate for permission to take Jesus's body, it was given, in spite of the fact that the crucified were not allowed to be put in a private tomb or buried by relatives, but were cast into a common grave.

Did Pilate, then, hope that he was still alive? My feeling that he did is confirmed by a letter he wrote to the Emperor Tiberius in A.D. 32. The original is in the Vatican Library. It is possible to acquire copies of it at the Library of Congress in Washington, D.C. Pilate wrote:

To Tiberius Caesar. A young man appeared in Galilee and, in the name of God who sent him, preached a new law, humility. At first I thought that his intention was to stir up a revolt among the people against the Romans. My suspicions were soon dispelled. Jesus of Nazareth spoke more as a friend of the Romans than as a friend of the Jews.

One day I observed a young man, among a group of people, leaning against the trunk of a tree and speaking quietly to the crowd that surrounded him. They told me he was Jesus. This was obvious because of the great difference between him and those around him. His fair hair and beard gave him a divine appearance. He was about thirty years old, and never before had I seen such a pleasant, kind face.

What a difference there was between him, with his fair complexion, and those wearing black beards, who were listening to him. As I did not want to disturb him, I went on my way, telling my secretary, however, to join the group and listen.

Later my secretary told me that he had never read in the works of the philosophers anything that could be compared with the teachings of Jesus, and that he was neither leading the people astray, nor an agitator. That is why we decided to protect him. He was free to act, to talk, and to call a gathering of people. This unlimited liberty provoked the Jews, who were indignant; it did not upset the poor, but it irritated the rich and powerful.

Later I wrote a letter to Jesus asking for an interview at the Forum. He came. When the Nazarene appeared I was taking my morning stroll and, looking at him, I was transfixed. My feet seemed fettered with iron chains to the marble floor; I was trembling all over as a guilty person would, although he was calm.

Without moving, I appraised this exceptional man for some time. There was nothing unpleasant about his appearance or character. In his presence I felt a profound respect for him. I told him he had an aura round him and his personality had an infectious simplicity that set him above the present day philosophers and masters. He made a deep impression on all of us, owing to his pleasant manner, simplicity, humility and love.

These, worthy sovereign, are the deeds that concern Jesus of Nazareth, and I have taken time to inform you in detail about this affair. My opinion is that a man who is capable of turning water into wine, who heals the sick, who resuscitates the dead and calms rough seas is not guilty of a criminal act. As others have said, we must admit that he is really the son of God. Your obedient servant, Pontius Pilate.

The man who wrote this letter after queries had been raised about Jesus's activities, even though he did not want to jeopardise his position or make an enemy of Caesar — to whom the angry Jews would have reported him — may nevertheless, having been unable to save him when he was brought before him, have arranged the execution in such a way and time that, unknown to his enemies, Jesus might survive the ordeal.

Contrary to usual Jewish custom, the body was not laid in a grave and buried, but was placed in a spacious, airy rock cave in Joseph of Arimathea's private garden, the entrance to which had to be blocked by a large stone. (It is said there was a connecting tunnel to Joseph's house, possibly an alternative exit in troublous times.)

However that may be, John tells us that the rich man Nicodemus also came, bringing "about a hundred pound weight" of myrrh and aloes. A prodigious amount — to help heal the wounds? It is interesting that in 16th century England two folk charms were used when gathering sage and verbena, claiming for these herbs the distinction of having grown first on Calvary and helped to heal Jesus of his wounds.

Scientists state that the perfect negative on the linen Shroud of Turin could only have been 'burned' into the cloth by a split second radiation. It is my belief that this was a split second cosmic radiation which helped to re-energise the spent, unconscious body.

Jesus reputedly told his disciples that he would rebuild the temple (of his body) in three days. They had no idea what he meant. They had all scattered, except John, the only one who presumably saw the body taken by Joseph of Arimathea and his friends. They all assumed he had died, which was why, when he appeared to them in the Upper Room they were afraid, and thought him a spirit.

But Jesus told them he was no spirit, that a spirit does not have bones and flesh as he had. He showed them his wounds and, asking for something to eat, ate broiled fish and a honeycomb. On another occasion he had made a fire on the lake shore and was cooking a fish.

The fact that he 'appeared' in the Upper Room when the door was reported as locked is something an adept, master or *avatar* can do at will, while in the physical body. Swami has done this innumerable times — even living with a family for two days while fully active 600 miles away.

On one occasion Baba 'appeared' and delivered a woman's baby, doing all that was necessary, including washing and wrapping the infant, before 'disappearing'. The night staff, who had not thought the baby due, were astonished when the woman said she had been delivered of her child by "the one in the red dress with a mass of black hair whose picture is on the hospital walls".

Incidentally, I wonder how many people remember, or know of the visitations to one Lloyd Tester of a mysterious stranger who simply called himself 'The Wayfarer'? The record of these conversations, together with an unusual, beautiful photograph of the stranger, which I have in my possession, was printed some fifty years ago, but has recently been reprinted in booklet form.

I am tempted to quote a brief excerpt which explains the removal of the stone from the tomb entrance:

I do but remind you of this, son, that you may see what occurred after the Crucifixion of the Master Messenger . . . Even here there was no miracle, unless it was a miracle that his few closest friends (who had begged the body and laid it away from the angry people) watched over him and waited patiently and confidently for the return of the spirit to the body, and then straight away led him back through the secret passage which connected the tomb with the house of its owner, Joseph of Arimathea.

Here they were met by that most wretched of all men, poor Judas, who in his distraught state of mind thought he saw the ghost of his betrayed Master returning from the dead, leaning on the arms of two men, whom he took to be his accusers. This was the unbearable point at which his reason snapped.

With a frenzied shriek he dashed along the passage leading to the tomb, and with the abnormal strength of the maniac he dashed himself against the obstacle that seemed to bar the way to freedom. With terrible shrieks and curses, and the strength of ten normal men, he forced away, all unaided, the heavy sealed stone that closed the entrance to the tomb and with the terrible howl of a madman rushed away to the place

33

where he met his own destruction.

I tell you this at some length for your own enlightenment. It was not that there was any need for undue secrecy (except in the minds of a few faithful friends who still feared the power of the authorities), but that it was his wish to withdraw for a time from the scenes of strife.

The spirit did but pass for a short time, to return again to the scene of his earthly sojourn. Again and again he appeared to his chosen ones, showing even the most sceptical the marks of his murderers, proving that it was the same body, the form they had known and loved so well.

What of the stories of his final disappearance in a cloud or mist? These accounts simply do not tally. Matthew does not even mention it! Another Gospel puts the 'disappearance' on the very same day as the Resurrection! While another says that Jesus was quite often with the disciples, giving them instructions for the future, for forty days.

Earlier in his ministry, when his enemies threatened to stone him, it is said that he simply "disappeared out of their midst", that is, became invisible. What is evident, however, is that he left them, and went elsewhere. So where did he go?

There is a great deal of evidence in ancient histories and chronicles that he continued his mission by travelling, in stages, to the East, to find the lost or scattered tribes of Israel.

After the destruction of the Assyrian Empire, only a remnant returned to Palestine. The other ten tribes had been dispersed eastwards and were to be found in Persia, Bactria (Afghanistan) and beyond the Indus in Kashmir, that beautiful region in the Himalayas west of Tibet known as 'heaven on earth'.

To this day there are those who call themselves Ben-e-Israel, the sons of Israel. There are numerous works, both ancient and modern, which attest to the Israelite origins of the Afghans and the Kashmiris.

Various very early histories, such as the *Bhavishya Mahapurana* written in Sanskrit, state that Jesus, accompanied by Mary his mother, and Thomas, after staying some time in Damascus, took the long caravan route across northern Persia, where he preached, converting many, and earned the name of "the healer of lepers". This teaching pilgrimage took several years, travelling ever towards the East.

In the 'Acts of Thomas' and other sources, Jesus, Mary and Thomas stayed in Taxila (now in Pakistan) whence they continued towards Kashmir. But Mary, not being able to bear further the hardships of the journey, died at what is now the small town of Murree, which was so named in her honour, some 30 miles from Rawalpindi. Her tomb at Pindi Point is an important shrine to this day. In 1950 the tomb was repaired, thanks to Khwaja Nazir Ahmad, author of the book *Jesus in Heaven on Earth.*

Jesus went on into Kashmir through the valley known as 'the Meadow of Jesus'. This beautiful green valley with wooded slopes is still inhabited by the Yahudi race, descendants of the tribes of Israel. Thence to what, when interpreted, means 'the place where Jesus rested'. And then to Srinagar, the floating capital of Kashmir, set among its lakes at the foot of the Himalayas.

He was, in fact, retracing the route by which he had returned to Palestine after his lengthy travels and studies in India, and elsewhere, during his younger years, when preparing for his ministry, according to the manuscripts in the Himis monastery, where he stayed for some time on that first journey.

The king, Raja Shalevahin, was much struck by this distinguished, pale-complexioned figure dressed in white. When questioned, Jesus told him (according to the *Bhavishya Mahapurana*) that he had proclaimed his ministry in a country far beyond the Indus and had been made to suffer. He had preached on love, truth, and purity of heart, and for this reason was known as the Messiah.

He said his mission was to "purify religion". The Raja befriended him in many ways and promised obedience to his teachings. Towards the end of his earthly life Jesus lived simply, beside Lake Dal, but multitudes were drawn to him, to hear his message, and to be healed.

It is stated that at a ripe old age Jesus asked Thomas to continue his work, and to place a tomb over the exact spot where he should die. The simple tomb lies, oriented east—west, in the crypt of a shrine called 'Rozabal', meaning 'Tomb of the Prophet', in the centre of Srinagar.

A very ancient carved tablet shows two footprints indicating the exact location of crucifixion scars. The shrine is visited by those of all faiths, and members of one family have been its custodians for 1900 years.

It is also stated in ancient chronicles that Thomas did as he was bid. After revisiting Taxila, and Mary's tomb, he travelled south throughout India, preaching, founding communities in Kerala and finally coming to Madras, where the present Cathedral of Saint Thomas was built over his tomb.

To this day, Hindus, Muslims, Buddhists and the Ben-e-Israelis revere the great pale-skinned Prophet who came from Palestine in the far west bearing the scars of crucifixion; who healed the sick and gathered to him the multitudes, whether kings or beggars, and who stated that he had come "to purify religion".

It can be understood, therefore, in view of the above and much else besides, why I was anxious to ask Baba one question. So I said:

"Swami, there's something I've wanted to know for a long time. Did the physical body of Jesus recover in the tomb? I mean, it wasn't a materialised body of spirit — in the same way that Yogananda's Master showed himself to him in fully materialised form three months after he had been buried?"

Swami replied, "No — the <u>physical</u> body. No spirit materialised body. The physical."

"Ah!" I said. "Then, did he journey to the East, continuing his mission, to Kashmir?"

"Yes — and he also travelled to Calcutta, and Malaysia."

"Then is it the body of Jesus which was buried in the Rozabal Shrine at Srinagar in Kashmir?"

Swami nodded, and said, "Yes", so simply, with an upturned inflexion in his voice, as if waiting for the next question, his eyes never moving from mine, with such gentleness.

Of course I wished, in retrospect, that I had asked more questions. But he had told me what I really wanted to know, and I was satisfied; and also happy that it was so. And when one really thinks about it, many questions that leap to mind regarding past events are of academic interest compared to the here and now, and the living reality of the Divine Principle Incarnate at this most crucial period of the planet's evolutionary history.

I knew, too, that Ron had a most important and momentous question he wished to put to Swami, and which I will leave him to describe in Book Two. I will only say that we left that interview in a daze . . .

36

# 5

# DID WE FAIL?

*I am always aware of the past, present and the future of every one of you."*

... Sri Sathya Sai Baba

My husband, Ron, and I felt so overwhelmed and blessed when we emerged from that interview – the third in three days, and such a vital one to us – that we were scarcely conscious of what was going on around us. As we joined the rest of the group which had been patiently waiting in the outer room, Baba took a basket from the corner and piled little packets of *vibhuti* into everyone's hands. Ron and I received fifty-nine of them between us.

Professor Kasturi says Baba materialises about one pound of this fragrant sacred ash every day, which is not 'brought' from anywhere but literally comes from his body. But each year at the Dassehra Festival, in Puttaparthi, Baba puts his hand into a small, very light, upturned urn held by a devotee, such as Kasturi, or Dr Gokak, or the scientist Dr Bhagavantham, or the 90-year-old Sri Karunyananda, and an endless stream of ash pours out over the small silver statue of his former body, Sai Baba of Shirdi.

When one hand tires he uses the other (during the changeover no ash falls), until there is ash 10 inches deep on the floor around the seated statue. This is later gathered and wrapped in paper packets. Kasturi once worked out that Baba must have materialised at least five or six tons of *vibhuti* over the years — and he wrote that several years ago.

Much that was said in that private interview described in the last chapter cannot be related, being of a personal nature. But Swami's last words to me were, "You go on writing — that's good." There was something else, however, which filled us with elation mixed with considerable confusion.

This was on a Saturday. Baba was apparently going to Bombay for a few days on the coming Tuesday morning to his beautiful Dharmakshetra set on a hill on the outskirts of that gigantic city. Our friend Vemu Mukunda told us, "Ask Swami if you should go to Bombay." This, of course, was something which would never have entered our own minds.

But, during that interview, Ron did ask, a little tentatively, "Swami, we're getting old and came to India only to see you. Should we come to Bombay?" Swami considered this, and in a tone which suggested we could really do as we wished, said, "Yes . . . yes, come with me to Bombay." Suddenly feeling all at sea, I asked, "Should we stay in a hotel?" (At that time, only our fourth day in India, we did not even know in what part of that vast city Dharmakshetra was.) Again Swami considered. "A hotel? Yes, if you like," and then added, "Or I'll look after you."

It was said so casually, and we did not know what this really meant. Nor did we know that on these visits he usually takes a small party. Even had we known, there was no reason to think we would be included.

At the end of the interview, which had been a long one and had to be brought to a close while we were still speaking about the animal kingdom, Swami got up and said, "We will talk more of this in Bombay . . . "

Those words will always haunt me. How many times have I come out in goose pimples at the thought of them! We were such 'raw recruits'. Anyway, even the thought of being on the same aeroplane as Swami (there being only one flight daily between Bangalore and Bombay) elated us. In a state of euphoria we rushed off by auto-rickshaw that afternoon to the airline office to see if they could change our booking from Wednesday January 30th (the day we had booked to leave) to Tuesday the 22nd. To our dismay we were placed 125th on the waiting list! As the office was closed on Sunday, we were told to try again at 4:30 on Monday afternoon.

Would 125 people suddenly cancel? During Monday? Were we behaving like teenage camp-followers? Having heard that 200,000 are apt to gather when Swami is in Bombay, and there were various functions, including a wedding that he had to perform, how could we really expect him to find time for Peggy and Ron, two elderly folk from England? I had visions of being lost in the crowd. Nor would our friend Vemu be with us. Vemu suggested I should ring up Shri Indulal Shah, in Bombay, who could possibly put us close by Dharmakshetra (though probably on concrete, he added.)

But how could I ring him if we had no idea whether we'd get on the aeroplane till the last moment? Nor did we see how we could get back to Bangalore, even if we arranged for extra money for additional return fares. We realised we might well be stranded in Bombay for days, waiting for our flight home – the same precious days when Swami would be back in Bangalore. And the idea of leaving after such a few days, perhaps never to return, and without even going to Puttaparthi, seemed dreadful.

Of course we had not yet learned that one cannot rationalise where Swami is concerned. One must just trust. Also, one has to realise that every word Swami utters has significance, however casually spoken. He had said, "Or I'll look after you." The word 'or' was the difficulty! Would he, or wouldn't he? And with 125 people on the waiting list? Somewhere inside me I had the feeling of being a nuisance – although this is wrong.

Baba has since come in a dream to show me that I must renounce the 'unwanted' complex of my childhood, and the feeling of being less worthy than others. (In other dreams since our return he has given me incomparable blessings.) He has said that no one dreams of him without his willing it. So whatever is said, shown, acted, conveyed or taught in a dream of him is valid.

But the main reason why, by late Sunday night, after a long discussion, we finally decided to abandon the seemingly vain attempt to go to Bombay was that we were so full up, spiritually, after our interviews and overwhelming experiences that we felt we simply had to have a little time for "our souls to catch up with our bodies."

There had to be a breathing space, to think, plan future work for Swami, thoroughly to soak in all we had been told. (Incidentally, I doubt if Ron could have stood it physically at that juncture, with all that would have been involved in such a rush. And my temperature was still quite a bit above normal.)

That evening, in our hotel room – our beds littered with sheets of diary notes – we were unexpectedly visited by Mr and Mrs Balu. He is a director of the Coffee Board of India, also a most gifted artist. His wife is a novelist and journalist and an expert in every kind of beautiful craft.

Both are most delightful and lovable people who had, with their three sons, become faithful devotees of Baba for some three years, though they said it seemed like three hundred years. I know exactly what they meant. We had previously been taken to meet them at Mr Balu's office, by Vemu, and were later to spend a most rewarding evening at their home – while Swami was in Bombay.

The next morning, Sunday, we sat with the crowd under the banyan tree for the first time since our arrival, having been till now in Swami's garden. Among all the Indians were several Americans, a party of Scandinavians, a contingent of Italians, and many other nationalities from both East and West.

When Swami moves slowly along the aisles he is aware of everyone. He is 'working' with everyone, inwardly, even (and perhaps especially) when he appears to ignore people. He has said: "You may be seeing me for the first time. But you are all old acquaintances for me. I know you all through and through." And when he looks at you, even briefly, that look is indelibly printed on the mind for ever afterwards.

This morning he inspected the bookshop, and was driven through the gates, possibly to see his herd of cows which he personally superintends with loving care. We, too, have been dairy farmers at one period of our lives, and were keen to visit the herd. As we were staying at Brindavan all day, we later walked down the road, first to gape in amazement at the enormous and architecturally unique Sri Sathya Sai Arts, Science and Commerce College for over one thousand picked students; and then down to the cool, spacious cowshed in the farmland behind.

Even the cowsheds, here and at Puttaparthi, are in Swami's colours of pink and blue. On each of the pale blue sliding doors was the symbol of the combined religions, which is indeed everywhere – the symbol of universality. The cows were so peaceful and contented, and the white-coated students in charge of them absolutely quiet and meticulous.

Everything Swami does is significant and has a message. When the cows were to move to their new home from their original quarters behind his residence, we were told that Swami arranged a procession through the village. First came the flute players. Krishna was once a cowherd boy and is always depicted playing his flute. Then came Swami leading the first cow, decorated with flowers, followed by sixty students, each leading a cow, calves following mothers. A group singing *bhajans*, lively sacred songs, brought up the rear. I wish I could have seen this lovely procession in their honour.

While sitting eating our sandwich lunch in the shade we were most struck by a group of college students wielding pick-axes to remove the large granite rocks beneath the sand, probably to extend the lavatory building. Although the sun was at its height they never once stopped this heavy work for a moment during the hour we were there. (And in a country where the educated never used to soil their hands or do manual labour.)

I was also struck by the obvious routine of one of the 'street dogs'. There are always three or four of these attractively shaped brown or fawn hounds which come into the *ashram* and lie around in the sun. This one went to a door of the bookshop, cocked its ears expectantly, and immediately a hand appeared to put its 'lunch' outside. Nothing is overlooked under Swami's jurisdiction. No wonder my proffered biscuits, to my surprise, had only been accepted out of politeness, as it were, not hunger!

Also, earlier that day, we were told to see the saintly old Professor Kasturi in the little room behind Swami's house where he lives when Baba is at Brindavan. We were to discuss Ron's article which he had shown to Swami at the first interview, and other matters. When we told him he would probably live to be a hundred, he just gave his beautiful smile and replied, so simply, "If Swami wants me . . . " It was a touching sight to see this 83-year-old ex-chancellor of a university, a most gifted and famous writer during his long life, squatting barefoot on the edge of a low camp-bed, the little room stacked with papers, and his few clothes hung on a peg.

While Swami was in Bombay this tall, fragile, most devoted man did us the honour of coming to talk to us for two and a half fascinating hours in our hotel bedroom. We shall always be grateful to him, and for the wonderful stories he told us about his earlier years with Baba who was only twenty-two years old when he 'caught' the 50-year-old professor who had previously made fun of him in the humorous magazine he edited — until he met him!

Vemu and the Fergusons returned about four o'clock that afternoon, to prepare for the concert they were giving that evening in the large students' hostel in which some students were to be 'back-ups'. Flo joined me in the crowd waiting for *darshan*. Being Sunday, *bhajans* were being sung most attractively to the accompaniment of a hand-drum and little tinkling cymbals. The singing only stops when Swami finally sits in a chair under the great tree in front of the Krishna statue, and gives the signal for the closing *bhajan* and the 'waving of the flame'.

Swami returned to his quarters, but as he was almost immediately going to the concert, Flo and I lined up with others to see him. As he passed us he smiled, and said to Flo, "Does it fit?" referring to the *sari* he had given her the day before, and which she was wearing.

Mr. Balu had asked if we could attend the concert, but alas, exceptions cannot be made to the rule that no women are allowed in the boys' hostel. But Ron was given VIP treatment. Because his leg would have been uncomfortable sitting in the lotus position on the floor, a chair was provided for him quite near to Swami, who smiled at him sweetly as he came in. Ron was the only European among an audience of about a thousand, comprised of students and a most elite gathering of teachers, professors, scientists, artists and writers.

Flo and I had been chatting in the car, but returned in time to hear Swami's voice giving a discourse after the concert, and the *bhajan* singing which ended the evening. It was a glorious, still, balmy night when Swami came out, with a crescent moon and a very bright star just beside it, in a deep turquoise sky. As he walked slowly by, Swami looked at it and remarked, "A pity the star isn't a little higher!" (to make the exact Muslim symbol.)

He passed on, always giving out so much love to all. One is bathed in that fantastic aura. I wondered how one could ever bear to leave that beautiful, peaceful, quiet place, and the sight of him, or the nearness of him. Unbidden tears swelled in my eyes. Yet he says: "I am wherever you are. It is only this body which is here."

It is difficult for most people to understand or to <u>know</u> omnipresence as a fact, even when it is demonstrated to be so, by personal experience. Swami spoke about this to Dr John Hislop. He asked Hislop, "You know Swami as the *Avatar*?" "Yes." "No doubts?" "No doubts whatsoever." "Your own experience is that Swami is omnipresent." "Yes, that is my direct experience."

"Yet," said Baba, "when you leave Swami at Brindavan and arrive at your hotel you think of Swami as being at Brindavan! You see, it is not easy to know the Omnipresent *Avatar*. Of course, there are always some who know. Not every blossom opens to the sun when it rises. Only some are ready. There is the factor of ripeness. Not every fruit on a tree is ripe at the same time."

This omnipresence has been demonstrated to me (and, of course, to thousands of others), sometimes by a small remark. For instance, at a later date, he smiled and said to me, "You were depressed the day before yesterday." And for reasons I will explain in due course, I had been — in the hotel.

What is it but omnipresence when there is perhaps some inner problem, and Baba comes in a dream to elucidate it? I could cite so many examples of people I know personally who experience direct contact with him, in any part of the world, either by visual sight (materialisation), voice, clairvoyance, dream, by appearance of *vibhuti*, and so on. But as this is a personal record, I am merely recounting my experiences.

Next morning, Monday, was the Fergusons' last day before returning to California. We all went to morning *darshan*. I had written a little note to Swami explaining our reasons for staying in Bangalore, asking Vemu to give it to him if he was able to see him before *darshan*. But it transpired later that Vemu had not been able to give it, though Swami doubtless noticed it in his hand. (But then Swami knows what is in a letter <u>at the time it is written</u>.)

When he came to the men's section he called Ron and Maynard forward from where they had been standing by the compound wall. He had a message for Maynard, and then said to Ron, in the sweetest, gentlest way, "So you're not coming to Bombay?" (Actually, Ron is a little deaf, and cannot be certain whether he said this, or "Are you coming to Bombay?" But it was the former he reported to me immediately afterwards.)

Thinking Swami had seen our note, he replied, "No, Swami. We decided to wait till you come back. You <u>are</u> coming back?"

"Oh, yes," said Swami. "I shall be back on the 28th. Four days in Bombay and two in Gujerat."

When Ron told me afterwards that Swami was going on to Gujerat my heart sank. But as it turned out, Swami did not go to Gujerat, and returned on the 27th. I did wish Ron had said we were 125th on the waiting list! But we had made our decision.

If we had failed in some way, Baba gave no sign of it. When Maynard went to touch his feet, and Swami saw Ron's clumsy efforts to do likewise with his stiff leg, he said with such understanding and love, "Don't bother. Here's my hand." Ron kissed it, and Swami put his hand under Ron's elbow and gave him a strong hoist up.

Later, in Bangalore, we said farewell to the Fergusons. When I kissed Flo neither of us could speak for the lumps in our throats. We had known one another for only a few days, but sharing the <u>experience</u> of Baba brings people very close together, for it is unique. Then we set off once more to the airline office to revert to our original booking for the 30th.

I could not help asking, "If we weren't taking our names off the waiting list would we have got a ticket?" But try as I might, I could not make the man at the desk understand this complicated English grammar, full of subjunctives. So we shall never know . . .

From time to time I still hear Swami's voice saying, "We will talk more of this in Bombay." Whenever I mention it Ron asks why I go on tormenting myself about it. Yet I think, as it later turned out, that we did right in the circumstances. I was happy to hear Mr. Balu agree when we spent an evening at his home during the rewarding and moving days to come. And Swami kept the most beautiful surprise for us up his sleeve . . .

# 6

# OUR CUP OVERFLOWS

*"I am granting things out of Love; My Love will never diminish.
I have no desire of any kind. I talk of Love, I guide you along the
Path of Love. I am Love."*

. . . Sri Sathya Sai Baba

Our good angel, Vemu Mukunda, saw to it that our days in Bangalore, while Swami was in Bombay, were filled with memorable
events and meetings, even when he could not be with us. We owe
him a lifelong debt of gratitude for his more than generous care of
us, regarding it as an insult if we so much as pleaded to pay our
share of taxis — even when he took us the 220-mile round trip to
Baba's birthplace, the little village of Puttaparthi on the River
Chitravati, where the immense, beautiful *ashram* of Prasanthi
Nilayam now is.

This was a most moving experience which I will not describe at
the moment, nor the fascinating and instructive hours we spent
with Kasturi, Dr Gokak and Mr and Mrs Balu, for I feel that the
very many readers of *Two Worlds* who have written to say they
"can't wait" for the next instalment will want to know what

transpired when Swami returned to Bangalore from Bombay on the Sunday, January 27th. To our consternation this was the day that Ron woke up with all the unpleasant symptoms of 'flu, and had to remain in bed, feeling really ill!

I trudged the streets to find a chemist open on Sunday, for we were quite out of aspirin. When I returned I prayed fervently, "Swami, Swami! Please make Ron all right for tomorrow!" For we had only two more days left, being booked to leave Bangalore for Bombay on Wednesday morning. How dreadful if Ron were to be bedridden during our last days.

But to our immense relief and Ron's astonishment, he fell into a deep sleep — and woke at four o'clock perfectly well! It was the shortest attack of 'flu he had ever experienced in his life, for in the past it has laid him low for days on end. Of course we should not have been astonished, for had I not appealed to Baba?

So next morning we were at Brindavan for *darshan*, under the banyan tree. Hundreds of students came out through Swami's gates, as usual, and eventually Swami himself. Apart from speaking to an elderly Westerner who had newly arrived (and I fancy was an old devotee), he ignored most of the men's section and came to the women's. When he came down the aisle where I was sitting he stopped and stood close in front of me, and asked (as if he had just remembered something), "Oh! Where is your husband?"

I knelt up and made a gesture towards the men's area. "Over there, Swami." I was thinking, where else could he be? But this was Swami's way of letting me know he knew that Ron had been ill yesterday — letting me know that he was checking, as it were, that Ron had been able to come.

Bringing my palms together again I realised I had gently cupped both his hands in my own, but he did not mind this 'breach of discipline'. "Very happy, very happy," he smiled, his eyes already scanning those nearby as he slowly moved on. How I longed to ask if we could see him once more, to say goodbye! But I did not need to utter the words, for when he returned to the house, and Vemu had a chance to say we were leaving Wednesday morning, Swami replied, "Yes, I know. I've just spoken to Peggy." But I hadn't uttered a word about leaving!

That afternoon we had to go to the Air India office to confirm our flight from Bombay to London on the Thursday — only to find our names had been removed to the waiting list. We had not confirmed early enough. We had delayed this on purpose as we were determined not to leave India till Swami had come back, in case his return might be delayed for some reason. So we booked provisionally on a flight via Rome at 5 a.m. on the Friday, but were told to come back the following afternoon. (Oh, how complicated modern travel is compared to 'the old days' when it took half an hour to obtain a 10-year passport, not several weeks, and once a seat on an aeroplane was booked there was no further messing about with local confirmations or delayed flights!)

I confess I felt very depressed that day. I wrote in my notes: "I feel I will almost die if we can't say goodbye to Swami and thank him, ask his blessings on our work in England, ask one more question, touch his feet once more . . . " My heart yearned unbearably for 'one more time'. It was a physical pain in the depths of my solar plexus.

Later, I began to pull myself together. How greedy can one be? Had we not already been blessed more than we could possibly either have deserved or expected? Had we not been granted two group interviews and two private interviews in three days? Had not Ron been privileged to attend the concert and share the rapt attention of a thousand Indians and listen to Swami's hour long discourse and sweet singing voice?

What about the hundreds at *darshan* who had no word, perhaps for weeks, even months? This was a test. I had to accept with grace and equanimity that there would in all probability be no 'last time'. With this acceptance came a certain tranquillity. Though deep down a quiet hope lingered, it was with a different state of mind. If it was to be, it would be. If not, we had every reason to be content.

Next morning, Tuesday, Swami stopped to have a word with Ron at *darshan*. "How are you?" he asked kindly. "Very well, Swami." "When are you leaving?" "Tomorrow morning," Ron replied. "Can we . . . ?" But Swami has a way of passing by without causing the slightest injury. Ron never got out his request. Vemu said later, "I think Swami is having a game with you. He told me he would see you, but didn't say when. Perhaps it's a test of some kind." (So Vemu thought it was a test, too.)

It was a hectic day, with many visits. Both Vemu's brothers, one a consultant anaesthetist, the other owning a printing firm, had extended loving hospitality and assistance, and we were touched to receive parting gifts from them both. Vemu's 86-year-old father, too, inspite of just having experienced a most severe heart attack – and given up for dead – received us in his home, looking the picture of health, thanks to Baba's help in effecting an almost miraculous recovery.

This venerable old gentleman chatted away, reminiscing about 'the old days' when he met the then Prince of Wales, in 1926. I think it made his day when Ron told him that his father was a friend of his, and the Prince had often come to their home in those bygone days, together with his brother who was much later to

47

become King George VI.

Then there was another frustrating, endless wait at the Air India office because the clerk with whom we had an appointment to see about our tickets had been called away to attend to a sick relative. Eventually Vemu turned up there, to say it was arranged to meet up with Mr and Mrs Balu so we could all go to 4:30 *darshan* together.

So while the men coped with the problem of our Bombay—Rome —London flight, I dashed back to the hotel by taxi to change back into my *sari*. Finally, the five of us, squashed hotly into the car with the driver, made it to Brindavan on time. Mrs Balu and I took our places, not very near the front as the place was crowded. Would Baba even notice us? Yet I felt calm, resigned, and content to be inconspicuous. But as Swami passed, some several yards away, he looked — and there was a sudden quick little smile. My spirit soared. "That was a beautiful little smile," I whispered to Mrs Balu.

After *darshan* there was to be the singing of *bhajans* in Swami's house, led by the students. When Vemu and Mr Balu joined us they said, "Swami says you can come in." How gratefully I followed Mrs Balu as she led me through the women's entrance into the house to where the ladies of the *ashram* and singers were already seated in the women's section.

The men, and the students, were out of sight in a long room just inside the glassed verandah entrance, and Baba was talking to them. Then he sat in a chair by the open verandah doors and the *bhajans* started, the first cadences sung solo, and then repeated by all voices to the fascinating musical accompaniment and finger-cymbals which Baba also uses at these times with enjoyment.

The students sang beautifully. One in particular sang a solo introduction so musically and with such feeling and artistry that it sent shivers down the spine. From the brightly lit interior one saw the trees gradually become black silhouettes against a deep turquoise sky, as we sang and clapped our hands to these invigorating rhythms. Sometimes Swami leads the singing himself in his beautiful voice, but not on this occasion.

At the conclusion *prasad* was handed round for everyone to eat, which I can only liken to tasty cheese straws without the cheese. I was given so much that I put most of it in my Indian canvas string bag and ate some every day for the next two weeks.

Soon Swami took a reluctant leave of the gathering, and as he slowly mounted the wooden, winding stairway from the hall, turned back twice to say a further word, as if the intense love and devotion focused on him from every heart present drew him back. Mrs Balu grabbed me. "Quickly!" she whispered. "This is where we women have something over the men. We can see Swami pass along the gallery . . . "

We quickly withdrew to an interior room with a partly boarded up gallery above one end. Everyone's eyes were raised to it. One could have heard a pin drop in the silence, followed suddenly by a strange sound — the simultaneous indrawing of breath of every woman there at the first glimpse of red at the end of the gallery. It was like a sudden breeze through the trees on a still night.

When I saw the red robed figure pass slowly and silently by, as if lost in thought, hands folded, head slightly bent, I was filled with such intense compassion for his 'aloneness' that tears filled my eyes. Here was a being who worked twenty-four hours a day, every day, all his life, without respite, for humanity; and never more so than when he was alone, unsleeping (for he has said he does not sleep) during the night hours, concentrating on the thousands of supplicating letters from all over the world, and much else far beyond our ken. Mrs Balu whispered, "Whenever I see him passing along up there I always feel he is returning to heaven . . . " Was that to be my last glimpse of him?

In the car returning to Bangalore Vemu said, "There will just be time in the morning to come over for *darshan* before we go to the Aiport." Oh yes, please, just one more opportunity to see him come out of those gates towards the crowd, one more chance that he might pass close by . . .

So that night we packed up, paid the hotel bill, and said farewell to the pathetic old night porter in his ancient army uniform which proudly bore four medals from the War in Burma. Whenever Ron saw this brave old man with failing sight, eking out his days for a pittance, they exchanged brisk salutes, which delighted both.

Early next morning we set off for Brindavan, with our luggage in the car, for the last time. On the way we stopped to get a garland of fragrant white blossoms which I hoped to get a chance of offering to Swami if he came near enough to my place in the crowd. As usual, when one is anxious about the time factor, the level-crossing gates were closed near the approach to Brindavan! Eventually a train puffed by and we hurried on. Of course the front places in the *darshan* crowd were all taken!

A nice young American offered her place in the front row when she learned I was leaving. But I couldn't deprive her of it. She had a beautiful flower she wanted Swami to touch and bless for a friend. I was sure she would gladly make room for me should Swami approach near enough to speak to. We waited patiently, all eyes on the distant archway through which Swami would come.

But instead, a small white figure suddenly appeared — running! In a moment we could just make out that it was Vemu. He was hurrying towards the men's side, then changing course towards the women's side, and beckoning frantically. <u>Could it really be for us?</u>

("Well, where are they?" Swami had asked, a little mischievously; and at Vemu's blank expression added, "Peggy and Ron. I'm waiting!") We could hardly believe it, for he was definitely beckoning to us, unable to pick us out in all that crowd of people, and hoping we would understand, stand up, and come.

There was no doubt about it as he approached nearer.

With beating hearts we extricated ourselves, I from among the women and Ron from among the men standing by the compound wall, and went as fast as we could, Ron limping with his damaged tendon, across the large expanse towards the gates of Swami's garden. Vemu urged us on, "Hurry! Swami's holding up *darshan* for you!"

I expected to go through the women's entrance, to the patio, where we had been before, but no sooner had I entered the patio, thinking Swami would be in the interview room, than Vemu called me out again. "Not in there – up the drive!"

So up the drive we went, white-coated students on either side, to the main verandah entrance with a huge circular pattern of coloured flower petals outside. And there, flanked by several important looking men in business suits, was Swami, with a big smile on his face, coming forward to meet us. We just fell at his feet, completely overwhelmed.

I had flung my carrier bag on the ground as we approached the verandah. And I havn't the faintest recollection of what became of my garland. I must have held it up with my right hand while I knelt down, to keep it off the ground, for Vemu says that Swami literally unpeeled my fingers from around the string, taking it and handing it to someone nearby.

Then he materialised *vibhuti* for us, and a man stepped forward with a piece of paper in case we wanted to wrap it up. I ate some, and kept the rest. This time it was very pale, very fine, and very fragrant. (It is now in a little container in my private shrine. Sometimes I take a little, but not much, because I want it to last forever.)

As Swami led us into the house, he turned to the important looking men and said to them, loudly, and with a big smile, "She's a great writer," in a tone as much as to say "Put that in your pipe and smoke it." They looked somewhat astonished – but not as astonished as I was. I could scarcely believe my ears.

And then we were in the private interview room – where Ron had broken the glass table – alone with Swami, almost too overcome to speak coherently. <u>He was all love.</u> All tender concern, all quietness, and as if he had all the time to spare and we, for those precious minutes, were the only people in the world. It is ever so.

And that was when he told me, smiling, "You were depressed the day before yesterday." I could only nod. He <u>knew</u> that was the day I had written in my notes that I felt I would almost die if we didn't see him once more! And he had planned this glorious surprise — perhaps to test our inner reactions in the meantime? Was that the meaning of that quick little smile at *darshan* last evening?

Swami spoke about some private matters, and brought to an end once and for all a deep problem and situation which had persisted for more than seven years and which he knew all about before Ron brought it up at our last interview. This shadow was removed from our lives merely by the serious utterance of five words, which he repeated, looking into our eyes. Swami never wastes words. Five words were sufficient. The problem no longer exists.

We asked if he would help with what we wanted to do in England, and he said he would. He was "very happy, very happy" with what we had in mind. "And will you help with my monkey mind?" I asked, remembering his joking words about my "mad monkey" mind at a previous interview. But now he shook his head with a smile and reassured me, "No, you are very controlled. Very patient."

Ron asked about meditation, which he has always found difficult in the accepted sense. (Actually, he is a person who is in a perpetual state of meditation.) Swami said it was the <u>heart</u> that was most important, in <u>all</u> things. "The heart, the heart . . ." He brushed aside our words of gratitude for having blessed us so much more than we deserved, with a gesture and turn of the head which could have meant 'what of it?'

His love surrounded us. I never voiced the question still hovering around my mind: "Had we failed in not going to Bombay?" Even though it had seemed impossible to get there in the circumstances, Swami could have made the impossible possible. Yet he had filled our cup to overflowing by this sudden, totally unexpected honour of calling us — a very inadequate elderly couple — up to the verandah before all eyes, to give us this last interview and blessing, the surprise he had kept up his sleeve.

There is no limit to his giving. The only limitation is in our own capacity to receive. The current is always switched on, always available. It is the bulbs that are faulty . . .

It was hard to tear ourselves away. I went down and lifted the hem of his robe back with both hands, and gently kissed his foot, and then his small hand, for the last time. My longing had been granted . . . I have no recollection at all of what Ron was doing at that moment. Probably touching Swami's other foot in farewell. Yet there is no farewell — only to the physical form. He is ever-present.

In the verandah I turned and saw dear Kasturi, palms together in greeting, literally beaming from ear to ear, so delighted for us. Unable to go to him, we could only return his greeting in the same fashion, and beam back with eyes full of happy tears. A student smilingly handed me my bag which I would have certainly left behind, money, tickets, passport and all. I could tell by his expression that he understood so well how I felt.

Choked, and in a state of bliss which I had never before experienced in seventy years of rich living, we hurried down the drive, through the archway flanked by college boys, across the long stretch of sand where the crowd still waited patiently, and with a delighted Vemu calling back, "We must hurry. You can have a good cry on the 'plane."

Thus we left that sunlit scene of colour, fragrance, peace, quietness, warmth, and the ineffable radiance which surrounds the small, unique, red robed human form of the *Avatar* who is the Embodiment of Divine Love, and is forever enshrined in our hearts.

# 7

# THE ABODE OF GREAT PEACE

*"The life of Sai, the message of Sai, the ideals Sai holds forth, the lesson that Sai teaches the world, are all enshrined in one word – LOVE."*

... Sri Sathya Sai Baba

After that totally unexpected and quite overwhelming final interview there was just time to return to our Bangalore hotel to change, regretfully, from a graceful *sari* into linen slacks before Vemu hurried us to the Airport. We exchanged the warmest of farewells till we were to meet again in England. Our gratitude for his constant care of us was impossible to express in words.

It was only our bodies that went through the necessary motions, in the way one functions in a blissful dream, unaware of how one moves from one place to another. And then we were flying over the mountains and valleys to Bombay. We were quite incapable of speech.

Bangalore and Brindavan were behind us, perhaps forever, but our breathless spirits were still within the radiant aura of Baba's love. The last vision of the red robed, smiling figure waiting for us in that fragrant, colourful, tranquil setting was superimposed on the drab scene of the noisy airport. A schizophrenic experience, being in two places simultaneously, our souls separated from our bodies, unable to catch up with the hasty transition from vibrant reality to the mundane world which seemed so shadowy and unreal.

We were still in this semi-dazed state when we were suddenly clasped in the arms of a little woman who had fought her way through the crowd at Bombay Airport. It was our Parsi friend, Shernaz. It had been she – then a total stranger – who had been instrumental in the miraculous healing of my doomed leg when I had appealed to Baba's photograph which had lit up in dazzling light in my bedroom at home, three years previously. Though living in England, she has a flat in Bombay and had come to meet us.

Perhaps our having to take a flight home a day later than we had originally booked was 'arranged' for a purpose, for it enabled us to visit Baba's beautiful Dharmakshetra after all – where we might have been with him the previous week.

Now, however, in the company of Shernaz's niece and her husband we were able to be taken over it at leisure, with every symbolic detail explained to us by the extremely nice warden, Mr Rao, who appeared from nowhere as soon as we had climbed the winding path, leaving our shoes at the top in the place provided. (Merely to be barefoot again, on Swami's hallowed ground, brought Brindavan that much closer.)

This unique, circular building on a leafy hill rises in the shape of a pure white lotus surrounded by a small moat of clear water, symbolising the purified heart. *Dharma* means Righteousness or Right Living. *Kshetra* means Field or Arena – the arena of conflict between man's lower and higher natures. The circular prayer hall and sanctuary beneath the lotus dome is called *Satya Deep*, meaning the Flame of Truth, approached by a bridge of nine ascending steps over the water.

Every measurement adds up to the sacred number 9, the immutable number of the Godhead, for however many times it is multiplied the result always adds up to 9 (18, 36, 45, 54, 63 and so on ad infinitum). Creation, symbolised by 8, decreases each time it is multiplied, and must eventually merge with God. For 8 multiplied by 9 adds up to 9 (72).

There are 1116 apertures round the prayer hall, for purifying air to pass through, 18 petals to the lotus dome which contains Baba's apartments; the column outside, symbolising all the religions with the opening lotus at the top, is 36 feet high; the whole structure took 108 days to build; and even the bus which brings people to it is number 333!

When Baba laid the foundation stone in 1967 he materialised a copper plate out of the air, with mystical emblems on it, and laid it at the base of the foundation. Dharmakshetra is a highly charged place of pilgrimage serving all faiths, and is also the headquarters of the Sathya Sai Seva (service) Organisation for the Bombay area, which does immense welfare work of every kind.

The inside is simple and beautiful, the central painting in the Sanctuary being two hands clasping the Lamp of Truth with a tall, unwavering flame. Also in the building are some small rooms for Baba's guests, a room where he serves his party with food, and a little kitchen adjoining it. Here, Mr Rao told us, Baba loves to lift the saucepan lids, examining and stirring the contents to see that all is well for his 'children' (Baba often cooked for the whole family when he was but eight years old.)

Down the hillside we saw the schoolrooms, library, large hall, and workshops equipped to teach trades such as printing, engineering, carpentry, electrical work and so on, where young drop-outs can have free tuition. These boys were busily engaged at the various machines, with happy faces in this quiet, happy atmosphere. Our Parsi friends were tremendously impressed, indeed fascinated, asking Mr Rao endless questions, and obviously surprised that the Parsi New Year is celebrated there, as well as the feast days of all the major religions.

But the most moving and memorable visit had been to Puttaparthi – the faraway village in the valley of the winding River Chitravati where Sathya Sai Baba was born, with the given name of Sathyanarayana, to the Raju family at sunrise on November 23rd 1926. As the birth became imminent the household were often awakened at midnight and in the early hours by the musical instruments in the house playing melodiously, as though by unseen but expert hands. No one could explain this strange phenomenon at the time . . .

The 110-mile drive from Bangalore was itself a fascinating experience. The entire countryside reminded both of us, more and more as we progressed, of what Palestine might have been like two thousand years ago. White oxen or water buffalo patiently ploughed little rice paddies; a small boy quietly herded about three hundred cheerful goats to new pastures; young women in bright *saris* walked gracefully with tall jars on their heads, or planted out fields by hand, in rows. Once we had to pull up to allow a tribe of lively grey monkeys to cross the road. We pestered Vemu to identify the unfamiliar crops – which Westerners only recognise in the setting of supermarkets and greengrocers.

There was one spacious, bustling little town, and little villages of thatched cottages in the shade of great trees, lakes, and always the terracotta earth. Then we turned off the Hyderabad road towards the distant granite mountains. The road became narrower, more bumpy, up hill and down dale, fording streams. Until more recent years the last part of the journey had to be made by bullock cart, but still people of high and low estate flocked in their thousands, whether state ministers, politicians from Delhi, scholars, scientists, holy men from the Himalayas, foreigners, the rich, the poor, and the sick. And so it goes on, in increasing numbers.

Suddenly we glimpsed Sai Gita, Swami's beloved elephant, conversing with her *mahout* under a tree, and we knew we had arrived! On the left, an avenue of trees led up to a statue of Krishna with a white cow and calf, placed in front of the pale blue doors of the model cowshed, with the emblem of the combined religions on them, as at Brindavan. Further along, we passed the splendid High School, the Elementary School, the fine Arts Science and Commerce College, and the students' hostel similar to the beautiful one at Brindavan.

Finally, the little village and open square. But first we turned down to the right, to the river, and got out on the hot sand at the water's edge. At most times of the year the Chitravati consists of a huge expanse of sand. Today there was a large lake of calm water, and on the far side a group of women busy with their laundry work. Overcome with a feeling of awe and reverence, we took off our shoes and waded in the cool water. It was as if we had travelled back in time, and were immersing our feet in the ancient Sea of Galilee. A smiling cherub-faced little boy gazed up at us, with palms together in greeting, repeating, "Sai Ram, Sai Ram!"

Just such a little boy Swami had been, swimming, laughing, full of fun, never telling on the big bully boys who resented his amazing knowledge in school — without ever paying attention — and who held his head under the water, or dragged him along the sand, tearing his one and only white shirt so that he had to pin the tears together with cactus thorns. The little boy who could not join the Boy Scouts because his family were too poor to provide the uniform . . .

Yet a boy unlike any other — who performed miracles at two and three years old, was called "our *guru*" by the people at five, and *Brahmajnani* (he who has all knowledge and wisdom) at six! It is not possible to write here of his astonishing boyhood, of his sweetness and compassion for people and animals, of his teaching at ten years old, of the spiritual songs he composed, the dramas he wrote, directed and acted in at twelve, and much, much else, for this can be read in Professor Kasturi's splendid four volumes of his life, under the title *Sathyam Sivam Sundaram.*

But all this was in our minds as we cooled our feet in this sacred river, and we could not prevent the tears filling our eyes. Along these sands, as a young teenager, Baba took his devotees of all ages, for there was no room elsewhere, even though they built him a constantly enlarged rustic temple or *mandir*.

Daily miracles, which are his very nature, took place here, including the playful ones like making a ball of sand and tossing it to a child to eat — for it would turn into something warm and delicious as the child caught it. Swami has always liked to talk and teach along the banks of rivers or the sea shore in many places, and always, it seems, he cannot resist materialising anything and everything he wills from the sand. Even recently, in June 1980, on a visit to Kashmir, he sat on a sandy patch in Lieutenant General S.P. Malhotra's garden and materialised gifts for his host and hostess. Fortunately someone present had a cine-camera, and we have seen the film of this happening.

Then our friend Vemu interrupted our reverie by saying, "Look! There's the 'wish-fulfilling tree'." We looked up at a high rocky promontory just beside us, rising some 150 feet. Almost at the top was a green tamarind tree with a little red flag on it, rising from among the large boulders. The young Sathya would ask his friends what fruit they wanted, and whatever fruit they asked for would appear on the branches, an orange on one, an apple on another, a mango, banana, or whatever was requested. Indeed, Baba has done this, sometimes, when stopping for a picnic on a car journey, for those travelling with him.

But I was thinking of the evening when the young Baba, returning from the sands with a group, had levitated to the top of the rock and called, "I am going to show you the Vision of Light." "Suddenly," wrote C.N. Padma, who was present, "there was a great ball of fire like a sun, piercing the new moon dusk. It was impossible to open the eyes and keep looking. About three or four of the devotees fainted and fell."

At a later date, when Baba was visiting a family in Mysore, he granted their *Brahmin* priest a vision, and the priest did not recover consciousness for several hours. While on another occasion, when talking to a retired health inspector about God, Baba showed him the Flame emanating from his forehead. The inspector was similarly so overcome at this magnificence that he did not recover consciousness for seventy hours, and alarmed his children.

Baba is careful now, for our physical bodies are far too weak to stand certain spiritual experiences which are 'too much to take'. Dr V.K. Gokak once asked Baba if he would ever show him his True Form, and Baba replied, "You would very quickly wish me back in the form you know." I can say, speaking purely personally, that experiencing the close presence of Sai Baba fills one up

57

with such a sensation of unprecedented bliss that breathing becomes quite difficult.

We tore ourselves away from the contemplation of this scene and drove slowly up the village street in search of somewhere to leave the car in the shade of the high *ashram* wall, almost pushing aside noble, sloe-eyed white oxen and avoiding hens marshalling their chicks to safety. The sandy street was flanked on one side by little open shops, many full of fruit. A tape-recorder was playing *bhajan* music. The actual birthplace of Swami has been replaced by devotees with a beautiful shrine to Shiva which we entered through wrought iron gates.

With bare feet, avoiding the stone which was too hot to walk on at midday, we went through the big archway over which are the words "You are in the Light. The Light is in you. YOU ARE THE LIGHT", and entered Prasanthi Nilayam – the Abode of Great Peace – and into another world!

Because Swami was absent, and residents were indoors at that hour of the day, we had the place almost to ourselves. It was beautiful. Tall cyprus type trees rise heavenwards. The only sound in the silence was the breeze rustling the eucalyptus leaves, and the pigeons softly crooning on the ledges of the tall lotus statue with its five-sided base bearing the emblems and quotations from five major faiths, surrounded by a moat of cool water.

An avenue of trees leads up to the enchanting, colourful building in traditional Hindu style which contains the Temple Prayer Hall, interview rooms and so on, while Swami's own rooms are above, surrounded by a balcony on which he appears early every morning after the still earlier rituals have taken place. This commences with the chanting of the long-drawn-out AUM twenty-one times, before dawn, the sound reverberating from perhaps a thousand throats across the valley to the mountains.

On three sides of a huge quadrangle are long three-storied blocks with communal covered balconies along their length (in places, three blocks one behind the other), providing simple accommodation for 10,000 people. Since our visit a further round building has been erected for Westerners, also providing Western food. All this, of course, is totally inadequate during certain festivals, or the All India or World Conferences of the Sri Sathya Sai Organisation, or on Baba's birthday (which he himself has no interest in, but consents to celebrate purely to please his devotees.)

Over a quarter of a million people assembled from all over India and from a vast number of countries for the Fiftieth Birthday and World Conference in 1975, and on these occasions every square inch of ground is occupied by makeshift tents and the flat roofs of buildings are crammed. His High School, Secondary and Primary

Schools, the College and its hostel are also utilised.

On the occasion of the World Conference and Birthday in November 1980, although only two or three delegates were allowed from each Sri Sathya Sai Centre, 12,500 delegates attended from all over the world, from some fifty-four countries, including Russia and Japan. A quarter of a million people covered an area of 100 acres equipped with water mains and drains, roads and electricity.

Moreover the State Administration of Andhra Pradesh had recently brought a hundred villages around Puttaparthi under a new administrative region named Sri Sathya Sai Taluka. The birthday celebration that year was for these villages, to inaugurate a new era of love and service in this spiritual revolution.

On the fourth side of the quadrangle is a huge canteen and various offices, behind which we saw devotees laying a road of square granite slabs; while behind Swami's garden, set into the rocky hillside, is the fully equipped hospital which serves the surrounding countryside. Baba supervised the construction (as he does everything), watching over the devotees who, standing in long queues along the slope of the hill, passed from hand to hand metal, stones, bricks, water, mud, mortar, and everything needed.

But what took our breath away was the great Purnachandra Auditorium in the sandy quadrangle itself — a magnificent hall holding some 35,000 people. The front, with its domes, balconies and beautiful architecture painted in blues and pinks, against a deep blue sky, is dreamlike. The interior measures 220 feet by 140 feet without a single column to support the roof — the only example in the whole of Asia — so the hall looks vast, for as everyone sits on the floor there are no chairs to spoil it. Both sides, moreover, between carved columns of saintly figures of all religions (including a carving of Jesus on the Cross), can be rolled up, thus opening it to the air, and for the benefit of all those outside.

On the right of the platform are beautiful murals of the Ten Hindu *Avatars* going back into past ages, concluding with the major *Avatars* — Rama (11,000 years ago), Krishna (5,000 years ago), and the Kalki *Avatar* on the white horse of ancient prophecy, Sathya Sai.

On the other side are equally beautiful murals of the Buddha with his disciples, Krishna with Arjuna, Jesus leading his sheep, Zoroaster with his disciples round the Eternal Flame, and a lovely picture featuring the star and crescent moon (as it is forbidden to Muslims to depict their Prophet or their God), with the teachings of each written below in five languages.

Some of Baba's pithy sayings are written round the Hall. For example: "Seek out your faults and others' merits." "Love lives by giving and forgiving; self lives by getting and forgetting." "The heart is the Temple of God." "Grace is proportionate to exertion." "God is Love; live in God." "The pure heart is the inner purpose of all discipline." "The secret of happiness is not doing what you like, but liking what you have to do." "Instead of digging 4-foot holes in 10 places, dig 40-foot in one. Concentrate on the chosen path." "Follow the Master; face the devil; fight to the end; finish the game." "Recognising one's errors is the beginning of wisdom." "Shed just one tear; I will wipe a hundred from your eyes."

Experiencing this sacred place, and Brindavan where we had been so blessed, and in the contemplation of beautiful Dharmakshetra in Bombay, the Sivam in Hyderabad, the Sundaram in Madras, the 3,400 Sai Centres of service to humanity in India, and all those in some fifty-four other countries, increasing every year, the colleges for both men and women in Puttaparthi, Brindavan, Anantapur, Jaipur, Bhopal and in Gujerat, spreading through every State, the High Schools, Secondary Schools, Elementary Schools, and Kindergartens, and some 14,000 Bal Vikases (education in human values) for children, and so much else, we could but echo the words of R.R. Diwaker, Chairman of the Gandhi Peace Foundation, former minister in the Government of India and a State Governor, scholar and writer, when he said on Baba's fiftieth birthday:

"Once Swami was a village urchin . . . Now we assemble from the four quarters of the globe and what do we find? Philosophers and politicians, educators and legislators, scientists and technologists, the rich as well as the poor, the ignorant as well as the learned, and from all nations, and all religions. If this is not a living marvel and a miracle, I would like to know what is."

# 8

# FROM BETHLEHEM TO BRINDAVAN

*"There is only one religion: the religion of love."*

. . . Sri Sathya Sai Baba

In spite of all the commercialism, the eating and drinking, and the fact that a large section of the population in the Western world nowadays tends to disregard the significance and meaning of the Christmas Festival, nevertheless a real spirit of goodwill is in the air, and noticeably so.

There is a kind of magic about Christmas. The subtle and silent drawing nigh of angelic hosts is sensed, however dimly, or unknowingly, whether we celebrate Christmas in the wintry north or in the sunny climes under the Southern Cross.

Perhaps, unconsciously, it is a return to our childhood when we knew that fairy stories were true; that the *daivic* kingdom of nature spirits really existed (as indeed it does); that there was Good and Bad, with capital letters; and that the Prince would appear, on a white horse, wielding the Sword of Truth.

Yet even among Christians of so many kinds and multifarious sects there is diversity of opinion about the central figure on which this festival is based. Theological gymnastics have all but obliterated the Man of Nazareth who walked over the mountains of Galilee and Judea with a handful of semi-illiterate disciples, often sleeping rough, yet making such an impact on both rich and poor, patrician and peasant, that the priests plotted to get rid of him.

In this scientific, materialistic age it is the fashion even among some clergy to dismiss the Bible miracles as myths, and to present Jesus as an inspired teacher of truth and morals, an example and ideal to which to aspire in a humanitarian sense, but whose teachings are almost impossible, if not quite, to put into practice in the jungle we have made of the world.

The sermon on the Mount seems a far cry from war in space, the megaton bomb, political blackmail by particle-beam transmitters, lasers, deadly microwaves, chemical and biological warfare, cybernetics, international terrorism, or bases on the moon.

Yet anyone, whether professed atheist, agnostic or materialist, cannot fail to marvel that a youngish man, whose ministry lasted only three years, in Palestine, a tiny outpost of the Roman Empire (for the travels in Tibet, India, Persia and Egypt are mentioned elsewhere than in the orthodox Bible) made an astonishing, astounding impression lasting just on two thousand years!

Just imagine if, in those days, people had had film cameras; if the public discourses and even private talks had been tape-recorded; if people on the other side of the world could have heard his voice on long-playing records; if, when he spoke in the Temple and elsewhere "as one having authority", his words had been retained on tape or film . . .

Supposing books had been published in several languages during his earth life, with documented evidence from those who had personally experienced instantaneous healings, phenomenal happenings, clairvoyant visitations; witnessed the multiplying of food for thousands, materialisations, transfigurations, bi-location, miracles of astonishing kinds, and the raising to life of those whose bodies had begun to decompose. And supposing, too, that his great aura of love had been tested by a scientist expert in Kirlian photography, and the wonders he performed witnessed and attested to by institutions of psychical research.

Just imagine, you might say, if only that had been possible! As it is, you say, we have only his reported words: "Blessed are those who have seen and believed. But thrice blessed are those who have not seen and yet believed."

Yet today all these things are possible. And it is because all these things are now possible that I believe we are able to be so much closer to understanding the 'nature' of Jesus, who was called the Anointed One – the Christos.

Now? you ask, how can that be? For this reason: that every single phenomenon and happening mentioned above has been and is being demonstrated by One who is on earth today, in the human form of the *Avatar* of this Age, Sathya Sai Baba.

One of the differences between the most saintly of holy men and an *avatar* lies in the fact that the powers of the former have to be acquired and developed by long training and spiritual disciplines, and which have to be kept up if those powers are not to fade (which they inevitably do); while an *avatar* is born with them. They are his very nature.

The powers that are miraculous to us are normal to him. His will is sufficient. He has only to will something to happen or to appear, for instance, and it happens or appears, or disappears. An *avatar* is no medium, dependent on another entity or higher power in another dimension. He IS the higher power.

Baba says: "My miracles are part of the unlimited power of God and are in no sense the product of *yogic* powers which are acquired. They are natural, uncontrived. There are no invisible beings helping me. My divine will brings the object in a moment. I am everywhere."

The word "brings" in this connection can be, with all respect, a little misleading for although there are occasions on which Baba apports or teleports objects, he has complete power over the elements and atomic particles so that he is able to transform one object into another simply by blowing his creative breath on it. This phenomenon occurs constantly.

Incidentally, Dr V.K. Gokak, when we were privileged to visit him in his home in Bangalore, told us of an amazing teleportation which had taken place at Prasanthi Nilayam. He had been with Baba at one o'clock to discuss certain matters connected with a festival which was to take place, I believe, that evening. At three o'clock he had occasion to go to Baba's room again. To his utter astonishment he found the room piled high with covered buckets containing food, masses of them.

"But what is this, Swami?" he asked. "How did all these get here?"

Baba smiled and answered, "Not by human means. The van that was bringing them is in trouble. It wasn't going to arrive." Baba had teleported the entire contents of the van!

An *avatar* assumes human form in order to take human evolution a step higher, to usher in a new age, when the need for intervention is very great, as indeed it is today. "In order to save someone from drowning," says Baba, "one must jump into the water" – that is, incarnate.

"I came in response to the prayers of saints, seers and seekers," or, as the Krishna Form stated in the *Bhagavad-Gita*, "When virtue declines and evil flourishes . . . to save the good and destroy evil-doers, to establish righteousness and truth, I am born from age to age." But in this present Kali Age, says Baba, it is not a question of destroying evil-doers. The scale is too great. It is a question of destroying evil, not by force, but by love and transformation.

The same divine principle has been made manifest in all *avatars*, minor and major, but in varying degrees. Jesus, the Master of the Masters, was the vessel in whom a ray of the divine spirit was made manifest to fulfil a certain *avataric* mission.

Baba says: "Jesus was a master born for a purpose, the mission of restoring love, charity and compassion in the heart of man." When we asked, "Was Jesus an *avatar*?" Swami replied, "Yes." But he has qualified this statement by saying that Jesus had some divine powers, but not the full powers (the sixteen *kalas* or attributes) of a major *avatar.*

There have been only two previous *Purna Avatars* (fully divine incarnations) — Rama, 11,000 years ago, and Krishna, 5,000 years ago, when conditions in the world were very different to what they are today. We are now privileged to live, at this momentous period in our history, when the third *Purna Avatar* is in our midst, for our sakes.

Sai has said: "Rama, Krishna and Baba appear in different dress, but it is the same entity, believe me . . . I am new and ever ancient. I come always for the restoration of *Dharma* (righteousness), for tending the virtuous and ensuring them conditions congenial to progress, and for educating the 'blind' who miss the way and wander into the wilderness.

"Some doubters may ask, 'Can *Paramatma* assume human form?' Man can derive joy only through the human form; he can receive instruction, inspiration, illumination only through human language and human communication . . . The decline in *Dharma* is so acute a tragedy, the intensity of affection that the Lord has for good men is so great, that He Himself comes.

"The Lord is Love itself. He comes in human form so that you can talk to Him, move with Him, serve Him, adore Him, and achieve Him, so that you can recognise your kinship with Him. I declare that I am in every one, in every being."

Naturally, there are certain similarities in all *avatars*, whether major or minor, the chief of which is all-embracing, universal self-less love. It is for this reason that Sathya Sai Baba declares that "the birthday of Jesus must be celebrated by all mankind, for such Masters belong to the whole human race." (And as Yogananda pointed out, "Jesus was born an Oriental to bring East and West together.")

Characteristically, it is at the *ashram* of Sathya Sai Baba that the Festival of Christmas is celebrated with pure devotion to the ideals, life and teaching of the one he always calls "the beloved Jesus".

Not only are plays beautifully produced and performed about the immortal Galilean but, on Christmas morning, before dawn breaks, a torchlit procession of singers winds its way through the streets and in the extensive *ashram* grounds (usually at Brindavan), culminating in the 'waving of the flame' of a thousand candles — a moving and impressive sight which sets the tone for the day.

As so often, Swami feeds huge numbers of the poor and needy. (At certain festivals he also gives a *sari* for each woman and a *dhoti* for each man, but whether he does this also at Christmas I am not certain.) Always there is an inspiring discourse on Jesus and his mission. It is a truly holy, and happy, day, but in the right way.

"It is not by festivity and fun that you can celebrate Christmas," Swami has said. "Celebrate it rather by resolving to put into practice at least one of the ideals he enunciated, or (by) endeavouring to reach at least one of the goals he placed before man.

"Let me call upon you to give up, in memory of this holy day, two evils from your mind: self-praise and scandalising of others. Adopt one habit as yours: the habit of loving service to the distressed. If you spend all your time and energy merely to pile up worldly comfort and sensual delight, you are disgracing this human existence.

"You consider this habitation of yours as your body; no, it is the Temple of God. God resides therein. Keep it clean, fresh and fragrant through developing compassion and love. Christ's birthday is when he is born in each person's heart. It is only on that day that one is entitled to celebrate Christmas."

Baba has spoken so much about Jesus, but it is possible here to give only some excerpts of his many discourses on this subject. For example: "It is the destiny of man to journey from human-ness to divinity, as he has already journeyed from animal-ness. In this pilgrimage he is bound to encounter various obstacles and trials.

"In order to smooth his path and help him overcome these troubles, sages, seers, realised souls, divine personalities and Incarnations of God appear among men and illumine the path. They move among the afflicted, the seekers who have lost their way or strayed into the desert, and lead them into confidence and courage.

"Certain personalities are born and live out their days for this very purpose. They assume birth for a cause. Such guides, exemplars, and leaders appear among all peoples and in all lands. They inspire faith in higher ideals, and teach, as if their voice is the voice of God, counselling from the heart.

"They teach that multiplicity is a delusion, that unity is the

65

reality. They instruct others that each one is really three people: the one he believes he is, the one others believe he is, and the one he really is.

"Jesus had no attachment to the self; he never paid heed to sorrow or pain, joy or gain; he had a heart that responded to the call of anguish, the cry of peace and brotherhood. He went about the land, preaching the lesson of love, and poured out his life as a libation in the sacrifice to humanity.

"Jesus could assert that his life was his message, for he lived among men as he advised them to live. Everyone has to start his spiritual pilgrimage, proclaiming he is a servant or messenger of God and trying to live up to that high and responsible status. This is the stage of *duality*.

"Then he progresses to discover the divine within himself, and realises that God is his precious heritage, which he must claim and utilise. That is the stage when one feels he is a son of God, of the same nature as God.

"Finally, he merges in God-consciousness. This is the essence of all religious disciplines and teachings.

"When Jesus proclaimed that he was the messenger of God he wanted to emphasize that everyone is a messenger of God and has to speak, act and think as one . . .   When progress is furthered, Jesus asserted, each one can recognise all as sons of God, children of God, brothers and sisters of oneself . . .   Finally, knowledge ripens into wisdom, and the goal is reached when one realises 'I and the Father are one'.

"Jesus has shown the way in clear terms. He announced very early in life that he had come to illumine the spiritual path. He had the Light within him. Jesus was the name he was known by; he was honoured by the populace as Christ, for they found in his thoughts, deeds and words no trace of ego. He had no envy, or hatred; he was full of love and charity, humility and sympathy . . .

"The name Jesus itself is not the original one. He was named ISA. In the Tibetan manuscript at the monastery where Isa spent some years the name is written as Issa. The name Isa means the Lord of all living beings." I-sa or Sa-i both mean '*Ishvara*, the Eternal Absolute'. (For those who do not know, *Sai* is pronounced as two syllables, not as is often assumed, like 'sigh'.)

The Tibetan manuscript referred to by Baba is the one discovered by the Russian, Nicolas Notovitch, who had travelled widely in Afghanistan, India and Tibet in the late 1880's. In his book, first published in 1890, he tells the fascinating story of his travels which culminated in an 'accident'. Thrown from a donkey on a steep mountain path, he was obliged to recover at a Buddhist monastery at Himis, in Leh, Ladak, then the western region of Tibet and now the northernmost part of India at an altitude of 14,500 feet.

During his travels Notovitch had heard tales of a saint from the West who had been revered by the Hindus and the Buddhists. While convalescing, he was shown a copy of a manuscript describing the life of this saint known as Issa, the Indian equivalent of the name Jesus.

The story in the manuscript not only paralleled much of what the Bible says about Jesus, but also included his life from the age of twelve to thirty as well, which, for some strange reason, has been completely omitted from the four New Testament stories (selected from many) that we have — although covered in the Aquarian Gospel.

Originally written in India and later brought to Tibet, the manuscript had been set down in the ancient Pali language shortly after merchant caravans brought the news of the crucifixion of Isa.

The original manuscript was located in the Mt. Marbour monastery near Lhasa, capital of Tibet, with copies at several of the country's major monasteries. The copy, in Tibetan, shown to Notovitch by the monks, was translated for him and included in his book, *The Unknown Life of Jesus Christ.*

In 1922, Swami Abhedananda, who had travelled much in Asia, Canada and America, went to Himis, saw the manuscripts and wrote about them in his Bengali book of Travels, *Kashmiri O Tibbetti.*

In 1925, the Russian artist, Nicholas Roerich, also visited the monastery and wrote about the manuscripts. And as recently as 1975, Professor Robert Ravicz, Ph.D., of the California State University at Northbridge, visited the monastery. He was told by the head abbot that the documents could be studied, but it would necessitate living in the monastery for a long time, and learning classical Tibetan.

The original manuscripts in the Pali language, in the Mt. Marbour monastery near Lhasa, have doubtless disappeared during the destruction of the monasteries by the Chinese following their invasion and annexation of Tibet in 1957. However, a friend who recently visited Himis Monastery was assured that these manuscripts have been safely hidden in caves.

Baba has verified and filled in these 'missing years'. At an age when it was customary in those days for a betrothal to be arranged, Jesus avoided this and set off with a merchant caravan travelling East. Baba says that he arrived in India at about sixteen, and that his mother, Mary, had sold household possessions to help him in his journey. Nevertheless, he was practically penniless during his travels, often having only one meal a day. He wore a simple *dhoti* of the type seen in India today.

Swami also said, in reply to questions posed by Janet Bock and reported in her book, *The Jesus Mystery*, that Jesus attained Christ-consciousness at the age of twenty-five in India, when he was able to proclaim, "I and my Father are one."

"After experiencing this identity with the Father," says Baba, "he returned to his own country." He returned to Palestine through Tibet, Afghanistan, Persia, and areas which are now embraced as part of the Soviet Union and, by the time he arrived in his native land, he was in his twenty-ninth year.

That was why his cousin, of almost the same age, had no idea who he was when he approached him on the banks of the Jordan. John only knew, psychically, that this was the One he had been waiting for, the One of whom he had said: "There is one coming, the latchet of whose sandals I am unworthy to unloose."

But let us leave the past and return to Brindavan. A friend of mine, who edits the magazine *Heralds of the New Age* in New Zealand, wrote of her personal experience as follows:

> For those far from home Christmas was one of unique delight when, bridging the years between Bethlehem and Brindavan, Sai Baba spoke of the beloved Jesus, his purpose and his life.
>
> Surrounded by a vast human family, Swami saw to it that joy and brotherhood prevailed among the many overseas devotees gathered at Brindavan that Christmas Day. Dinner (vegetarian, of course) was a festive time, set round a Christmas tree. Song filled the air that early morning. Devotees walked singing through the streets. As the familiar strains of 'Silent Night' flowed out, its harmony renewed again the wonder and peace of Christmas.

As Baba so often proclaims, "There is only one God, who is Omniscient; only one caste, the caste of Humanity; only one language, the language of the Heart; *only one religion, the Religion of Love.*"

68

# 9

# SAI BABA AND THE ANIMAL KINGDOM

*"God is in every creature, so how can you give such pain?"*

... Sri Sathya Sai Baba

These words, quoted above, should be written up over every factory-farm building, every experimental and research laboratory, every slaughterhouse — and indeed every home, for in our human conceit we look upon ourselves as superior beings with the right to abuse, exploit and torture the 'inferior' to suit our selfish ends.

The truth is that we <u>ought</u> to be superior beings, having, as it were, 'worked our way up' through the mineral, vegetable and animal kingdoms of nature and now, slowly and laboriously, are in the process of ridding ourselves of our animal tendencies and striving to take the next step towards the fully human, the super-human, and the divine.

Sathya Sai Baba says: "Birds and beasts need no divine incarn-ation to guide them, for they have no inclination to stray away from their *dharma* (right living, self-disciplinary rules.) Man alone forgets or ignores the goal of life."

Despite our greater mental, intellectual, emotional and imaginative capacities (or could it be because of them?) the violence, hatred, aggression and cruelty of so many humans is never found in the animal kingdom.

The devotion of domesticated animals to us, and that of wild animals and birds to each other, often puts us to shame. How many people die of a broken heart, as these are known to do? And with what selfless dedication animals and birds look after an afflicted or blind companion or mate . . . Even despised rats and mice have been seen leading a blind companion by a straw in their mouths.

I will always remember the Canada goose which carefully guided his blind mate to a safe winter harbour near San Francisco. That gander never ceased to feed and care for its mate's every need, even disobeying the strong migratory instinct to fly north for the summer, for he would not abandon her. The pair became the wonder of the townspeople — until some heartless humans decided to have that loyal and loving gander for a barbecue supper . . .

The blind goose, bereft, was taken into care, but it is doubtful that she lived, for wild geese and swans pine to death when some hooligan human kills their mate.

When talking to his young students Baba said, "I derive much *ananda* (bliss) watching 'wild animals' in their own habitat. Their movements, their relations with others of their own kind, their free uninhibited lives are very attractive to behold.

"They do not grieve, lamenting their misfortune, comparing their fate with that of other denizens of the forest. They do not clamour for fame. They do not plan and prepare to earn positions of power and authority over other animals. They are not eager to accumulate possessions that are superfluous.

"When we consider these traits we are led to conclude that they are leading lives of a higher grade than men. Men have the extra qualifications of education; they have the moral sense, and the capacity to judge and discriminate. But yet they are caught in the coils of greed. Greed is the seedbed of grief."

And in a letter written from a game park he visited in East Africa in 1968, Swami wrote: "We spent the night in the wooden houses over the trees. In that area were very big lions, cheetahs, zebras, bison, giraffes; and many other kinds of wild animals were freely moving in thousands. The way in which these various animals were moving about with mutual co-operation and adjustability appears to suggest that they are better than human beings in the present day world, where humanism and human-ness are altogether dying out.

"The scenes where these wild animals were moving together, eating together, drinking together, and licking each other with friendly feelings, appears to me to teach a lesson even to human beings. <u>In all of them godliness was clearly visible.</u>"

Always, Baba urges us to remember we are human beings. "Each of you has struggled upward from the stone to plant, from plant to animal, from animal to man. Do not slide back into the beast. Rise higher to divinity, shining with the new effulgence of love."

Yet it would seem that human beings have slid back, not into beasts, but into becoming devils incarnate where the use and abuse of the animal kingdom is concerned. What is licensed, and sponsored, in the name of 'research' — especially 'behavioural research' involving years of mental anguish (so often merely to satisfy, it seems, some sadistic curiosity the results of which benefit no one, or are known to any intelligent child) — would land the ordinary citizen in gaol for a long time.

But it is not my purpose here to detail the sickening cruelty perpetrated on hundreds of millions of highly intelligent and sensitive creatures, whether in the cause of medicine, or psychology, industry and commerce, cosmetics, pesticides, accident research, chemical and bacteriological warfare, defence, aerospace programmes, nuclear and laser research, war wounds, and so on. The catalogue is too long.

How astonished and horrified human beings would be if those above us in the spiritual hierarchy, the great masters, teachers, the Christed ones, instead of extending loving aid in answer to our pleas for help, used and abused us in some cruel sport or experiment of their own devising! To whom and what could one aspire? To what aspect of divinity, with or without form, would one turn for comfort, guidance, understanding, advancement and, above all, love? Yet Man is the Christ among animals . . .

The Tibetan master, Dwhal Khul, has told us: "Man is the initiating factor here, and to man is committed the task of leading the animal kingdom towards liberation — a liberation into the fourth kingdom, for that is the sphere of its next activity." As Baba has said: "All life may aspire to human birth."

Baba has also confirmed that man is incurring "very bad *karma*" for his immoral, unethical and unspiritual treatment of the kingdom just below us on the evolutionary ladder. <u>Of what use to torture the foot in an attempt to benefit the hand?</u> All life is one, indivisible, though in diverse forms. "The Universe is the body of God. All creation is the vesture of God," says Baba. "Love God, and you see God in every creature."

To those who, while considering themselves spiritually-minded, sometimes put forward the fallacious viewpoint that animals were placed on earth for man's use (meaning abuse, and to eat), Baba states quite categorically: "Animals did not come for the purpose of supplying food for human beings. They came to work out their own lives in the world. When a human being is dead the foxes and other animals may eat, but we have not come to provide food for those that eat the dead body; we have not come for that purpose. Similarly, man eats the animal, but the animal has not come to provide man with food. But we have taken to eating meat as a habit." (When Baba says "we" he refers, of course, to human beings in general, for even as a small child he would not remain in a house where flesh was cooked.)

Incidentally, it is estimated that in one year alone Britain imported groundnut protein from India to the equivalent of a year's ration for 13,000,000 children – and all to feed tormented factory-farm animals which never so much as see the daylight until they are carted off, in fear, to be slaughtered.

By feeding this valuable food to a vast animal population a loss in protein value in excess of 80% is incurred in the end product. This same food, either in its original form or by simple processing for direct human consumption entails a loss of only 10 to 15 per cent. Without this mania for consuming the corpses of countless millions of our gentle, vegetarian 'younger brothers' there would be enough food for all of us – and a great deal of disease would be eliminated.

Because his life is his message, Sai Baba's every action, however small, sets an example and teaches us something. His love, consideration and care for animals is revealed continuously in small, unobtrusive ways, as well as in larger enterprises and in all his teaching that there is only ONE LIFE – that the One became the Many . . .

As a simple example, Professor Kasturi says that years ago Baba took a small party for a few days up to Horsley Hills, 3,800 feet above sea level. Twice a day he led them to some beauty spot for spiritual teaching. Food had to be carried up from the small hamlet below, and a buffalo at the bungalow helped to transport water from a well in skin bags slung across its back.

When the day came to leave, Baba proposed they walk down together. In fact, says Kasturi, he suggested they should see who could run down the fastest, Baba being a good athlete when young, and never at any time assuming the 'dignified' pose of so many 'holy men'! Then he said, "Wait, I will be back in a minute," and disappeared.

Being curious, they quietly followed him – and found him taking leave of the buffalo. He was talking to it, and patting it affectionately, saying, "You have done me good service, *Bangaru* . . . " (a coveted term of great affection, meaning golden one). No one else, of course, had given a thought to the patient, willing animal. Only Baba.

The following incident, apart from being a touching one, demonstrates the close relationship Baba has with animals, and his knowledge of every soul, human or other.

In the village of Bikkatti in the Nilgiri Hills lived a dog called Kuttan, meaning 'the lame one'. I quote Kasturi's words: "He was a very old, loving dog, yet alert where strangers were concerned. Baba, on visiting the village in 1962, walked down the carpets laid out for him. Kuttan strained at the leash by which he was held lest he bounce on Baba. But Baba stopped and patted him, and asked that he be let loose, saying, '*Bangaru*, leave him alone – he is a pure *atma* (soul).'

"So Kuttan followed Baba up the dais, sat and listened with him to the *bhajan* singing, and later followed him into the kitchen where Baba, after blessing the food, asked that Kuttan be fed first.

"When the dog finished his meal, he walked up the decorated dais and stood beside Baba's chair, watching the long lines of villagers having their food. After a while Kuttan placed his head upon Baba's footstool and, within a few minutes, breathed his last.

"Everyone felt he was a pure soul; and he was buried near the dais, in a shroud of flowers." How wonderful that Baba gave this loving, lame old dog, that he knew to be 'a pure soul', such a blissful passing into the next sphere of life!

There may be some who are unsure whether individualised animals (and birds) retain their personality and individuality after physical death. Baba leaves us in no doubt, as the following story demonstrates. It also demonstrates his love, care and concern for the individual, whether human or animal, and also his omnipresence whenever there is a cry from the heart.

My friend Jean, whom we first met at the Sathya Sai Centre in Wellingborough, Northamptonshire, wrote down at my request the details of her experience. I quote her words:

"It was a little over two years ago and we had recently lost our two pet dogs within a short time. One was aged fifteen, the other twelve. We decided to give an unwanted dog a home as we greatly missed our two pets. On inquiry at a local dogs' home we were given a list of available dogs. As an afterthought we were told, 'Then there's poor Emma . . . ' I asked if 'poor Emma' was also a dog, and was told she was.

"As soon as we saw Emma I knew she was special. Her hindquarters were very weak. She seemed terrified to move. We were told she had been very badly treated by her previous owner. She could not eat, and hardly lapped up milk – but we took her home with us.

"In due time she became a beautiful dog, physically. Mentally, however, the scars remained. If we had to leave her in the house she went hysterical, and would tear furniture, carpets, and even doors to pieces. Loud noises terrified her.

"We did everything possible for her and gave her all the love we could. But it seemed to no avail. She was so psychologically damaged that two years later we had to have her put to sleep.

"We were heartbroken. That night I mentally called Sai Baba and asked him to let us know in some way if her tormented mind was healed. I fell asleep.

"Sometime later I became aware of a feeling like electricity flowing in the room. I then saw Sai Baba standing there with my dog by his side. He spoke softly to her and she ran to me, then back to his side. He spoke to her again, and this time she sat in front of me and I stroked her.

"I gazed into her eyes and she looked completely calm. After stroking her I noted all the previous nervousness seemed to have disappeared. Sai Baba just smiled. Then he and the dog disappeared."

Jean adds: "When I had tried to mentally contact Baba before, he had always replied. I am at first awoken by a feeling like waves of mild electricity flooding the room. Also he has provided the complete answer to whatever problem I am asking about. From these experiences, I became convinced of his omnipresence and his great compassion."

Compassion indeed, not only for this tormented dog, whose mind had been healed after leaving her physical body, but also for Jean who had first shown true compassion in taking 'poor Emma' to her heart. But the scars from her previous ill-treatment had proved too deep to be eradicated in this life.

In this case, Baba brought the dog in a completely materialised form so that Jean was able to stroke it and gaze into its eyes. I have had such ample proof, myself, that so many animals of various descriptions are alive in the world of spirit; and how many times, too, have owners of dogs, even cats (and indeed horses), been saved from accident or fire by being roused or protected by animals which had passed from this life some time previously.

Baba has had no less than fourteen pet dogs over the years, always in pairs. Jack and Jill were the first. Baba says they used to fast every Thursday (a sacred day) as if by some holy compulsion. And they could never be induced to eat flesh.

Jack slept at the head of Baba's bed and Jill at the foot. After three years of being in his presence Jack's 'voluntary work' of keeping urchins away from cars which had to be parked some distance from the Nilayam, led to his undoing. Unaware that he was lying underneath the car, the occupants drove off, nearly killing him.

He mustered enough strength, said Baba, to drag himself back to the Nilayam, and with a final effort pulled himself onto Baba's lap. With his eyes glued on Baba's face and his tail shaking feebly with joy, he concluded his earthly life.

Jill could not live without him, and followed him in a few weeks. Both bodies are buried in the quadrangle of the *ashram*, and a structure for growing a holy plant was erected over their mortal remains.

There followed Pomeranians, Chitty and Bitty, and Lilly and Billy. Then came cocker spaniels, Minnie and Mickie, and Honey and Goldie. And in due course there were the Alsatians, Rover and Rita, and Tommy and Henry.

These animals received the tenderness and love of Baba in great measure, as did a horse he once owned – and stags, deer, rabbits, peacocks, camels and all kinds of birds. There is also a huge walk-in aviary. I have already mentioned in an earlier chapter that we saw many animals and birds in Swami's woodland garden at Brindavan. But his 'animal orphanage', where animals of all kinds, large and small, live in free, natural conditions, is in the forest close to Puttaparthi.

Kasturi gives an account of a most fascinating, and typical, event which occurred when Baba was fourteen. A young Englishman, a sub-divisional officer, was being driven along in a Jeep through the forest on the other side of the wide River Chitravati. When they reached a point exactly opposite the village of Puttaparthi the Jeep suddenly stopped, and nothing would make it go.

Finally the driver said, "There is a wonder boy in Puttaparthi who materialises holy ash just by waving his hand in the air, and it will cure anything, even the Jeep!" As he was completely stranded the Englishman agreed to let the driver go to the village, while he remained in the vehicle.

Eventually the driver found the boy and begged for some holy ash, but Baba said, "No. I am coming myself to the Jeep," and walked across the river, which was mostly sand, with the driver.

Glancing into the back of the Jeep, Baba saw the body of a tiger which the Englishman had shot just two hours previously. Addressing the Englishman in a tone of authority, the young Baba told him:

"I stopped the Jeep at this place – for this is the mother of three two-week-old cubs who at this very moment are wailing and crying out for her. GO BACK! Recover those cubs and give them to some zoo where they will be looked after. And do not again shoot wild beasts, for they have not injured you. Why do you go in search of them, surrounding and laying traps to catch them? Shoot them instead with your superior weapons, such as your camera. That won't maim or kill them."

The Englishman was so deeply impressed by this young boy that he immediately obeyed, told his driver to turn round (for, of course, there was nothing wrong with the Jee,), went back and rescued the cubs which he put into proper care, and never again shot an animal except with his camera, which he actually found more adventurous.

All this became known when one day, some time later, this Englishman turned up in Puttaparthi, looking for young Baba. His conscience had been so touched that when the tiger skin came back from the taxidermist he found himself unable to live with it. He had brought it, and laid it at Baba's feet as a gesture to prove his conversion.

This occurred at a time when a larger 'temple' was under construction for the growing numbers of people who flocked to Baba, and there was one woman present with a photographer. She begged Baba to sit on the skin in meditation pose, and gave him a rosary to hold. Baba good-naturedly obliged her, though he says he had never held a rosary or ever sat in meditation – then or since. This actual photograph is reproduced in Dr Sandweiss's book, *Sai Baba, the Holy Man and the Psychiatrist.* And this is why Baba has a tiger skin in his possession, which has puzzled some people.

(Incidentally, there is now no necessity whatever for women to wear the so cruelly obtained furs of animals when simulated furs of all kinds are so excellent and attractive – and untainted by blood and suffering. It is to be hoped that no sincere devotee of Sathya Sai Baba would do so, but substitute compassion in place of vanity.)

I have wondered if the episode of the orphaned tiger cubs was one of the reasons which later prompted Swami's animal orphanage, especially as Kasturi tells us that his beloved elephant, Sai Gita, was only eleven days old when she came to him! I have a charming photograph of Swami playing with her when she was small.

The relationship between Swami and this now large elephant who adores him is a very special one. When he leaves Puttaparthi great tears roll down her trunk. People say: "Baba must have gone. Look at Sai Gita." But if he is to be at Brindavan for any time, Sai Gita is brought to be near him.

Baba says he can call her from a distance of five miles, and she will immediately come to him in a straight line. When he feeds her with a basket of fruit she places a garland over him with her trunk, goes down on one knee, and always, it seems to me, she likes to place the tip of her trunk on her Lord's feet.

Richly caparisoned, she proudly takes part in festivals. And when Swami has been away she becomes aware of his presence again long before she sees him, and trumpets loudly. Baba has to calm her down, fondling her great trunk and telling her, "That's enough, Gita. That's enough."

In the compound at Brindavan many trees were removed because, it is said, the monkeys insisted on jumping on to Baba's shoulders when he came out to give *darshan* to the people. Now, the monkeys keep to his garden.

I cannot resist including in this chapter the remarkable incident connected with a cat which lived in Assam, North-Eastern India, for it is a wonderful demonstration of Baba's omnipresence.

It occurred on November 24th 1972 when a party of some ninety pilgrims had made the long journey from Assam to Putta-parthi for the birthday celebrations. As Baba walked among them, giving out packets of *vibhuti* to each one, he suddenly turned back to a young woman he had already passed, and threw her two more packets, saying, "These are for the cat."

Who was this lucky cat? Naturally, everyone wanted to know what lay behind this unexpected gesture. The story the young woman, Lakhi, told was an astonishing one. Apparently she had rescued a young stray cat hiding in a drain one wet night, took it home, and called it Minkie. But her elder sister, a nurse in the hospital, did not at all appreciate Lakhi making a pet of this cat. The last straw came when, while preparing dinner for some guests, Minkie succumbed to temptation and ran off with a bit of fish.

This resulted in the poor creature being taken by the scruff of the neck and being beaten with a long stick. As it yelled in pain, however, every picture of Baba in the house (and there were sixteen of them) swayed violently, and several fell down with a loud crash.

Thinking it was an earthquake, the guests ran out into the court-yard. But the two women realised that only Baba's pictures had fallen – no others. "Baba is angry with us," they cried, "stop!"

Both of them were now in tears as Lakhi lifted Minkie onto the table. The poor cat began to shake herself to ease the pain and, as she did so, puffs of fragrant *vibhuti* emerged from her fur and fell thickly on the table! The guests had come in again and they, too, witnessed this. The fragrance which filled the room announced Baba's presence – or omnipresence.

More than six months had passed since this had happened in Gauhati, Assam – but Baba remembered as he passed Lakhi in that large crowd, and turned back to give her extra *vibhuti* "for the cat".

The implications of this story are difficult for most people to grasp or come to terms with. Omnipresence is one of the divine attributes. Because Baba's human form is in India we tend to think of him as being in India. But this is an illusion.

Neither is he mind reading when he tells one of events in one's life, or of dreams one has had, or one's innermost thoughts, or, indeed, even of conversations one has had in one's own home thousands of miles away.

He explains it like this: "It is not that I first enter your mind, probe it, then come out and tell you. Actually, I am always residing in your mind and so I am fully aware of all that goes on therein at all times. There is nothing hidden from me."

I leave readers to ponder on this. The incident of the cat is merely one of thousands of examples of Baba's omnipresence.

Of course, being very human, one is tempted to wish that Baba would make more than pictures fall in some of the revolting experimental institutions throughout the world. But change cannot be brought about in this way, as well-meaning saboteurs have found when they attack some laboratory. (The laboratory wherein a monkey had been made pregnant with human sperm was broken into, and the pregnant monkey died. But, doubtless, this horrible experiment will be made again.)

Some unthinking people say: why does not Baba do something about the starving millions in the world, or about this, or about that? But who caused these ills? Humanity. Alleviating the effects cannot cure the cause of human misery and the possibility of self-destruction on a world scale.

To remedy the consequences of man's wrong-doing overnight, as it were, would merely mean that the wrongs would start again the next morning. It is in the heart of humanity that change must come. And this is part of the *Avatar*'s mission.

The former Prime Minister of India, Shri Morarji Desai (who has been to Prasanthi Nilayam and shared the platform with Sai Baba) banned the exportation of monkeys to foreign laboratories, thus saving at least 20,000 of these near-human creatures a year — much to the anger of experimentalists in the United States who have tried every devious means of getting this decision reversed. (Also, no doubt, the "middle men", for the price charged for a monkey when it finally reaches its miserable destination is 200 times more than the fellow gets for trapping it in the jungle.)

Ironically, it was the devious behaviour of the U.S. Primate Steering Committee in falsely denying that monkeys were used by the military for neutron bomb and radiation experiments which clinched the ban, when Indians finally learned details of these horrible experiments. The International Primate Protection League reported:

"Amidst all the sordid intriguing of petty men, one figure stands out . . . Shri Morarji Desai, a man of principle, did what he thought was right . . . Invincible and incorruptible, he stood by his decision, confounding and exasperating those seeking to deviate him from his principles." (Bangladesh has followed suit.)

Mr Desai also placed a ban on the extremely cruel export of frogs' legs, but, alas, it has been impossible to implement the ban while restaurants in Europe and the United States insist on catering for the depraved appetites of overfed gourmets. Thus, yearly 5,000 tons of live frogs have their legs cut off just below the waist. Unfortunately, this does not kill them, but merely leaves them helpless, to die slowly. As 5,000 tons of frogs would normally consume 450,000 tons of food in the year − mainly undesirable insects and pests − insect infested crops then have to be sprayed, at much cost, with noxious and polluting insecticides which further upset the balance of nature.

I only mention this revolting trade as but one small example of how human beings create their own ills, and that of the planet, by wrong thought, wrong action and, above all, by lack of LOVE.

One must, however, pay tribute to dedicated organisations in the uphill struggle for animal rights. Each one of us can help, even in small ways, often by just keeping our eyes open. Let me give you one very small example.

A Canadian magazine asked to review my books and sent a copy of their publication. In it I noticed an article about horse meat accompanied by a photograph which does not bear describing. I sent the article to the World Society for the Protection of Animals. Their excellent field officers discovered the photograph did not emanate from Canada and traced it to a certain abattoir in Toulouse, France, which in 1978 slaughtered 148,000 horses, most of these wretched animals having travelled from Poland, or been shipped from the U.S.S.R. The appropriate action regarding this slaughter-house is now being taken and I am "thanked" for raising the matter. It is I who give thanks. My small part took just five minutes and a postage stamp.

Now I deplore people who visit a place or country for a few weeks and then imagine they know all about it. But I am entitled to give my personal impressions while in Bangalore.

I was struck very forcibly by the quietness and total lack of apprehension in all the various animals to be seen everywhere, despite the alarming, constantly hooting traffic. Placid donkeys grazed on sidewalks or, having eaten, stood head to tail dozing, either awaiting collection or until deciding to return home.

Unhaltered, untethered ponies even grazed on the sparse grass between a dual carriageway. I watched one pony walking sedately along the pavement. When it came to a garden gate it pushed it open and walked up the garden path. In poorer quarters, of an evening, cows lay outside their owner's door, quietly chewing the cud or eating a bundle of hay. Outside a row of shops four cows were being milked on the pavement — which would have been a strange sight outside Woolworth's in Tunbridge Wells. A couple of beggars, sitting on the path one night, were sharing their meagre fare with a street dog.

But what struck me most of all was that never once, during our stay, did I ever see a stick used on any draught animal, or hear so much as a harsh word or a raised voice — in stark contrast to the rough behaviour in our own markets.

When we watched water buffalo, cows or white oxen being washed in one of the lakes in Bangalore, each animal, when finished, walked home by itself, irrespective of passing cars. The sense of peace and communal living between humans and animals seemed very marked, and this also applied to the children who appeared to accept animals as part of daily life (and not as objects to tease or torment as, alas, in some East European countries).

In our hotel we were always surrounded by a group of dining room staff whenever we sat down for a coffee. Had we seen Baba? was the main question. But they were amazed that we, Westerners, were vegetarians. In an effort to offset the more unsavoury influence creeping in from the West, I explained that the most progressive people in the West were giving up eating meat because they had come to realise it was wrong to kill and eat our fellow creatures, and it was also much more healthy and prevented many diseases.

They were all ears for our mini-discourses, the more educated translating for those who did not understand English. Doubtless, other people probably thought we were a strange couple!

I often feel 'homesick' for the sight of all those noble-faced, sloe-eyed white oxen with their tall horns, painted in gay colours with flowers on top. We can all learn from each other. But our main task on behalf of the animal kingdom, which Baba loves so much, is to remember always his words: "Love God and you see God in every creature."

# 10

# THE PRACTICE OF ONENESS

*"Man's inhumanity to man expresses itself in the form of natural catastrophies, like earthquakes."*

... Sri Sathya Sai Baba

These words of Baba, quoted above, are all the more significant when coupled with his words to us in one of our interviews when we asked him about the planet.

"There will be physical repercussions due to man's growing selfishness. Minor adjustments to the planet, and a certain clear out."

And: "The world is the body of God. There is a cancer in the body and it must be removed."

Indeed it must. The picture appears to be overwhelming and awe inspiring when looked at as a whole. But we have to remember that however large the canvas of the total picture, it is made up of millions of individual brush marks. If even a reasonable percentage of the darker brush marks become transformed into light the entire picture would present quite a different appearance.

We are all cells in the body of God. But do we ever stop to think, or feel this oneness and what it really implies in our day to day life? Aren't we apt to accept it (if indeed we do accept it), along with our acceptance of the Fatherhood of God and the Brotherhood of Man, as a fine principle that we "believe in" but which changes our behaviour or affects our living, thinking and outlook scarcely at all?

How often, for example, do we think kindly of the myriad little lives for which we are responsible within our own bodies? This may seem a strange thought at first, but we are "the imperfect gods" in whom they live and move and have their being. But has this ever occurred to us?

These little lives, with their own forms of consciousness, are working incessantly, for every second of their life cycle — growing, reproducing, fulfilling their appointed tasks, attacking and repelling foreign or unwelcome visitors, rushing to the scene of any injury or accident to repair the damage as quickly as possible, so often struggling in adverse conditions against pollution, incorrect feeding, even poisoning, and every kind of abuse of their environment as it reacts to our undesirable emotions, whether of fear, hatred, envy, anger, anxiety, or unrestful imbalance.

No wonder they sometimes become weakened and overcome by some virulent invader. Or they become anti-social rebels against prevailing conditions; go on strike, or organise greedy and selfishly motivated groups at the expense of the community as a whole.

When we constantly and thoughtlessly abuse all the little lives whose consciousness is attuned to doing their very best against all odds, is it not adding insult to injury when we become angered by the malfunctioning of our body?

Man is the macrocosm of this microcosm composed of the mineral, plant and animal kingdoms from which he draws his roots. Each kingdom advances the consciousness aspect to a greater stage of perfection, and demonstrates a larger sensitivity and responsiveness. Each manifests a fuller revelation of the hidden and inner glory. Man is the link between the three lower kingdoms and the three higher ones pertaining to the soul life, which is the One Life.

It is understandable, then, that the human kingdom, being the fourth and middle one of seven, is perpetually on a metaphysical see-saw, as it were, torn between form and spirit, body and soul. The less evolved human identifies almost exclusively with the body, while the more evolved human struggles to identify with and react to soul consciousness and contact — to become what he inherently is, that is to say, divine.

Any seeker or aspirant, therefore, however humbly treading the spiritual path, is involved in the responsibility of raising and helping the lower, the sub-human, kingdoms on their upward path. And this includes the myriad living microscopic beings of which our bodily vehicles are composed.

Few people really believe in the power of thought, yet thoughts possess an energy little dreamed of by the unaware, the unthinking, or the materially orientated. Dr Frank Baranowski pointed out to the students of the Sri Sathya Sai Arts, Science and Commerce College that the electrical energy released by one burst of anger is sufficient to light a two-cell flash bulb for three months. This remark by a scientist should force us to reflect.

Thought can and does affect what we call matter. (It must never be forgotten that matter is materialised spirit – or God.) Negatively utilised, as in black magic, or as demonstrated recently in Russia, it can stop the heartbeat of an animal or kill a bird in flight. Or, as demonstrated by Dr Remy Chauvin of the University of Strasbourg, it can accelerate or slow down the radioactive disintegration of a uranium isotope.

Similarly, we all have the potential to heal our bodies, if we are sufficiently attuned to the reality of Oneness. It is extraordinary what can be achieved by projecting loving, encouraging thoughts to any part of our bodies which needs help in conquering some adverse condition. Even cancer has been 'self-healed' in this way, without outside treatment. By infusing the living cells working on our behalf with increased energy and light, they 'take heart', and respond to what is, in the final analysis, an outpouring of love.

The key word is, of course, LOVE. "If you develop love," reiterates Baba, "you do not have to develop anything else." It is as simple as that, for God IS Love. "Love God," said the Nazarene, "and your neighbour as yourself."

Yet how difficult we find it to put this simple truth into practice! "Man is ill; but he is resorting to remedies that cannot cure," says Baba. "People admire the phenomenal advance of science. But the advance has been from fear to greater fear, from destruction to more destruction.

"In prehistoric times men killed each other using bows and arrows; now they kill entire populations with the help of atom bombs; this is praised as remarkable advance!

"The scientist cannot stop the rise of greed and hate in the human heart; he can only forge the weapons they require and improve their lethal efficiency. Man lives in daily dread of extinction as a result of the discoveries of science; for, any moment, the storm of hate may rain bombs on their homes. Science has deprived man of self-confidence. He is not sure of even himself. He is afraid of himself for, at the slightest provocation, he is transformed into a wild and vicious beast."

It is unfortunate that in describing the degraded behaviour of humans it is customary to liken them to beasts, or some particular animal. While, on the one hand, animals can develop truly selfless devotion and amazing intelligence and reasoning powers when encouraged by a loving relationship with humans, no animal, whether wild or domestic, deviates from its *dharma*, as Baba has pointed out, or decimates its own species. Indeed, one understands the sentiments expressed by Michael Bentine when he was asked in a television interview what he was most afraid of. He replied, "The depths to which human beings can sink."

It is not animals that we fear in this day and age. It is against humans that we lock and bolt our doors and windows, and fear to walk the streets at night in case of attack. In fact our best protection from humans is an animal — the dog!

When we see on our television screens fanatical mobs screaming and clamouring for blood, massacring their fellow creatures and daubing their victims' blood on walls and cars with their hands (incited by "religious" leaders!) it is indeed a misnomer to refer to them as "animals".

Sathya Sai Baba says: "By mere human form one cannot be called a human being. It is only when that human form has got the divine qualities that derive from the fact that they are created by God that he will be entitled to be called a human being."

Man's inhumanity to his own species, through his crass inability either to understand or to practise Oneness, overflows not only in his inhumanity to the animal kingdom but towards the plant and mineral kingdoms as well. As a highly evolved Red Indian chief said quite recently, "Wherever man goes the Earth hurts."

Not content with injecting high-powered explosives into the bellies of whales (what are left of these sensitive and intelligent animals), man detonates hydrogen bombs in the belly of the earth. He causes imbalance and huge empty caverns by draining its 'black blood', pollutes the air and the seas, poisons the soil, destroys animal and bird life, not to mention our greatest benefactor, the worm. Man maltreats and denudes the plant kingdom to such an extent that it is said that the vast Amazon Valley will become a desert in time, denying us vital oxygen.

Baba say: "Nature is God's vesture. The Universe is the 'university' for man. Man should treat nature with reverence. He has no right to talk of conquering nature or exploiting the force of nature. He must proceed to visualise in nature its God."

There is nothing wrong with science. The word merely means knowledge. It is the uses to which science is put that is so often indefensible. As the great Mahatma Gandhi said, "One of the things that will destroy us is science without humanity."

Similarly, there are things that we ought not to know! It often occurs to me that those who brought eventual catastrophe to lantis are reincarnated today, indulging in a blacker art involving, for example, the transplanting of the living brains of monkeys into the heads of dogs — or deliberately breeding a variety of loathsome and lethal diseases to let loose on mankind, in the name of "Defence". How true is the old saying, "Whom the gods destroy they first make mad."

None of these obscenities would be possible had we, as human beings, any real awareness or conception of Oneness, and the inter-relationship of ALL THAT IS — that is, God, the One in Whom we live and move and have our being.

Science and scientists will ever remain helpless in the face of the One Reality — the soul. And as Sai Baba says, nothing exists, in whatever form, which is not ensouled.

Neither can science ever produce a formula, mathematical equasion or diagnosis to explain the experience of beauty, or the magic of a piece of music, or bliss, or inspiration, and certainly not of love. Yet one comes across ludicrous attempts to do so by scientific minds which seem incapable of understanding the obvious. The following incident is a small example.

In Russia a hedgehog was found with a broken leg on a country road by a woman doctor. The good woman took it home, set the leg, and cared for the little animal till it was fit, and then gave it to her grand-daughter who lived 48 miles away. However, Topa (as they had named the hedgehog) refused to eat and became so sluggish and miserable that the girl reported that she had released it in a forest.

Two months later, Dr Ushakova found Topa sitting on her door-step. This little hedgehog had walked 48 miles to return to the person who had saved it and cared for it, and who has now let it stay. But what happens? Soviet veterinary scientists are now busily engaged in trying to discover more about the 'homing instincts' of hedgehogs. Irrespective of the fact that the animal was not returning to its natural habitat. The answer is to be found in one word: LOVE.

It will ever remain a mystery to scientists how a much loved dog which got inadvertently lost in the Arizona desert managed to walk 2,000 miles over the most fearful terrain, including the Grand Canyon. Enduring intense heat and thirst, and later extreme cold in the snowy mountain ranges, this dog did not give up till it flopped down, exhausted, emaciated and bleeding, beside his master's car 2,000 miles to the north. No wonder we speak of dogged determination!

85

In this age of the scientific "explosion" and our intense desire to tabulate the most superficial aspects of phenomena — the physical — have we not sacrificed the subtle areas of consciousness and perception since the 18th century when reason began to be worshipped in the West?

If ours is the most cerebral age in history, why is it also the most destructive? Why, in this century, have we defiled and polluted the earth and its atmosphere and decimated animal life more quickly than in all the preceding millennia of man's existence? Does reason in isolation plunge us deeper and deeper into unreason?

Yet it may well be that an understanding of sub-human intelligence will become a factor in helping us to save ourselves from ourselves and to become truly human. Although plant intelligence has been officially recognised, plants are organically far from us and therefore less embarrassing than the recognition of animal intelligence. And I repeat . . . embarrassing.

Gandhi said, "The appeal of the lower order of creation is all the more forceful because it is speechless." (Though Baba has said that he understands the languages of animals, adding that it is "often far sweeter than that of humans.")

But it is embarrassingly forceful now that it has been proved and demonstrated that although animals cannot speak with the tongue (except instances of imitation), many domestic ones not only listen to and understand the language of their owners (as children do), but can also learn, with the aid of an abacus (the counting frame children have) and a blackboard, to do addition, division, subtraction and other more complicated mathematical problems more quickly than I ever could! This is not telepathy, for often the answer has not been worked out by the teacher.

Of course dog owners well know that many words have to be spelt out rather than spoken, like w-a-l-k or d-i-n-n-e-r for example, if they don't want their dog to react immediately. But in the 102 or thereabouts known cases of animals (horses, ponies, dogs, and at least two cats) which have been taught the alphabet and the foot, or paw, tapping system of communication by their owners, it has been proved that they think, reflect, feel, and have opinions about day to day matters, and a wide variety of subjects both ethical and even philosophical — even about death.

If this is doubted, the remarkable book, *The Talking Dogs*, by Maurice Rowdon (Macmillan, 1978) will remove that doubt to a considerable extent. The author stayed for some time with Frau Heilmaier, her dog-school teacher Dorothy Meyer, the Saluki dog Belam and the poodle Elke II, in Bavaria. He states: "What I witnessed was to change my life . . . The discovery that in many respects animals have a moral integrity, truthfulness, and compassion superior to our own was an even greater shock."

Often, quite apart from their school lessons, the dogs would interrupt the humans' conversation by coming up and sitting in the tapping position when they wished to say something. Equally, when a subject was being discussed, the humans would say, "Let's ask Belam or Elke what they think about it." The dogs would respond — and sometimes teach the humans an uncomfortable lesson!

Belam's 'wife', Keesha, never wished to learn. But Belam's puppies by her were keen to learn tapping at three months old. Yet it was Belam, the proud father, who gave advice and instructions as to which of his children was the most advanced in intelligence, which should start first, and knew them all by name and character — for animals vary as much as humans.

Incidentally, anyone who has experienced astral projections will know that when meeting and talking to animals in the out-of-the-body state one hears their spoken words although their mouths do not move. This is, of course, communication by telepathy, but the thoughts behind the words are being transmitted from the animal's consciousness.

If certain animals, then, can learn the alphabet as quickly (and even more quickly) than children can, and also learn the tapping code for the letters — though the results are quite often phonetic spelling, as with children — and moreover when the answers to questions are thought out and sometimes totally unexpected, animal intelligence of a high order is demonstrated as a fact. And this is to many people an embarrassing fact.

In the past I have often criticised Dr Christian Barnard, the pioneer heart-swop surgeon, for transplanting hundreds of living dogs' heads on to the necks of other dogs, in the spiritually unacceptable cause of enabling a few humans to stay a few days or weeks, or even months or a year or so, longer on this planet. Now at last it would appear that Dr Barnard is seeing a glimmer of light, for quite recently he wrote:

"Last year a Dutch animal breeding centre sent me two chimpanzees as a gift. I killed one and cut its heart out. The other wept bitterly and was inconsolable. I vowed never again to experiment with such sensitive creatures, and the memory of that weeping chimp has remained with me." (The hospital staff were haunted for days by the heartbroken chimp's crying.)

But what creature is not sensitive? I have never forgotten two earwigs which my young son and I rescued from drowning a few years ago. We laid them on a table and thought they were dead, but soon one of them recovered. The first thing it did was to go to the other one and, with its feelers, it kept on stroking its head and fussing round it in obvious distress and concern. Finally, the second one showed signs of life. When fully recovered they went off together.

Does nuclear age man, if he is not to destroy himself, or continue to massacre his fellows, have to learn from a humble insect? There is only one way to stop or curb the rot. That is by teaching, spreading, and, above all, practising LOVE which is the recognition of ONENESS.

If it be thought that I have laboured the kinship of the human and animal kingdoms it is because it is vital to our progress and our survival that we recognise that the basis of life is inter-relationship on all levels, in all kingdoms. And these include the subtle kingdoms of the ethers, the angels of the air and water, the nature spirits and *devas* on whose co-operation we depend, and whose alienation, by our own actions, can create havoc and catastrophe.

We reap the fruit of our actions. Some words of Baba's are quoted at the beginning of this chapter, and I will repeat them here: "Man's inhumanity to man (and all kingdoms) expresses itself in the form of natural catastrophes, like earthquakes." And, "God does not decree these calamities (such as earthquakes, floods, droughts, famine, epidemics) but man invites them by way of retribution for his own evil deeds . . . "

". . . So, finally, if the *Avatar* brings the calamities mentioned by you to an immediate end, which I can, and do when there is a great need, the whole drama of creation with its *karmic* law will collapse. Remember these calamities occur not because of what God has made of man, but really because of what man has made of man. Therefore man has to be UNMADE and REMADE with his ego destroyed and replaced by a transcendent consciousness, so that he may rise above the *karmic* (law) to command . . . The *Avatar* leads the people themselves to a higher level of consciousness to enable them to understand the truth of spiritual laws so that they may turn towards righteousness and steadfastly work for better conditions.

"This will relate them back to nature and the *karmic* law of causation. They would then transcend the cycle of cause and effect in which today they are involved as victims, and thereby command and control the natural forces to be able to avert the calamities you mention."

The questioner asked, "You mean that you are presently raising the consciousness of mankind to a Godlike condition to enable them to command their own destiny?" Baba replied, "Exactly. They would become shareholders of my *sankalpa shakti* (divine will power). I have to work through them, rouse the indwelling God in them and evolve them to a higher reality in order to enable them to master the natural laws and forces.

"If I cure everything instantly, leaving the people at their present level of consciousness, they would soon mess up things and be at one another's throats again with the result that the same chaotic situation would develop in the world."

It is the realisation of the indwelling God, in all creation, which is so vital; and in our present stage of duality, when the observer feels separate from the observed (whether other humans or other kingdoms of nature) it is by love and loving service that we can best bridge the gap, one could almost say the chasms which divide us.

Love is not sentimentality. Rather is it the experiencing of compassion which allows us to feel the essence of all forms of life. Through love we can blend with the aspiring consciousness of the animal, the plant kingdom, the very stones under our feet — and of human beings, however strange they may appear to be. Baba tells us: "There is nothing in the world that has no heart, which is incapable of feeling joy or grief." Whatever we do against others, in all the kingdoms, we do against ourselves. That means the Indwelling God.

Our next door neighbour often presents us with a test! Someone said to me not long ago, "How can I stop becoming intensely irritated with the woman next door?" I suggested that she could try, in imagination, to see a little nugget of gold deep inside that person, and to realise that it was part of the very same piece of gold that was within herself — the gold of God. This seemed to be an entirely new thought, and she determined to try practising it.

"Love," says Baba, "will awaken the compassion of man towards all God's children, human and animal; it will fill him with wonder and amazement at the handiwork of God, and he will see Divinity everywhere and in everything." And Baba himself has given the most touching lesson, so moving in its utter simplicity, when in his former body as Sai Baba of Shirdi.

A lady made a plate of sweets for Sai Baba of Shirdi, and a dog ate them, whereupon she drove off the dog with blows. She then carried another platter of sweets to Sai Baba of Shirdi, but he refused them, saying that he had eaten the sweets she previously provided and his hunger was satisfied. The lady protested, saying that this was the first time she had offered them, so how could he say he had already eaten them? But Baba replied, "You offered them to me before and when I ate them you beat me."

In this way he gave a lesson that he was omnipresent and that there was only one life. It was the epitome of ONENESS.

# 11

# OMNIPRESENCE

*"Call Me by any Name. Picture Me in any Form. For all Names and all Forms are Mine. I am everywhere at all times."*

. . . Sri Sathya Sai Baba

It is only by one's own experience, and sometimes learning of the experiences of others, that one <u>knows</u> the above quotation to be absolute truth. I have proved it to be so.

"I am always aware of the past, the present and future of each one of you," declares Baba. Long before we come to know of the *Avatar*'s presence in the world in human form, he is ever aware of us, for he is the Resident in every heart, whether we know it or not, whether we accept or reject.

Manifold are the ways and methods by which he draws us or makes his Presence known. Sometimes it is in quiet, subtle ways. Sometimes in a dream. Sometimes by various phenomena, or an appearance, or a vision. Sometimes as a direct response to sincere prayer, or an anguished cry from the heart to God. "I respond equally quickly no matter what Form and Name of God you adore and worship."

This startling truth takes so many diverse forms that any attempt to describe them would be entirely beyond the scope of this small volume. Readers must refer to others, far more competent, who have known Baba for many years, some of whose books appear in the Bibliography. In any case, as Howard Murphet has pointed out, "Writing a book about him is like trying to enclose the universe in a small room." It is an impossible task, for Baba has so rightly said: "No one can understand My mystery. The best thing you can do is to get immersed in it . . . Dive and know the depth. Eat and know the taste."

However, I cannot resist mentioning two or three examples which demonstrate dramatically the truth of Baba's words: "Call Me by any Name . . . " The first (which includes the second), is drawn from Alvin Drucker's fascinating contribution to the 1980 'Golden Age' volume.

Al Drucker is a former aerospace engineer, adviser to the United States Air Force, the Federal Aeronautics Administration, NASA, and the National Academy of Science. Later, he trained as a natural healer, specialising in acupuncture, homeopathy, herbal medicine and psychotherapy, and for ten years he has been teaching holistic health classes and conducting a community clinic in natural healing in California. How did this change of vocation come about?

He had invited a friend to come on a flying outing in a small 'plane to see the breathtakingly beautiful Sierra Nevada mountains. A turbulent storm was predicted for the next day, but he thought that if they did run into bad conditions he would quickly turn back to the calm coastal weather. But it was not to be.

After forty-five minutes he realised he must turn back from the storm which suddenly confronted them — but when he did so, it was only to find that black turbulence streaked with lightning had closed in on them from behind as well. .The little 'plane was like a toy boat lost in the surf of the seashore, at one moment sucked down towards the 12,000 feet high peaks, at another drawn up again, and thrown this way and that.

For two hours he battled to maintain control. His friend had lost consciousness through lack of oxygen and appeared lifeless however much he shook him. In desperation he called, "Mayday! Mayday!" on the radio, but it was a futile hope. Even if he had been heard, what could mere man do in the face of these angry elements? He was lost. Every ounce of energy had gone in this long, unequal struggle. The fuel was ebbing, metal fabric ripping, and strands of steel support cables snapping.

It was then that he called out to the Almighty, "Oh God, please help me! I can't fight anymore . . . Please come and save me! I don't want to die." After that anguished cry he became calmer and added, "Do with me as you will. I am yours."

And then he put the 'plane into a shallow dive . . . If he saw the ground before they hit it he would use the last of the fuel to attempt a crash landing. Otherwise it would all be over very quickly.

Suddenly a voice came loud and clear, booming through the cabin speakers which must have been left on from his last radio attempt an hour before.

"Aircraft in distress, can you hear me?"

Al Drucker says that though the voice was strong and firm there was such a wonderful quality of gentleness and caring in the sound that he choked with tears. It was as if an angel had been sent to guide them home. He fumbled for his microphone, but never switched it on, for the voice immediately said:

"You needn't reply. Don't worry, I will guide you down safely . . . You are about 75 miles from Reno Airport. Don't worry. You'll make it." In a sure, calm tone the voice kept up a constant stream of directions to avoid the worst cells of the storm, and giving the height of unseen landmarks beneath him so he could keep enough altitude to clear them. But 75 miles? There was only enough fuel for 20, perhaps even 10 minutes at full throttle!

Then came the final instructions: "If you stay on your present course you will break out of the clouds in 12 minutes and see Reno Airport straight ahead. Start your final descent for landing. I will be fading out with this transmission. Goodbye, and good luck!" And the voice was gone, without ever having identified itself.

Drucker says, "At this point there was no longer any question in my mind that we were in God's hands. He had heard my cry and was bringing us down safely." All went as predicted. In exactly 12 minutes he saw the Reno strip. As the little 'plane touched down in a flurry of snow, his friend woke — and the engine burned its last drop of fuel. A sudden clearing in the storm had permitted the airport to open just before Drucker's emergency call for permission to land.

There was no flight service station with a radar in the direction from which they had come which could have brought them into its field. "It's a miracle you're alive!" they said. The worst storm of the season raged for five days. There was no possibility of returning home.

Now comes the sequel. At the first opportunity, after hurried repairs, they shovelled four feet of snow off the 'plane, and having no clothes for such intense cold, headed south to the Mexican border and a milder climate.

Now it so happened that his friend knew of a *yoga* academy in Tecate, just over the border. That evening they made their way there to see about the possibility of staying overnight.

It was the home and *yoga* centre of Indra Devi, a very old devotee of Baba. A group of people were just finishing singing *bhajans*. When Drucker saw the picture of Baba, without having the slightest idea who it was, he says, "I felt an immediate, overwhelming flood of emotions. I knew there was some connection between the red robed figure and the voice that had rescued us so dramatically from the storm."

He asked about the picture and was told it was of Sri Sathya Sai Baba who lived in southern India, and he was told many unusual stories that sounded similar to his own.

But how could this man in far off India suddenly appear on the aircraft radio over the Nevada mountains at that critical moment? Yet the feeling of the connection was so strong that he knew he would have no rest till he went to India to find out the mystery of the voice . . .

"From the first day of that fateful pilgrimage," writes Drucker, "I felt immersed in a sea of grace." Although there never seemed an appropriate moment to ask Swami directly, Baba arranged for the answer to come indirectly. Al was given a room to share with what he thought a strange companion for a Westerner – a very humble elderly Indian who, after exchanging greetings of 'Sai Ram', said nothing.

Next day, however, he discovered the Indian spoke faultless English. After much persuasion and protestation he told Drucker how he had come to Baba, and it was through the latter's truly fantastic story that his own question was answered. The following, then, is what this Indian gentleman recounted.

He had been a State official, a follower and friend of Gandhi, a student in Britain during the Second World War. In later life he had come to devote his mature years in service to God.

Baba had drawn him into his fold as the result of an accident, though he was unaware of Baba's human existence at the time. Driving with his wife along a narrow mountain road he had to swerve violently to avoid another vehicle. His car plunged down the mountainside. As they were flung about inside the car as it rolled several hundred feet down the precipice, the last thing he remembered was hearing his wife crying out, "Rama! Rama!"

When he recovered consciousness he found himself, to his utter amazement, beside his wife who was propped up against a boulder. She recovered consciousness at the same time. Both were unhurt. But how had they got out of the car which was now a mangled wreck further down the mountainside? It was not only a miracle, but a complete and utter mystery.

Months later he happened to be on Government business in a

city where Baba was making a rare visit. Almost despite himself, he was drawn to the huge field where Baba was to give a discourse, and joined the gathering crowds of people. To his great surprise, a Sai volunteer approached him, saying he had been sent by Sri Sathya Sai Baba to direct him to a seat in the front line. Just as astonishing was the discovery that Baba had described him so perfectly that the volunteer had no difficulty in finding him among the gathering multitude.

When Swami appeared, he came up to him, now seated in the front line, and said to him, "Ah! You have come. You must thank your wife for your life. If she hadn't called Me you would now be dead. I pulled you both out of that car and set you down on the ground unharmed, even though you didn't think of Me once. But I have saved your life many times before without you even knowing it. Do you remember the Air Raid Warden?"

Suddenly a long forgotten memory returned of when he was a college student in London during the intensive bombing in 1940. Every night the siren sounded at the approach of German bombers. And every night he had felt too tired to go down to the shelter from his little room on the top floor of the building where he lodged, for he had a job as well as his college studies.

One night, after the siren had sounded, there came a furious pounding on his door. A gruff voice said, "Open up! I know you're there. Come down at once. It's the law!" Meekly he had opened the door, to reveal a tin-helmeted, red faced Englishman with a torch. "No time to get dressed. Come as you are. Come with me NOW!"

Still in his pyjamas, he followed the Warden quickly down the stairs. The Warden pushed him into the shelter, already full of people, and locked the door from the outside. In a matter of minutes there came a mighty, deafening explosion. The house had received a direct hit. When they were dug out of the damaged shelter the young student saw that the entire top part of the house had disappeared. He thanked God for his escape. His only regret was that the Warden who had saved his life must have been killed outside by the blast.

"Do you remember the Air Raid Warden?" Swami repeated. "I was the Air Raid Warden. I came to save you from that bomb. I have protected and saved you many times before in your life. Now you will come and be with me."

The astonishing thing (to us) is that in mid-1940 Baba was a very young teenager of thirteen who had just thrown down his school books in a remote Indian village, declaring that the work for which he had come must begin, and that his devotees were calling him.

94

Even then, forty years ago, he was already selecting and protecting his future devotees who, in time, would number tens of millions. Even then he was starting to gather them to him. When Al Drucker heard this story he immediately knew why Swami had put the two of them together in that flat in Prasanthi Nilayam at Puttaparthi.

Drucker adds: "At the end of the Summer Course at Ooty some years later, in 1976, Swami gave a historic talk highlighting his early life and mission. At that time he bid those of us present to return to our native places with the assurance that wherever his devotees are he would be present. He said, 'I have you and you have Me. In the years to come I will come in many manifestations of My form. Do not fear. Wherever you are, there I will be.'

"We know," says Al Drucker, "that he has been making good this promise to his devotees even before they come to him . . . Long before we even know of his existence in human form, and know of his world mission, and long before we recognise his immense effect on our own lives, he is already guiding, shaping, protecting, preparing us for the day when we come into his presence and start our real work. That is the wonderful gift of grace that we have all inherited by our good *karma.*"

The third example I would like to give centres around a lady called Mrs Bhat who, at the time, lived in Mysore. Her husband, Mr K.R.K. Bhat, was a senior executive in the insurance world. Her experience is included in Howard Murphet's meticulously researched book, *Sai Baba, Man of Miracles.*

It has often been thought, erroneously, that Hindus have many gods. This, of course, is not the case at all. These are merely aspects of the various attributes of the One Formless Supreme Absolute. Thus in front of a college, for instance, you may find a statue of Saraswati, goddess of the arts and sciences, of wisdom and learning, in the same way as Christians, notably Roman Catholics, have many patron saints. Prayers are addressed not only to Jesus the Christ, but to his mother, Mary, or to Saint Francis on behalf of animals, St. Anthony for that which is lost, St. Christopher for safety, and so on.

Thus, in the prayer room of Hindu households you find various pictures depicting saints, and personifications of the divine aspects of God. Mr Bhat was more inclined towards the Lord Krishna, but both his widowed mother and his wife were devoted to Lord Subramaniam, described as the personification of the highest possible state to which the law of evolution leads, and "who tends the spirit and growth of aspirants". He is depicted standing in a chariot, holding a spear-like object, with a cobra coiled round him.

Now way back in 1943 the young Mrs Bhat developed cancer of

the uterus. An operation was advised though there was no certainty of it being successful. However, her mother-in-law who was staying with her son and his wife at that time, was strongly against it. She told her son, "Lord Subramaniam cured your father of cancer without an operation, and he will cure your wife."

So strong was her faith that the young couple agreed not to have surgery. Instead, fervent prayers and devotions were carried out daily in the little shrine room to invoke the help of Lord Subramaniam. This continued for six months, mainly, as time passed, by the mother-in-law, for by this time young Mrs Bhat was confined to bed, gradually growing thinner and weaker.

Then one night, when lying half asleep, Mrs Bhat suddenly saw, in the dim light of the moon, a large cobra circling her bed. Much alarmed, she switched on the bedside lamp and woke her mother-in-law who was sleeping in the same room as the husband was away on business.

A search was made, but there was no sign of any snake. Thinking her daughter-in-law must have been dreaming, the old lady went back to sleep. But when Mrs Bhat finally turned out the light, she again saw the cobra by her bed — and almost immediately the snake took the form of Subramaniam, just as she knew him from the picture in their shrine room. He seemed to be floating above her. Then he touched her chest with his spear and she was drawn out of her body — an astral projection.

She found herself standing before him on the peak of a rocky hill, and at once knelt down to touch his feet. He began to talk to her, and asked her if she wanted to stay with him, or go back to the world. She understood that he was giving her the choice between continuing her earthly life, or 'dying'. So, thinking of her husband and her young children who needed her, she told Lord Subramaniam she wished to go back.

After further conversation he finally said to her, "You are cured of your illness and will soon grow strong. Throughout your life I will protect you; whenever you think of me, I will be there. Now go back."

"How do I go back?" she asked. He pointed to a long, winding narrow staircase which had opened near their feet, and led downward. She began to descend it, and then remembered no more till she found herself awake, in her bed.

Immediately rousing her mother-in-law, she told her the details of the experience. As soon as her husband returned home she told him too, and others in their family circle. From that night she gained rapidly in strength and health, and it was found that the cancer had disappeared.

She resumed her normal life, but now, in addition to her home duties and religious observances, she devoted herself to welfare work among the poor and needy, for God had given her back her life, and she was determined to use it fully in service to others as best she could.

Twenty years later, in 1963, Mr and Mrs Bhat first came to hear of Sathya Sai Baba and decided to go to Puttaparthi. Baba gave them an interview, and said to Mrs Bhat, "I spoke to you long ago – twenty years ago."

Greatly puzzled, she replied, "No, Swamiji, this is my first visit."

"Yes, yes, but I came to you when you were living in Mysore," said Baba, and he mentioned the name of the street in Mysore where she was living at the time of her cancer illness, when she had the experience with Lord Subramaniam.

Mrs Bhat was still utterly perplexed, so Baba took her a little way up the narrow winding stairs which lead to his quarters above the interview room, and told her to look down. Immediately she was reminded of the staircase leading down from the rocky peak on which she had been with Lord Subramaniam. The stairs were identical, and she was more bewildered than ever.

To help her understanding, Swami now waved his hand and from the air produced a photograph of himself in the chariot of Lord Subramaniam with a cobra circled around him. Now a light began to dawn on her. God can take any form, she thought. He had come to her twenty years before in the form she had worshipped, Subramaniam. Now he was here before her, in the form of Sathya Sai Baba. She fell at his feet, weeping tears of joy.

These three examples alone (and there are innumerable others) testify to the omnipresence of Sathya Sai, and prove the truth of his words: "Call Me by any name. Picture Me in any form. For all names and all forms are Mine. I am everywhere at all times."

When Alvin Drucker, about to crash his 'plane into the Sierra Nevada mountains, called out in anguish, "Oh God, come and help me!" it was Sai, then unknown to him in the human form, who 'heard', and immediately responded. It was his voice which came, out of the blue, to guide his deliverance.

When the Indian woman, with her husband, falling headlong in their car down the mountain side, called out beseechingly, "Rama! Rama!" before they lost consciousness, it was Sai, then unknown to them, who instantly responded and 'took' them out of the car before it landed far below in a mangled heap.

When Mrs Bhat and her family prayed earnestly and with sincere devotion to Lord Subramaniam to cure her cancer, it was Sai, then unknown to them, who responded and cured her.

Indeed, as Baba has declared, it does not matter what form or name of God we adore and worship, provided we have genuine love and devotion.

The implication in the incidents described in this chapter is almost too staggering for many people to grasp or absorb at first. Yet the truth of the following statement by Baba is inescapable:

"In this human form of Sai every Divine Entity, every Divine Principle, that is to say all the Names and Forms ascribed by man to God, are manifest."

## 12

# THE AURA CANNOT LIE

*"I want people to come, see, hear, study, observe, experience and
realise Baba. Then only will they understand Me and appreciate
the Avatar."*

... Sri Sathya Sai Baba

It seems a strange paradox that the country most advanced in the
science of parapsychology should be the Soviet Union whose
leaders are dedicated to the denial of God. "I looked for God in
space," said the first Soviet cosmonaut facetiously, dutifully
following the Party line, "but I didn't see him!"

What, then, did he see? Can anyone gaze out at the 100,000
million suns of our little galaxy of the Milky Way without seeing
God? Can anyone examine the tiniest flower, the smallest insect,
the miraculous microscopic life in a drop of water, or the mini-
universe in the atom, without seeing God?

The short answer, unfortunately, is yes. Such is the blindness
of the over-developed intellect, and the myopic vision of the
materialist which attributes all manifestation of whatever kind to
a mechanistic or even accidental cause, with a small 'c', that it

99

takes a child's simple mind to ask the one question which these persons cannot answer: "But what caused the cause?"

Yet today, with its extensive programme dealing with wide-ranging phenomena which come under the umbrella of para-psychology, including telepathy, psychism, thought power, telekinesis, and so on, the Soviet hierarchy is treading on dangerous ground.

In this instance I am not referring to the obvious dangers inherent in utilising occult powers for the ignoble purposes of warfare, espionage, destruction and subjugation. I refer to other discoveries which are being brought to light through the researches and inventions of Russian scientists, and which must, eventually, 'endanger' the whole bigoted ideology of atheistic materialism.

In particular, the brilliant Russian invention known as Kirlian photography has produced a 'camera' capable of photographing the aura around every living thing. This must, in due course, prove beyond all doubt not only what occultists know to be the etheric body — that is, the subtle body which animates the physical body (and which scientists like to call the "bio-magnetic energy field radiation") — but also the fact that this separates from the body when physical death occurs.

Of course, those people gifted with clairvoyance, in varying degrees, do not need such proof. C.W. Leadbeater was a highly gifted clairvoyant, and in his fascinating book, *Man Visible and Invisible* (Theosophical Publishing House, Madras), he includes 26 colour illustrations of different types and variations of auras, painted from direct observation.

These include those depicting various emotions such as fear, jealousy, anger, depression, love, affection, altruism, spirituality, etc. and vary from the savage up to the adept or master. The latter, he admits, is so extended and beautiful that no artist has a hope of reproducing it adequately.

Naturally, gifted people vary enormously in their perceptive abilities. Some see only the health aura, others that of the emotional and mental bodies, while others perceive the spiritual qualities, and the state of a person at any given time. (It is interesting that a clairvoyant observed recently that when I was talking to her about Baba my whole aura became mauve — a colour associated with spirituality, which proved that even talking of Sathya Sai Baba has the effect of lifting one 'above oneself'.)

Dr Frank G. Baranowski, of the University of Arizona, has been able to see the aura since childhood, which is doubtless the reason why he became an eminent scientist in the field of Kirlian photography. He admits to having given over 9,000 lectures in all parts of the world on the results of his exploration into the recesses of the human mind and body, especially the aura or bio-magnetic field radiation which reveals, when photographed and interpreted, the traits of emotional make-up and the predominant urges of the mind. In other words, character and spiritual development. He has researched extensively in this field, and in clinical hypnosis.

To further his researches, Dr Baranowski travelled throughout India. Purely as a scientist he photographed over a hundred holy men. He found nothing very remarkable, for although the auras were sometimes a little larger than most, there was always an element of ego-oriented concern for their own organisations or *ashrams*. He was not very impressed on the whole.

And then, in July 1978, he arrived at the *ashram* of Sathya Sai Baba . . . Friends of ours happened to be there at the time, met him, and talked to him — although he seemed to be bereft of words. For the Kirlian scientist had come face to face with a phenomenon he could not explain, but which made him a changed man, wondering how he was going to "explain the unexplainable" to fellow scientists back home. It was the phenomenon of divine love.

The first morning, very early, when he saw Baba come out of his residence, Baranowski says he <u>shone</u>. He has written: "The colour pink, rarely seen, typifies selfless love. This was the colour that Sai Baba had around him. The aura went beyond the building against which he stood; this energy field reached 30 to 40 feet in all directions.

"Never having seen any aura like this before, my first reaction was to look for fluorescent lights which may have been shining on him. But as I watched, the beautiful pink energy pattern moved as he moved. Entranced by this remarkable sight, I barely heard the devotional songs that were being sung and, before I knew it, Sai Baba had gone."

On July 30th Dr Baranowski addressed the students of the Sri Sathya Sai College at Brindavan on 'The Phenomena of Man', illustrating his lecture with slides depicting in colour the human aura. That same evening he spoke again, to 665 teachers undergoing an orientation course. And this is what he said:

"I am very glad to be here this evening to talk to you on the phenomena of man. We are understanding more about man each day and about his most important aspect — that simple four-letter word, LOVE. I am sure you must have heard that some years ago a camera was perfected for what is called Kirlian photography, which takes pictures of the energy bands that surround the human body. With this camera we can photograph the aura of man, which very often extends beyond the limits of the physical body.

"The aura is generated by the inside of a person — the energy, the love, the emotions. It comes out clear in the pictures we can

101

now take. Since 1969 thousands of pictures have been taken and studied by means of bio-magnetic field radiation photography. We can now say whether or when a person feels love, extends love, and showers love.

"The halo around people is of pronounced colours; energy is white. When a person is full of love the aura around him is blue. And when the love is pronounced it becomes pink. When a person is filled with hate, the blue becomes red. These bands can be seen, too, by trained eyes after a series of exercises.

"Strange things happen to your body when you hate, and are in anger. So, scientific evidence tells us to love. Love is what you have to develop and share with others. We can, with our perfected cameras, now photograph five different types of auras — physical, psychical, moral, spiritual, and intellectual. They are basically five, but the auras can change colour as affected by the emotions.

"I have met over a hundred holy men in India. Too many of them are involved with their own personal egos. Their auras show mostly their concern for themselves and their institutions. So they are only a foot broad, or perhaps two feet. I am not a devotee. I have come here from America, as a scientist, to see this man, Sai Baba.

"I saw him, on Sunday, standing there on the balcony, giving *darshan* to the devotees singing below. The aura Swami projected was not that of a man! The white was more than twice the size of any man's; the blue was practically limitless; and then there were gold and silver bands beyond even those, far beyond this building, right up to the horizon. There is no scientific explanation for this phenomenon.

"His aura is so strong that it is affecting me, standing by the chair on which he is sitting. I can feel the effect. I have to wipe my arm, on and off, as you must have noticed. I am a scientist. I have given thousands of lectures in all parts of the world, but for the first time, believe me, my knees are shaking. The aura that emanates from Swami shows his love for you. I have met a number of holy men, but not one of them has made himself as available to you as he does. That is a sign of greatness.

"Many years ago we had a philosopher, Ralph Waldo Emerson, in the United States. He was once asked, 'What is success in life?' He replied:

" 'To laugh often and much, to win the affection of children, to find the best in others, to endure the betrayal of false friends, to make the world a little better place to live in than when we were born into it, by rearing a little garden patch, improving some social condition, or helping a child to grow healthier. To know that one life breathes easier since you lived. That is success.'

"Swami has given you this key to success — the simple four-letter word: LOVE. If ever I can use the phrase that I have seen love walking on two feet, it is here."

Dr Baranowski resumed his seat and Baba began his discourse. The scientist sat watching him with amazement. When the discourse ended, he asked permission to speak again.

"I have been watching Swami while he was addressing you," he said. "The pink aura manifesting was so vast and strong that it went even beyond the wall behind his chair. It filled this big hall, embracing all of you gathered here. I repeat, there can be no scientific explanation for this phenomenon.

"I have been watching him for a week now, as he walked among you, morning and evening. I have seen his aura, pink in colour, go into the person he is talking to or touching, and returning back to him. This is because we draw on his energy. His energy seems to be endless. It spreads everywhere, and can be drawn upon by everyone around.

"An ordinary man will soon get exhausted, going round as he does, among so many. I have watched him come to a little girl in a wheelchair, and tickle her. I was astonished at the aura of love that was all around him then.

"I was not brought up in any belief, though I am a Christian born and a Roman Catholic. The scientific community in my country finds it difficult to accept a god. It is not scientific, they assert. I am risking my reputation when I make this statement: two days ago, right outside this hall, I looked into his eyes. They have a glow inside them. It was clear to me that I had looked into the face of divinity.

"In my estimation he is exactly what he appears to be, what he wants you to be, what he tells you to be . . . love. That is what he is. I have spoken on platforms with President Ford of the United States, Queen Elizabeth II of Great Britain, and Queen Wilhelmina of the Netherlands. But I will never forget this experience. It is overwhelming in its impact."

Dr Baranowski's talk was later printed in the September 1978 *Sanathana Sarathi*, the *ashram* magazine. He told our friends that if a normal human being possessed the same amount of energy as Sai Baba, he would die. Yet he exists on practically nothing, and gives himself unsparingly day and night, year in and year out, his radiance never failing for an instant.

This radiance is all-embracing, making its impact equally on hardened intellectuals, scientists, cynical newspapermen, professors and the like — people certainly not given to emotionalism. On one occasion newspapermen were sent to study him, talk to him and, hopefully, to 'expose' him. To their editor's consternation they returned and said, "He is God".

Howard Murphet, whose spiritual search had for years been along very intellectual lines, tries to put into words something which he admits is far beyond language in describing his and his wife's leave-taking of Swami when returning to Australia. He writes, in *Sai Baba, Man of Miracles*:

"He was like a mother seeing her children off to boarding school, except that he seemed to be the essence of all the mothers the earth has ever known. The stream of affection that flowed from him was a river carrying one off into an ocean of love. In that ocean one's physical body seemed to vanish, and all the hard lumps of separate self, of anxiety and worry and deep-lying fear, were melted away. For those exalted moments one touched the edge of the infinite and felt the ineffable joy of it."

This is a beautiful attempt to express the inexpressible. I have tried, in an earlier chapter, to convey my own experience of that never-to-be-forgotten, breath-taking, all-enveloping bliss, although words are totally inadequate. For a non-gifted person like myself (though reasonably perceptive and receptive) the experience of being within the radiance of that amazing and unique aura of total love, both in private interviews or even being in his vicinity when he passes by, is one that neither time nor 'distance' can cause to fade. Indeed, his presence, or rather his omnipresence, fills one's life and being.

Something of this aura manifests around a certain photograph of him that one may have, as vouched for by countless people, including myself, all over the world. Sometimes the whole area becomes suffused with light, or blue rays shoot out from the forehead in the photograph, or a brilliant star, brighter than a diamond, appears on the brow.

I find the experience of Marilyn Rossner, a most gifted Canadian sensitive, extremely interesting. Marilyn is the wife of Dr John Rossner, an Anglican priest who is also a parapsychologist and professor of comparative religion at Concordia University in Montreal.

Marilyn herself is a professor of special education instructing teachers at Vanier College in Montreal who work with emotionally disturbed and impaired children. She has a daily television programme called *Beyond Reason* in which she exercises her quite amazing psychic gifts which have helped many people to find faith in God, in a society mainly motivated by rationalism and materialism. She also has her own Spiritual Science Fellowship with over five hundred members. Truly, she is a remarkable person.

When visiting India with her husband and a large group of professional people from Canada, she told Mr Balu about her experiences of Swami's aura, which he incorporates in his excellent book, *The Glory of Puttaparthi*. (We also met Mr and Mrs Balu when we were in India, as mentioned in a previous chapter.) He quotes Marilyn Rossner as follows:

"When I saw Sai Baba I noticed the aura behind his head was white and gold, with streaks of mauve. He was all energy – one with energy all around – one with the universal and cosmic energy. I would say that Sai Baba is bathed in an ocean of energy and his body merged with all this energy. When he talked, I saw pastel shades of colour emanating – shades of mauve, pink and blue. His words, 'Very happy to see you all!' were so full of love that I saw the colours form into a heart.

"His hand movements were spirals of energy. It was constantly in spirals. Suddenly there was a spark (like a spark of electricity), and there was a ring that he had made!

"I saw the figure of Jesus Christ superimposed on him . . . When he lifted his hand in blessing, I saw Jesus Christ again on his hand. When I saw him and the visions of Christ, on him, a voice said in my ear, 'Even if Jesus came as he was on earth now, who would believe him? No one." Marilyn added, "Sai Baba is an *avatar*. He is all love. He is all energy. He is divine."

She also tells how Baba astonished everyone by going to a woman member of the group and asking, "How is your leg? The pain?" No mention had been made by anyone of this woman's leg condition, but Baba knew. He looked at the blisters – and the woman confirmed later that all the excruciating pain in her leg vanished completely.

Dr John Rossner also saw Baba encompassed by a big energy field, so huge and extensive that Baba's figure appeared a tiny fraction of it. It proved to this priest, in his own words, that "Baba is indeed no ordinary person." His faith in him is total, not only through glimpsing this huge energy field, but through many experiences of Baba back home in Canada, including several instances of the materialisation of *vibhuti*, Baba's sacred ash.

Incidentally, two years before actually meeting Baba in India, he appeared to Marilyn in her sitting room in Montreal, and also in the television studio when she was 'on the air'. But I must not be tempted to deviate from the subject of this chapter – the aura which emanates from Sathya Sai Baba for those who have eyes to see. If there is one certain thing, it is that the aura cannot lie.

To those like the Russian cosmonaut who looked for God in space, Baba says: "In order to see the moon, does one need a torch? It is by the light of the moon that one sees the moon. In like fashion, if one wishes to see God it is by <u>love</u>, which is the light of God, that one may see Him . . . Start the day with love,

105

end the day with love — this is the way to God."

We are immensely privileged to be living at a time in history when this Being — described by Dr Baranowski as 'love walking on two feet' — is incarnate in human form. A small, slender form just over five feet high, but whose aura of love reaches beyond the horizon!

# 13

# COMING HOME

*"The Lord has to come in human form and move among men, so that He can be listened to, contacted, loved, revered and obeyed. He has to speak the language of men and behave like human beings, as a member of a species. Otherwise, He will be either negated and neglected or feared and avoided."*

. . . Sri Sathya Sai Baba

And so I come to the final chapter of my section of this little book, a section in which I have endeavoured to give a brief outline of a very personal pilgrimage and its impact.

Others, far more erudite, have written many books on the phenomenon which is Bhagavan Sri Sathya Sai Baba, and will continue to do so, for truly the Infinite cannot be contained in the finite, or his mystery understood, and certainly not explained, by the ant-like comprehension of humanity at our present stage of evolution.

A fish sees images of land, trees and sky, animals and humans. But however high it leaps out of the water it cannot know the reality of life beyond its own element or vision. One can only urge readers to delve deep into the four incredible volumes of Baba's biography written by Professor Kasturi under the title *Sathyam Sivam Sundaram* (Truth Goodness Beauty), and others listed at the end of this book.

Can one describe the sun to a blind man? No. It is only by feeling its blessed beneficent warmth that he knows that by its rays his very existence is sustained. "I am beyond the reach of the most intensive inquiry and the most meticulous measurement," Baba has said, and it is so.

God becomes man so that man may become God — by becoming aware of his divine origin and indwelling divinity. That spark, "which lighteth every man that cometh into the world", must be ignited into a flame. And Sathya Sai Baba is the torch. "You are the waves. I am the Ocean," he tells us. We can only marvel, and accept; be grateful that we are privileged to be on earth at this vital period of its history; and above all, learn to love and serve.

I am reminded of some lines I wrote in an article before I had become aware of Baba's presence in the world. I wrote: Why is it, I wonder, that the contemplation of beauty can often be so painful? Why, when the soul is uplifted and expands in silent rapture, consumed with the urge to embrace such beauty in an overwhelming love, does the heart ache with an indefinable sadness?

Have you tiptoed into a garden at dawn, spellbound by the diamond dewdrops that tremble on webs of gossamer on a summer morning? Have you stood, alone, among tall, still trees on a starlit night, longing for your kinship to be recognised and accepted by that living, breathing fraternity? Or endeavoured to capture forever that magical, elusive moment when the setting sun transforms a moorland lake into a shining sheet of glass, and in the serene silence, suddenly, comes the wistful, unearthly cry of a curlew?

Have you experienced such moments, and a thousand others of a similar kind, without a sense of sadness, a stab of pain, as if such magic and beauty were too much to bear because it hurts, like an invisible needle penetrating the soul?

One of the reasons, perhaps, is the ever present contrast between what should be, what could be, and what IS at this moment of humanity's experience in the schoolroom of Earth with its tests and trials, the sloth and weakness of the flesh, the conflicting desires of the higher and the lower natures.

For good reason those beyond the earth's orbit call it "the sorrowful planet", a veritable maelstrom of good and evil, of abysmal ignorance and high endeavour, of material lusts and spiritual aspirations, of horrific cruelty and much compassion, of great selfishness and willing service. The contrast of polarities is plain for all to see and to feel, while increased knowledge can easily become an intolerable burden unless balance and equilibrium are constantly maintained.

Is it because of this knowledge that, incarnating for a brief spell on this beautiful but sad planet which is struggling not only to survive the desecrations of man's insanity but to take a great leap forward in the coming new age, I feel this stab of pain (almost of guilt as a human being) in the presence of unspoilt natural beauty? That I am filled with awe and compassion, which is also pain, for such gifts of the Creator as a summer morning, the scent of a perfect rose, the brotherhood of trees, a shining stretch of clear water?

Or, could it be all this, and something else as well? Is not this all-pervading ache at such moments of rapture a deep nostalgia for our true home from which we came into incarnation and to which we shall one day return? I believe such moments unloose the soul's memory of that merging, that oneness of spirit which is not in doing, speaking, seeing, or in any activity, but in the fulfilment of BEING. And is it not, too, a deep nostalgia for the future, when love will rule?

Thus I had written, with an aching heart. And lo and behold, very soon afterwards it was made known to me that the Great Lord had come to the earth, as was so accurately prophesied over 5,000 years ago in the *Mahabharata* and other scriptures — yes, and in the Revelations of St. John — in "an inconceivable human form". The Kalki *Avatar* on the white horse; and also He who comes forth on the white horse, in a blood red robe, and who is called King of Kings and Lord of Lords, and from whose mouth issues the sword (the words) of Truth. How many times have clairvoyantly gifted people seen this figure, in vision, over Sai Baba's head!

The immortal words of Christopher Fry spring so often to my mind: "Thank God our time is now, when wrong comes up to face us everywhere, never to leave us till we take the longest stride of soul men ever took. Affairs are now soul size. The enterprise is exploration into God. Where are you making for? It takes so many thousand years to wake, but will you wake for pity's sake?"

If there is one attribute above all else which speaks to me of Baba's Divinity it is his sublime PATIENCE. It is written that Jesus looked on the city and wept. At that moment he was overcome by his Humanity, and one cannot but help weep with him.

But Baba suffers the world in a never-changing state of bliss though there is nothing of which he is not aware. Neither is he in the least swayed or affected by the adoration of millions or the criticisms and calumnies of the ignorant who have never set eyes on him or read his teachings, or experienced HIM.

His love is all-embracing. Only the Divine in a human form can demonstrate and be both Perfect Patience and Perfect Love

109

personified. Yet I always remember the last lines of a little poem he sang at the commencement of one of his discourses: "I alone know the agony of teaching you each step of the dance . . . "

Dr Baranowski has written: "Perhaps of all the miracles I witnessed in India, no miracle is as great as the miracle of one man giving so much love to so many people." That love teaches, encourages, sustains, kneads, pounds, purges, transforms, burns away the dross, and finally reveals the golden nugget of divinity hidden within the heart of every being.

As my heart, in the past, had been pierced by the wistful, unearthly call of the curlew on a silent moor at sunset, so now my heart became triply pierced by the great glowing inward miracle of this Divine Love, which had been calling to me in the silence through all my turbulent life. For as Baba says:

"It is part of human nature that man desires to reach the presence of the Almighty, to see Him and be ever with Him, for deep within the human heart is the urge to reach the place from which he has come, to attain the joy he has lost, the glory which he has missed. Man is himself divine and so it is a matter of the deep calling unto the deep, of the part calling for the whole . . . "

Now there is no longer pain in the contemplation of beauty, but expanding joy! For all is HE — Truth, Goodness, Beauty. He is omnipresent. His human form may be in India — though he can and does appear anywhere at any time — but wherever I look I see him. In the sky, the sunshine, in the cooling rain, in the trees, in the flowers, in every bird and every creature, however humble. Ever conscious of his words, "I am nowhere absent", I greet all these manifestations with a silent, "Hallo, Swami" in my heart. One can never be lonely or alone any more.

He has transformed my life. And in time, if I let him, he will transform me — for has he not said: "If a person reciprocates My love from the depth of his heart, My Love and his love meet in unison and he is cured and transformed." The current is always there, always switched on. The light we are able to receive depends on the wattage of the individual bulb. Similarly, the sun is ever present, never ceasing to shine. It is only our local clouds which obscure its light and its warmth.

To endeavour to serve that Light which is incarnate as Bhagavan Sri Sathya Sai Baba for the rest of the years allotted to us; to play a small part in spreading knowledge of that Light; to try to live, in spite of weakness and frailties, as he wishes us to live; to love him in all people, in all the kingdoms of nature, in all the manifested creation, is our dearest wish. And, if he wills it, to return to serve him in the coming century when he takes the form of Prema Sai.

More and more, after leaving the physical presence, he fills and pervades one's whole being with his omnipresence. For me, he is the Mother of all Mothers in whose loving arms one longs to hide. He is the All-Powerful Father one implicitly trusts and obeys. He is the closest Friend, with whom one can share the deepest secrets of one's heart, for he knows one through and through. He is the manifested Unmanifest – the One who becomes the Many – at whose feet one cannot but fall, and to whose will one longs to surrender the last breath of the restricting mortal body, to come closer to him in the freedom of death.

Words of a very simple little poem flowed into my mind as the aeroplane bore us away from Bangalore over the mountains and valleys to Bombay, putting more and more illusory distance between my physical body and the 'inconceivable human form' standing there, shining in a glow of light, outside the verandah at Brindavan where we had taken leave of him. I can best describe my state as an agony of bliss, breathless, bursting. For after seventy years I had at last come HOME – and He was waiting for me with outstretched hand . . .

How small it is, the pale brown Hand
That holds the world!
How gentle is the mighty strength
That lifts Humanity from self-destruction!
In future aeons of Time,
When my struggling soul
Climbs slowly SAIwards,
Imbedded in my consciousness
To spur me on, will be the knowledge
That I looked into the Face, the Eyes of LOVE,
That once – nay twice! – I held and kissed
The small brown Hand of God.

111

# BOOK TWO

## by

## Ron Laing

*"This human form of Sai is one in which every divine entity, every divine principle, that is to say all the Names and Forms ascribed by man to God, are manifest."*

Sri Sathya Sai Baba
(World Conference, Bombay, 1968)

# AUTHOR'S NOTE

As this book is a collation of published articles in various magazines, which Sathya Sai Baba requested my wife and I to gather together in book form, there is inevitably some repetition. I have edited my section of the book as far as possible without spoiling the balance of the articles, but I am aware that there is still some repetition of event and quotation, albeit with a different slant and in a different context.

I ask the reader's indulgence for this and submit, in all humility, that since I am writing about the works and teachings of a *Purna Avatar* any repetition that has occurred may well be worth reading twice.

# 1

# THE LAST JOURNEY

I was born in hate, sixty-nine years ago. My mother rejected me at birth. She was a manic depressive and very unhappily married. I was a nervous and over-sensitive child. My only brother resented my intrusion into his world, and was forever bullying me and scheming to get me into trouble for offences I had never committed. My earliest memories were all unhappy ones – of Passchendael in the First World War when a hundred thousand souls were slaughtered in a single day for a stalemate position, of a fear of the dark and of attacks of 'croup' (an hysterical paralysis of the breathing tubes) as nightfall approached when I experienced the pangs of near suffocation; of disappointment on waking when I had an impulse to run to my mother's bed and jump in, only to find that when I did so she invariably got out. (I could not understand that.) And of the dreaded once fortnightly visits of my father from London to our country residence which usually led to intermittent periods of violent quarrelling with my mother, followed by periods of morose taciturnity when the emanations of hate and silent malevolence were so strong that I fled into the garden and climbed a tree to escape.

Ours was an affluent, upper class family in which to work was considered almost *infradig*. Life was taken up in hunting and shooting, in the killing of foxes and game birds. Even at this early age I sensed the social injustice and uselessness of the life, and the hypocrisy of speech and affectation of manners. I felt a total alien in an alien world. Yet I knew no other world, nor even that one existed.

Yet however dominating this childhood environment was, there was something in my spirit which never broke. I never really conformed and became a member of the family. I remained a solitary, introvert, and lonely child. Sometimes I sought the company of the dozen or so 'servants' in the house who seemed more natural and human than my family, but for this I was always upbraided.

I was educated at Eton and Cambridge University. My parents could scarcely have made a more inappropriate choice than Eton for one who was embryonically an individual and a rebel against orthodoxy. We were cast in a mould, and the tradition was so strong that it was virtually impossible to break out of it.

Here I had my first confrontation with Orthodox Christianity. Chapel going was compulsory, once daily on weekdays and twice on Sundays, and also 'prayers' every evening in the individual 'Houses'. On Sundays we also had homework on Theology. There was never a day off. As a result, chapel going became a monotonous chore; we sang and prayed by rote, through sheer repetition. I also sensed the Theology teachers did not believe themselves what they were exhorting us to believe. The preachers in the pulpit wore long faces, spoke in a deadly monotone, and had a sanctimonious look about them, almost as if they were conscious of being sinners themselves! So much of the teaching, too, was from the Old Testament, with its God of Wrath, rather than from the New, with its God of Love. The principle seemed to be to drill this dour brand of Judaistic Christianity into us, at whatever cost to the over-sensitive, by the use of fear and guilt.

In a word, wherever there was joy and laughter there was something amiss, wherever there was close friendship there was suspected homosexuality; the masters appeared to be forever on the lookout for 'sin'. If I scored a goal at football my impulse was to jump for joy, but if I saw a 'man in a dog collar' on the sidelines I desisted, with a sudden pang of fear and sin-consciousness. By the time I was eighteen I had come to equate the Church with sin and misery.

When my turn came for Confirmation I refused the rite. I cannot pretend that when pressure was brought to bear on me I was motivated solely by religious conviction; I became mulish and dug my toes in, and in the end I was left alone. But I think I was the only boy of about a thousand who refused.

My entry to Eton coincided with the death of my mother. Poor soul, she committed suicide. The family residence was sold except for a staff cottage which my father retained for me to live in during the holidays. He installed a housekeeper to look after me. She was a good woman who did her best, but she was highly class conscious and I was unable to communicate with her. She called me 'Sir' and treated me as if I was a budding 'gentleman', instead of the lonely, love-starved child that I was. I spent my time reading romantic novels or going to the escape world of the local cinema — that is, if there was a love story on. If there was a gangster film showing I did not go. And I went fox hunting — the tradition was so strong that I reluctantly conceded, but I did not enjoy it; I was always on the side of the fox.

And so a basically high-spirited youth with a zest for living spent his formative years, from thirteen to nineteen, either at school, indoctrinated into the concept of the Fall of Man and the belief that all men were sinners, or alone at home, in the escape world of fiction and the cinema, my only friend an Airedale dog. My poor parents, I love them now! My poor schoolmasters, I bear them no malice and I forgive them. They were the product of their times. Things have changed since then, but in those days they were the life-haters, the castrators who blighted more lives than they ever inspired.

At Cambridge I emerged a little from my shell. I made friends, including two very dear ones. (Alas, they were both killed in the War.) I worked hard and I played hard, except with girls; I was still too indoctrinated in the 'sins of the flesh' to approach women. Yet I was a virile youth and I suffered much frustration. It was not until decades later that I finally overcame my early conditioning, or so I believe, for at times I wonder if we ever do. I obtained an M.A. degree in Agriculture, and I led the Cambridge Judo team against Oxford. I never went near a church; the very sight of a church or a clergyman gave me the willies.

There followed a near half-century of ups and downs, of failure and success (although these are misleading terms), of following many trails and making many mistakes, of suffering and growth through suffering, but always I hope with sincerity, for this has been my one criterion. Yet, alas, I travelled throughout with maimed wings and a somewhat warped emotional nature.

On leaving Cambridge I made a tour around the world, journeying in North and South America, New Zealand and Australia, China, Japan, and India. At this time I was part Old Etonian, part roughneck, part seeker, and (in the later stages, after a relationship in Buenos Aires when the dam of my inhibitions was breached and the floodgates opened) part playboy — at one time playing polo in the Argentine or staying with the Governor-General of Australia in Melbourne, at another stoking my way across the Atlantic on a

117

cargo ship, or (to my shame) going fur-trapping with a Red Indian in the sub-Arctic regions of Canada; at one time sojourning in a Japanese monastery, at another living it up in the nightclubs of Shanghai. But I worked hard at the trip — I wrote thirteen volumes of diary and must have taken a thousand photographs.

In India I first experienced what Westerners call 'the magic of the East' — the lack of materialism and absence of hurry and bustle, the sense almost of timelessness. One could feel the spiritual heritage in the very atmosphere; it stilled one's nerves and put one in touch with one's soul. It was a strange experience for a young Westerner, accustomed to speed, aggression and competition.

In Delhi an inscription on a monument made a strong impact on me. It read:

> In thought, faith;
> In word, wisdom;
> In deed, courage;
> In life, service.
> So may India be great.

When I returned to England I had the words inscribed on a bracelet with a gold plaque and wore it around my wrist for a year or two until the time came when it seemed a little affected and I discarded it. For the words, "So may India be great", I substituted, "To increase the power of the spirit with sincerity". It seems strange that a young man with no belief in God and no religion should adopt this embryonic philosophy. Sincerity, it seemed to me, was all that mattered, along whatever path. It was a small beginning.

After fifteen months of travelling I returned to England. I was glad to be home. I felt I had seen the seven wonders of the world. I had seen the Rocky Mountains in Canada, the cherry orchards in Japan, the old imperial palaces in Peking.

But, for me, I still loved the English countryside best of all, with its twisting leafy lanes, its oak trees, its evergreen fenced fields and thriving stock, and its lovely old villages. I was of Rupert Brooke's generation. "Stands the church clock at ten to three? And is there honey still for tea?" Yes, I was glad to be home on my native soil. For me, England was still Shakespeare's 'sceptred isle — this blessed plot, this dear, dear land'.

Of course it had been a wonderful opportunity and a mind-expanding experience. I had encountered many different races and learned something of many different cultures. But people were much the same the world over. People were people. I had not noticed much difference between me, an Old Etonian, and the Red

Indian with whom I had slept on the snow in the Arctic in sub-zero temperatures to the glow of an all-night fire. I often wondered in later years if it had not been better to have stayed at home – to have started work, to have learned something of human relationships and the reality of ordinary living for, at twenty-three, in many respects, I was still as innocent and as naive as a child of ten.

In early manhood I made two disastrous marriages. Neither would have taken place had my childhood been normal. I can honestly say that when I married my first wife I did not believe that people told lies, married for reasons other than love, or could simulate affection beyond my sagacity to discern, limited as it was.

It cost me dearly, financially. I was not really guilty in either case, but I was no match for my sophisticated wives and their wily lawyers. For about five years it seemed that I spent most of my time in and out of solicitors' offices. Had it not been for these two misfortunes my estate today, owing to inflation and the unprecedented prosperity of the two companies in which I was compelled to sell shares, would be valued at several million pounds. Living as I do now, frugally and in a tiny cottage, I have no desire for wealth in a personal sense, but oh, how dearly I would cherish my lost financial heritage for charitable purposes!

During the first divorce I ran amok, spending virtually every night of the week for eight months in nightclubs, and drinking up to a bottle and a half of whiskey a day. It seemed the only way to purge out of my system the hatred that was in me. During the second divorce I sank into deep depression. I doubt if anyone who has not experienced deep depression can imagine what it is like. It is literally like living in hell, in a George Orwell world where God and human warmth do not exist. All sense of purpose deserts one. One's will to live goes; one wants to quietly lie down and die, like an elephant when its time comes. It is a victory to get out of bed in the mornings.

It lasted two years. Yet somehow I clawed my way out of it, and without resort to alcohol or drugs. I bought a cottage, furnished it, learned to hang curtains, to cook, to sew on buttons – things which 'servants' or my wives had always done for me – and I made a garden. This I have done several times in my life, and it is always therapeutic. Creative work is a spiritual activity. At the end of two years I had come out of the depression, and equally important, I had learned to live alone. I was grateful for the suffering, for through it I had matured and grown.

During the War I was a conscientious objector. To me, war was something one reads about in history books. It seemed inconceivable that it could happen again in modern times. I just could not visualise a civilised person from one country thrusting a bayonet

119

into the abdomen of an equally civilised person from another. And suddenly, from one day to the next, as if overnight, their instincts had become those of savages. I had known Germans, and often they seemed more cultured and humane than my own countryfolk. I simply did not realise how thin the veneer of civilisation is. To me the concept of war was absolutely horrific.

I was conscripted into Agriculture and bought a small farm, and here I lived and worked for six years in virtual total isolation. I was subjected to calumny and insults. I do not think I was a coward. I had shown courage on my world tour – in the Arctic my life had depended on a rifle, an axe and a box of matches without which I should have starved or frozen to death; and in China I had travelled a thousand miles up the Yellow River into bandit infested country.

One day I had found myself confronted by two Chinese soldiers who prodded me in the back with fixed bayonets. With a sudden flare of temper I turned and punched one flat with my bare fist. The other, dumbfounded that an unarmed man should do such a thing, simply fled. They could so easily have killed me.

My one friend during the War was an elderly deaf and dumb poet who lived near by. We became pen-friends and wrote to each other regularly. Through his love of poetry he opened up a new dimension in my life, and when he died he left me an anthology which he had compiled for his wife. It has been a source of inspiration to me all my life.

With hindsight I came to realise that my attitude to war was misguided. In man's present state of spiritual evolution evil can only be put down by resorting to means which are evil, however right the motivation. But at that time I did not recognise the existence of evil.

Ironically, this recognition came through an event which sparked my second divorce. Although even more disastrous financially than the first, it proved to be a blessing in disguise, for through it I eventually came to God. My then wife had an epileptic fit. It was clearly a case of 'possession'. I was suddenly aware of an evil force which made my hand shake. It was a complete revelation to me – if there was a force which men called evil then there must be a positive force which men called God.

I began to read and, one day, with considerable apprehension, I ventured into a church. It was the first time I had entered a church for fifteen years. It was a Catholic church. I was amazed. Here at least there was an element of joy, of the Life Abundant which Christ had preached. There was colour, too. The people were not dressed in black but in gay colours. They looked happy and relaxed, and when the consecration of the Host took place their faces were fixed on the High Altar with an intensity and apparent sincerity which amazed me.

For a year or so I read several books on Roman Catholicism. Then one day I read a book called *The Road to Damascus*. It was a compilation of accounts by a cross section of eminent converts to Catholicism, of how in their various circuitous ways, they had come to the faith. In one chapter a contributor told how he had taken the trouble to go to Palestine and stand on the shores of the Sea of Galilee where Christ had preached to the multitudes. Suddenly he broke into tears and wrote: "My soul was on its knees".

As I read that passage my soul, too, was on its knees. It was as immediate and as simple as that. In that moment I believed in the Divinity of Christ. I wept and wept — a cascade of tears flowed from me in a veritable catharsis of remorse and self-pity. It seemed that I shed a tear for every single day of my life, including the period of gestation in my mother's womb. But at the end of it I knew a peace which I had never experienced. "Come unto me all ye who labour . . . and I will give you rest." It was true!

In a flush of inspiration and spiritual awakening I joined the Catholic church. I had very little 'instruction'; my priest seemed to think I was 'ready'. I chose the Roman church because it was the original and seemed to me the most professional and authoritative.

For a year I was very devout. The rigid discipline was good for me. The confessional was good psychology, although I did not believe that priests had the power to forgive sin. A profound change came over me and I shall always be grateful to the Catholic Church for this. I even considered studying for the priesthood. I stayed for a time in a Benedictine monastery. The monks were clearly sincere. Many of them very lovable, with a sense of humour. I was surprised at the knowledge of the world they possessed — I had always thought of monks as men set apart.

In the end I decided against the priesthood. I felt that my place was in the world. I had joined the Church in a passion of excitement, but I now found that some of the dogmas perplexed me. I doubted my capacity to conform. In truth, all I really believed in was the Divinity of Christ.

It was at this time that I met my third wife — a loyal, stalwart, and balanced soul who has been my bedrock and my salvation for the past thirty years.

I returned to the land — I am a Virgo and a lover of the land. I bought a ruin of a farm high up in the Chilterns in Buckinghamshire, and converted it into a modern and efficient unit. I threw myself heart and soul into the work with total dedication and a complete singlemindedness of purpose. I worked a seven-day week and often a hundred hours a week. I never took a holiday. Starting from scratch, in ten years, I built up the highest yielding herd of pedigree Jerseys in the U.K. I doubled the fertility of the land and trebled the former milk production. It was a very happy ten years, with my new wife and close to nature.

But at the end of that span, although I still loved the life and knew every stone of my eighty acres of land, I felt an urging in my soul, a kind of spiritual restlessness. I had become a lapsed Catholic; Catholicism seemed irrelevant to the needs of a dairy farmer — a high creed for monks and celibate priests. The fact remained, I still did not know the answers to the basic questions: Who was I; Why was I here on this planet? And where was I going?

I was influenced, too, in my rejection of Catholicism by the experience of a friend, an eminent Roman Catholic writer who was invited by Pope Pius XII to write a history of the Roman Catholic Church for schools. He duly went to Rome to embark on research. He was given access to the inner Vatican Library. At the end of six months he returned to London, a deeply disillusioned man. It seems he had no idea of the amount of chicanery that had gone on over the centuries with such ancient manuscripts as there were, in order to make the texts fit the fabric of man-made theology which organised religion always becomes. It was perhaps as well that he died soon afterwards, for without his beloved Catholicism he would have been a lost soul.

The inner restlessness increased. After much procrastination I decided to sell the farm. It was a complete leap in the dark — I had no idea where my future lay. It was also a terrible wrench and sacrifice. Many times I nearly changed my mind. But as always the sacrifice proved to be a blessing. I threw away sixpence to pick up a shilling.

I bought a cottage nearby and set to work to write an autobiography, not for publication, but for therapeutic reasons. I felt I had overlived and needed time for my soul to catch up with me. It was an exercise in self-awareness and self-honesty.

It took three years and went to half a million words. I plodded away, six to seven hours a day, six days a week. It was often extremely tedious, and sometimes depressing. There were days when the words flowed, but there were many hours spent in deep soul-searching before I wrote a single sentence as I delved into myself for the objective truth. I was as ruthless with myself as I could be. Half way through I consulted a psychiatrist. After the second session he dismissed me, saying, "You are doing more for yourself than ever I could do; if only everyone would do this!"

It was like a giant clearing out operation. My aim was to become as far as possible a God-given identity rather than a child of

conditioning. As I wrote, it seemed that layer afte
(through lack of inner self-confidence) and ι
deception were being peeled off like skin until I
near the bedrock of my true being. As the band
wanted to start again, for I realised that what I had
beginning was simply not true!

I distilled out the difference between false and r
there is much false or endogenous guilt in a man who
unloved child. To what extent I succeeded is not for ι     judge.
I only know that my spiritual development grew apace from then
onward. At the end I felt liberated — the slate was wiped clean. I
was free to grow, to believe what I believed instead of what I
believed I believed. I was an individual at last, without the need of
a church or a *guru*. A first step was to become a vegetarian, and I
felt better in health for it.

At this time my wife and I moved to Sussex to give our son
(born in ideal conditions on the farm, when my wife was forty-
eight) a Rudolf Steiner education. Came a turning point in our
lives. Into the household came a housekeeper who developed into
a gifted medium, and for the following six years we had our own
Home Circle.

It was a wonderfully happy time. We experienced psychic
phenomena virtually everyday. It was no uncommon occurrence
to suddenly find a daffodil in our laps, or for a bunch of snowdrops
to descend from the ceiling and fall onto our breakfast plates. We
communicated daily with our friends and relatives in spirit, and we
made many new friends. My old deaf and dumb poet came through
and was overjoyed to speak to me in his natural voice. Also my two
dear friends from Cambridge, killed in the War, reminding me of
pranks we had got up to in our University days which I had actually
forgotten.

We were put in touch with our guides and given details of our
former incarnations. We came to understand how one incarnates
with what I term 'soul hang-ups'. In one life I had been a gladiator
in Rome at the time of Nero, had retired undefeated and been put
in charge of the 'sacred bulls' (probably connected with the old
Mithraic religion of Rome). No wonder, as a dairy farmer, I had
been so devoted to my cows, and particularly the bulls, and that I
had led the Cambridge Judo team!

Our medium, sometimes aided by ourselves, did much successful
'rescue work' of earthbound souls, and what a thrill it was to listen
later to these selfsame people expressing their joy and gratitude on
arrival at their true station in the world of spirit.

It was the first time I had had concrete evidence of an after-life.
Faith was no longer necessary; one becomes a 'knower' rather than

'believer'. I lost all fear of death. I became aware of the joy, indeed the bliss, experienced by those who dwelt in the higher echelons of spirit. At last spirituality became a happy thing. Teachers from spirit hardly ever used the word 'sin'; they preferred the word 'error'. The teaching was always of love, and more love. There was so much warmth and compassion in those who spoke to us. And humour, too! It gave a tremendous boost to my overall sense of well-being and to my inner self-confidence; indeed it transformed my life.

We were doubly blessed at this time by having the privilege of listening to the teachings of what, in my judgement, are one of the finest sets of tape-recordings from spirit in existence — the Abu tapes. The chief communicator had been an Egyptian priest 3,500 years ago. He dwelt in the fourth plane of heaven, and in order to reach us he had to don what he described as his 'astral overcoat'.

He was the gentlest, most compassionate soul I had ever listened to. In question and answer sessions he must have answered a thousand questions, and always with a clarity and lucidity which astounded us. He had the gift of helping us with our three-dimensional consciousness even to grasp dimly the meaning of transcendental matters for which our minds were not equipped, as if we had temporarily shifted consciousness to a higher level.

Concomitant with this happy phase I took up full time voluntary welfare work, at first with the Samaritans for a two-year period of training, and then with my own group, The Befrienders.

We were blessed at this time with a beautiful country property with a staff cottage which I converted into a hostel for our clients. In this way we were able to get to know them more intimately and give them more care than the Samaritans, who only did visiting.

During our first year's residence I made a garden, transporting matured shrubs and conifers up to twenty feet high with a tractor, and damming a stream which ran through the site to make a lily pond cum swimming pool, overhung by two weeping willows. From a bare plot of waste ground I now had a natural style garden that looked as if it had been in existence for a century. It was continually referred to and blessed by our friends in spirit, and I am sure it had a therapeutic effect on our clients. They drank in the beauty and imbibed the spiritual vibrations.

I took on literally the dregs of society, often those who had been rejected by the Social Services and even by the Samaritans as unhelpable. I had my failures, but more often than not I managed to rehabilitate those who came to us. I worked literally day and night, often listening with rapt attention for eight to ten hours at a time to someone's problems and going to bed at 4 a.m. with a feverish headache and a temperature from sheer exhaustion.

I developed a high degree of patience and a dogged determination never to give up. I came to think in terms of months and years rather than days or weeks. Two men, one a professional burglar, and the other a lifetime alcoholic, are now completely rehabilitated, but each took five years.

I had very little psychiatric expertise – I simply used the tools of commonsense and unrelenting loving-kindness, and it worked, often where the professionals had failed. I had always felt compassion for the depressed and the inadequate, probably because of my own failings, and I think my patients sensed this. They laid bare their souls to me and, after they had done so, however heinous the crimes they had committed, they still had a friend. This meant a great deal to them.

I was fortunate in having fifty acres of land, mostly forestry, and when jaded and exhausted in mind and spirit I used to go down to the woods and work in the forestry unit. Nature's healing powers came to my rescue; in a few hours I had recuperated. And often while undertaking this simple manual work a flash of enlightenment about the core of a person's problem would come to me as if out of the air.

I had a young woman who had been a heroin addict for fourteen years and in the hands of psychiatrists throughout. She withdrew from heroin in three months, and she is now a qualified social worker. Another was incarcerated in a mental hospital, having had five treatments of electrotherapy. She is now a qualified district nurse. The work was therapeutic for me, too. For ten years I had never given a thought to myself; I simply projected myself into the selfless service of others with a total dedication, and through 'giving' I 'received'.

But after ten years I had aged a lot; the work had taken its toll. I was sixty-five and reluctantly I gave it up. I tried my hand at writing articles. To my surprise, although some of my work was rejected (and almost invariably the pieces I thought the best!) the majority of my articles were published. It was fulfilling to feel that I was sharing with others such wisdom as I had acquired in the course of a full and adventurous life, both in the spiritual field and in other ways. It seemed like a final consummation in the autumn of my life. I did not expect much more. But it was not to be – there was another peak to the mountain.

After the death of our medium I rather lost interest in Spiritualism. Like all organised movements it seemed to be a little narrow, to restrict rather than to expand one's consciousness. It was an invaluable milestone on the pathway, but it was not the pathway. Spiritualism did much good work in proving the existence of an after-life, in rescue and healing work and, in rare circumstances, in providing good and valid spiritual teaching.

But I did not feel that those who communicated from spirit were all that high in the Hierarchy; sometimes it seemed to me that 'guides' knew less than the more evolved souls on earth. There were also many pitfalls. I read a little book called *Psychic Pitfalls* by Shaw Desmond (a Spiritualist but a stern critic of the movement) who had spent half a lifetime working with and studying the best known mediums of his day. He came to the conclusion that many messages were either coloured by the subconscious mind of the medium, or even tampered with by 'dwellers on the threshold'. One had to be very discerning.

The truth was that I no longer needed to belong to any movement or religion. I was a child of God and a citizen of the world, who believed that Love was the fundamental law of the Cosmos. God was Love. It was as simple as that. And I was comforted by the thought that some of the world's cleverest men, after a lifetime of intellectual analysis and philosophising, had reached the same conclusion — men like Einstein, Carl Jung, and Bertrand Russell.

At this point my wife told me of the One who is the actual embodiment of Love on earth — Bhagavan Sri Sathya Sai Baba. At first I dismissed the possibility. I thought: just another Indian *guru*. Then one day I took up Dr Sandweiss's book, *Sai Baba, the Holy Man and the Psychiatrist*. I had read precisely ten pages when I knew with certainty that this man was a Divine Being, transcendental. I knew it with a kind of 'soul sight'. I suppose I was 'ready', or as Swami says, I needed only a gentle tap with a hammer.

For eighteen months I read nothing but books on Sai Baba. I marked them, précied them, made copious notes on the quotations. And every day I felt more sure, and more steeped in reverence, awe, and amazement. There was nothing, absolutely nothing, that he did or said or taught that did not strike a chord in my breast. In fact if I had been asked to imagine God on earth it would have been an exact replica of Swami!

Here was a God-man who was the embodiment of Love itself in all respects. A God-man who put Love before everything, before all the sophisticated techniques of spiritual development. A God-man whose teaching proclaimed no rules or dogma except *Sathya* (Truth), *Dharma* (Right Living), *Shanti* (Peace) and, of course, *Prema* (Love).

A God-man whose concept of holiness was more wholeness than the piety and sanctimoniousness of so many of our Western ecclesiastics.

A God-man who was so intensely human, and yet so patently divine, who was one's mother and one's father and one's closest friend.

A God-man equally versed in the secular scene as the esoteric — friend of beggars and the downcast, inspirer and counsellor to Government ministers, interpreter to *Vedic* scholars!

A God-man who loved animals, and had owned no less than fourteen dogs, burying his favourite pair in a special place of honour in his *ashram.*

A God-man whose face was so gentle and so intensely lovable, yet had about it a sort of divine 'homespun' quality; I did not want my God to look like a saint on a stained-glass window, so ethereal as to be unapproachable by mere humans.

The time came when my wife and I felt we had to go to India. My wife had written a dozen articles which had created considerable interest in Baba, and I had done my share in lending books and talking to interested persons. Yet we lacked the authority of having ever seen him in person. Spiritually we longed to go, yet we dreaded the journey and the possible discomfort and hardship once there. We were old. It was mid-winter. I had a ruptured Achilles' tendon, and I had not been abroad or flown in an aeroplane for nearly twenty years.

It is my belief that when one is about to take a right course of action the Dark Powers impinge on one's mind all sorts of plausible reasons why one should not take that course. People telephoned us and warned us of dire diseases. Had we had injections? Had we got mosquito nets? We must be wary of pickpockets. One old friend even said the air trip would be a nightmare.

On a dark winter's morning in mid-January we set off at 4 a.m. for Heathrow Airport. It was a final pilgrimage of the soul. We went in faith — we did not even have injections. We did not take mosquito nets, and we did not take any medicines.

In the event the air journey was as smooth as a limousine — at 30,000 feet our jumbo jet was as steady as a rock and as spacious as a floating hotel. And once in India, the sun shone, the colours blazed, and we felt more sprightly than in England. I did not even see a mosquito. We did, however, take the precaution of boiling the water.

On the 17th of January 1980 a small group of us found ourselves standing at the corner of the College hostel at Brindavan, awaiting Swami's *darshan.* Suddenly there was a hush and the small red robed figure came floating across the sand. I stood rivetted. To my absolute consternation he came straight towards me and said, "Would you like some *vibhuti*?" I was speechless. He made two circular movements with his hand and poured a little heap of the sacred ash into the palm of my right hand. I stood agape and incredulous, with my palm outstretched. Swami said, "Eat it".

In a complete daze I ate it. We were then motioned to go to the residence.

I walked across the sand with more apprehension than I had ever felt in my life. Playboy and philanderer, sensualist, the loser of a fortune, neurotic and one-time depressive; and on the credit side, true seeker according to my misguided lights, successful farmer, dedicated welfare worker, and now a minor writer. True pilgrim, or neurotic sinner? I did not know, and I challenge anyone to know their true spiritual status. The first shall be last and the last first. I hobbled on with my injured ankle. I felt old, scarred by life. I was bald, toothless, rather shabbily dressed.

When my turn came for an interview I fell at his feet and broke. Forsaking etiquette I put my arm round him while he enfolded me in similar fashion. I looked up at him with tear-stained face and met his eyes for perhaps five seconds. I have never before seen such love and tenderness in a man's eyes. I nestled my cheek against his stomach. "I can't believe it, Swami," I managed to say through my tears, meaning that I could not take in the incomparable blessing to an old man of sixty-seven who had travelled 6,000 miles and was now in the arms of an *avatar*. It seemed like the last yard of a marathon odyssey of the soul, that I had reached the finishing tape and come home at last.

He turned to my wife and said, "This is a good man." I felt he had looked into my naked soul. He repeated the words, "This is a good man." I would rather have heard those words than if he had said I was a second Leonardo da Vinci.

Thus an old man from Tunbridge Wells in England met the *Avatar* of the new Aquarian Age, the founder of the new world religion, the Sai Religion of Love, embracing all the major faiths of the world. It surely says much for the universality of his love that he should take one such as I into his fold and within the orbit of his grace. My wife told me that I only just removed my old cricket cap (to ward off sunburn) in time, and that I had one sock inside out!

I had found my God at last. I had come home, into the arms of the mother I never had, but this time the Divine Mother. I had made the last journey.

# 2

# HIGHLIGHTS OF THE TRIP

In the fortnight that followed my wife and I had the incomparable blessing of three more interviews (four in all) with Sai Baba, and in addition many little chats at *darshan*. Our close friend, Vemu Mukunda, was enormously helpful — he arranged virtually everything for us, and with his almost superhuman energy kept us on the go every minute of the day. He was indeed a 'friend, philosopher and guide'.

Miraculously, Swami had arrived from Puttaparthi (110 miles from Bangalore) to Brindavan, only 14 miles distant, the day after we arrived so that we were able to stay in a reasonably comfortable and very economical hotel in Bangalore and motor over in a hired car each day to the *ashram*. Such were the blessings we received that I have often wondered if Baba timed this move to suit our convenience, feeling that we were a little old to face the austerities of the *ashram* at Puttaparthi.

*Darshan* is held under a circular corrugated iron structure through which grows a large banyan tree, and in the centre is a figure of Krishna playing his flute. About a thousand devotees sit in the lotus position awaiting Swami's appearance from his residence, about a hundred yards away across an expanse of sand.

He walks very slowly, almost floating rather than walking — (in fact, I got the impression of a flymo!) – with a grace and rhythm which I have never seen in a man.

*Darshan* consists in collecting letters from devotees with problems or sick relatives, uttering a word of encouragement here, giving a warm smile there, sometimes looking piercingly at a stranger as if gauging their past, present and future, sometimes healing, on occasion instantly, and of course materialising *vibhuti*, but never giving any indication which direction he will take or which corridor he will pass down next.

He seemed to work almost aimlessly, rather than in an organised way, as if he had all the time in the world, yet after a while one got the impression that he was a man with an almost limitless consciousness who worked in a thousand ways, and who never failed to see any real need in anyone present.

There was no need to be in the front row or anything like that, although some undiscerning people did push and shove a little to attract attention. In fact, one day I stood outside the *darshan* group altogether, against the *ashram* wall at the back, only to find myself motioned to come forward to speak to him.

The day following that ecstatic first interview we had a group interview at which Swami materialised many objects. My wife received a locket and a lovely *japamala.* She was spellbound. Two materialisations for her in one interview! When my turn came Swami produced a silver ring and, leaning over from his chair, placed it on the third finger of my left hand. He gave it a bit of a shove over the top knuckle, as much to say, "That will not come off." Indeed, it will not until the day I am cremated! I would not sell that ring for a million pounds. It was exactly what I wanted, and he placed it on the finger I hoped he would.

He was so loving, so gentle, so humorous, and so human; indeed, it seemed that he was more human than we 'humans' seated around him. Swami's divinity and his humanity do not co-exist: they fuse – the only way to describe it is to say that he is both humanly divine and divinely human!

The following day we had another private interview. Just my wife and I. It lasted a long time. We asked many questions. Swami gave us his undivided attention. Finally came the question which had perplexed and gnawed at my wife for a long time, and about which she had recently written an article: did Jesus die on the Cross?

There followed a detailed and absolutely specific reply. Jesus had not died on the Cross. The so called Resurrection was a physical recovery from his wounds. He had continued his mission in India and in Malaysia. He had finally died a natural death and was buried in Srinagar, capital of Kashmir.

We did not go into details of His 'death'. It is my belief that He may have died a clinical death on the Cross, but was revived in the tomb by a flash of radiation from Spirit, which possibly accounts for the impregnation of the Shroud of Turin with an exact replica of his wounds and visage. The Shroud is now accepted by both the Vatican and the scientific fraternity as authentic. But the point that Swami emphasised was that Jesus recovered in his physical body, and was not a materialised form.

So the very core of Christian belief, the Resurrection, rather than the immortal sayings of the Nazarene, was a myth. I had always suspected as much. To me it was the teachings that mattered.

As the reader can imagine, my wife and I came out of that interview in a daze. Why had two insignificant people from Tunbridge Wells in England been given such highly significant information? Why had we been so incomparably blessed with three interviews on three consecutive days when others, seemingly more worthy, had hung around the *ashram* for months, even years, without gaining a single private interview? I do not know the answer to that. I only know that it occurred.

A few days later Maynard Ferguson, playing the trumpet, and Vemu Mukunda, playing the *vina*, gave a concert in the students' hostel. It was a successful attempt to combine Eastern and Western music. At the last minute I was invited to attend. Unfortunately my wife was not allowed in because women are not permitted to enter the hostel. There was an audience of about a thousand, seated in the lotus position. With great courtesy I was given a chair on account of my damaged ankle. I believe I was the only European present in the audience, and it seemed to me to be an enormous privilege.

Swami attended. He smiled at me as he entered the large hall. The concert went well; there was a thunderous ovation at the end. Swami seemed to enjoy the experiment; he clapped his hands to th rhythm and afterwards manifested a ring for Maynard who had blown his heart out for the *Avatar*. Then Swami sang to us for a few minutes in his sweet, melodious voice, and finally discoursed to us for an hour without notes. He never uses notes.

There is a phrase in Dr Sandweiss's book, *Sai Baba, the Holy Man and the Psychiatrist*, about 'man's infinite capacity for doubt', which stems of course from the lower self. I arrived in India 99% certain that Sai Baba was an *avatar* and with 1% of doubt. As I looked about me at the audience while Swami discoursed that 1% vanished. No impostor could deceive such an audience. The students were dressed in neat white cotton suits, spotlessly clean. They were alert, intelligent, balanced and composed, dedicated, fervent, inspired; they would have made our undergraduates at Oxford and Cambridge look very second rate. So, too, the teachers – doctors, scientists, philosophers, poets, men of letters. All rapt with attention at Swami's words. No mere *guru* could have commanded such respect and reverence and love in such an elite audience. This was a God-man. For me it was the most magical evening of my entire life. My 1% of doubt has never returned. It was the moment of my total conversion, and since that day Sai Baba has completely filled my life.

Another seemingly magical thing occurred that night. I was reliably informed that Swami had discoursed in Telugu, yet his words came over to me in English! As far as I know, there was no interpreter. A man stood a few feet away, who appeared to be taking the speech down in shorthand, but he was not translating. I watched Swami's lips move and the words came out instantaneously. I can still hear the phrase: "Character, character, that is important in education."

Was I misinformed and was he actually speaking English? Or, had Swami performed one of his extraordinary miracles? There is a reported case where he was speaking in Telugu to a small group in his interview room, when it was pointed out to him that one member of the group did not speak his native tongue. Swami touched him on the head with the palm of his hand, and the man was immediately able to understand Telugu. In an instant he had transferred to him the mental faculty to understand an alien tongue!

Had something of this kind happened to me on that memorable night? I have never been able to clear the matter up to my satisfaction.

We did not see Swami again for five days. He left Brindavan for Bombay, saying he would return before we left for home. We decided to remain in Bangalore. Vemu Mukunda saw to it that we used those five days to good effect. We had a terrific schedule.

He introduced us to his family – to a younger brother who invited us to his home for a bite; and to an elder brother, a doctor, who presented us with a charming walnut container which we thought would be ideal for storing packets of *vibhuti*. At one meeting with Swami we had been literally loaded with about sixty packets of the sacred ash, and these we held very precious. We also met his old father, aged eighty-six, in his home. He was of the generation who regretted that India had ever become independent. He still seemed to be loyal to the Duke of Windsor!

One evening Professor Kasturi was brought to our hotel, and we had an exhilerating two hours with him. He is eighty-four, a saintly and intensely lovable old man, and full of humour! He is still regarded as one of India's leading humorist writers – in fact, thirty-three years ago, when he first became a devotee, he was the editor of a magazine similar to our own *Punch* which he called *Judy*, and at that time he wrote scathingly of Sai Baba, and caricatured him.

He is one of Swami's oldest devotees, and has just completed the fourth and most weighty volume of Swami's biography. In the 1950's, when he wished to start on the first volume, Swami told him he must wait a further six years, for at that time it would have read like something out of the Arabian Nights and would simply not have been believed.

He told us fascinating tales of the early days when there was only a handful of devotees who slept in one room with Swami and scarcely dared to close their eyes, for Swami did not appear to sleep at all and was liable to say something at odd times in the night which they were afraid of missing. So they slept like foxes, with one eye open. We deemed it a great honour that this saintly and now fragile old man should go to the trouble of visiting us in our hotel.

Another evening we were taken to Dr Gokak's house and had a very interesting two hours with this very eminent, Oxford-educated writer and scholar who is Swami's official interpreter. He is very intellectual and erudite, and a poet.

He told us candidly of his conversion some sixteen years ago when he had been a follower of Sri Aurobindo. It started with a very symbolic dream in which a rose (symbol of the heart) had consistently removed itself from a floral arrangement he was making on the tomb of that sage, and how he had just as consistently (and somewhat stubbornly) put it back. But nothing would keep the rose in its place. He enquired of a friend, learned in the interpretation of dreams and whose judgement he respected, what the possible meaning of this strange dream could be, and was told that he had become too intellectual and lacked heart, and love. He then asked himself, "How does one learn to love? What book can I buy?" Believe me, in sixteen years of service to Swami he had learned!

His story was really the story of the conversion of an intellectual who could not believe that anything transcended reason and logic. He was a hard nut to crack – it took five years. Doubts continually assailed him, and it was only when Swami explained to him in Sanskrit the meaning of his and of Sri Aurobindo's incarnations that he became fully convinced.

He told us how, many years ago, a small group of devotees formed a circle round Swami while he 'wrote in the sand' along the banks of the river at Puttaparthi. (It reminded me of Christ writing in the sand, although the circumstances were entirely different.) After waiting about two minutes while nothing happened Swami suddenly said, "Ah, now it is ready!" and proceeded to scoop out of the sand a two-foot solid gold statue of Krishna which was very detailed and very beautiful. He added jokingly, "If I had manifested a true likeness of Krishna you would have been very disappointed!" Dr Gokak asked Swami how he did it, and was told, "By will and imagination."

On yet another occasion we spent a wonderful evening with Mr and Mrs Balu. Mr Balu is a director of the India Coffee Federation, and a highly gifted artist. Before dinner he took us up to his studio and, although I am no art critic, it seemed to me that I was being shown paintings by an unrecognised genius of absolutely top calibre. There was a painting of a white horse in full gallop which showed an extraordinary degree of power and movement, and another which showed, symbolically, the fusion of science and spirituality.

He said the talent had only come to the surface since becoming a devotee of Sai Baba. There was one life-size collage of Swami which was so fantastically life-like that we simply started at it, as if mesmerized, for about ten minutes. The background was full of symbolism. I asked him how long the work had taken to conceive. "Oh, months," he said. In the bottom right-hand corner was a tiny figure of Sai Gita, Swami's elephant. I noticed nothing odd about it. Mr Balu took out a magnifying glass and said, "Look in the eye." I did so, and to my astonishment it was a tiny picture of Swami. Yet without the magnifying glass it looked like an elephant's eye. What a concept!

We had a lovely evening. Mr Balu's son drove us home. He said, "I have never seen two elderly people with so much joy about them." That pleased us greatly. There was already a rub-off from Swami's state of constant bliss.

To my dying day I shall never forget the festival of bougainvilleas which flowed like a streaming cascade along the whole length of Mr Balu's garden fence and massed along his balcony.

The day times were just as full, while Swami was away in Bombay. Vemu arranged meetings with editors. During the first interview the editor of the *Deccan Herald* said to me, "You look like a bust of Gladstone." It was the last thing I imagined I looked like, with no top teeth and very little hair. I replied, "It's strange you should say that. My great-grandfather, Samuel Laing, was in Gladstone's cabinet, and in 1860 was sent out to India to organise the railway fares." He was amazed.

He passed us on to a journalist who took details of our careers (somewhat inaccurately), had us photographed and gave us a write-up. Peggy was commissioned to write an article. The second editor, of a Spiritualist type of magazine, was very interested in her *Two Worlds* articles.

'Little' things happened as well as the 'big' things. For the whole seventeen days we had the feeling that we were in the grip of destiny. For example, one day at *darshan*, Swami called me out to ask if we were going to Bombay with him. It is the custom to kneel down and touch his feet. As I was about to do so he noticed that I had an injured ankle and was having difficulty in lowering myself. He made a gesture as if to say, 'Oh, don't bother', and then gave me a gentle heave to my feet. At that moment my wife hastily took a photograph only to find, later, to her great disappointment, that she had finished the film. The next day a stranger came up to me and said, "I took a photograph of you yesterday when Swami was helping you to your feet. If you would like a copy I will send one when you get home."

On another occasion another total stranger approached me à propos of nothing and said, "Would you like the name and address of an Englishwoman in London who runs a centre where *bhajans* are sung in English?" During one of our interviews I had asked Swami, "Would it spoil the sound vibrations if *bhajans* were translated into English?" He had replied, "No, the vibrations come from the heart!"

There was also one very amusing incident. We went to cash a traveller's cheque. The Indian bank manager was having a slack afternoon. He invited us into his office and proceeded to try to convert us to orthodox Christianity, while we, who had come from a Christian culture, tried to convert him to the world of Sai religion! He could not understand why two elderly people had come all the way from England to see Sathya Sai Baba. (He had recently come to Bangalore from Kerala.) We must have had an hour's discussion. He admitted he had never seen Swami. Towards the end of the conversation he played what he evidently believed was his trump card. He said, "This man has never raised the dead like Christ raised Lazarus." We countered immediately, quoting chapter and verse of the two known occasions when Swami had raised the dead. I think we won the day. The bank manager looked dumbfounded. He said, "I must go and see this man!"

But the highlight of the whole trip, apart from our interviews with Swami, was our visit to Puttaparthi, the birthplace of Sri Sathya Sai Baba and the seat of the main *ashram*, Prasanthi Nilayam. It was 110 miles from Bangalore and we covered this distance twice that day. It was swelteringly hot and the road was bumpy; indeed the last part, though recently improved, was little better than a bullock track. But it gave us an idea of the Indian countryside, and when we finally arrived it was like the last lap of a long, long odyssey to our true spiritual home. It was worth the discomfort a thousand times over.

On the way, as an ex-farmer, I drank in avidly all that I could see of the rural scene. There were many small lakes irrigating the paddy fields which despite the eternal sunshine did not seem to dry up. There were peasants planting by hand in the terracotta soil. Many of the crops I could not identify except the rice and maize, coconuts and grapes. There were granite hills, and many of the fencing posts and the trellis work for the grape plantations were shafts of granite.

We must have passed a hundred bullock carts and no more than half a dozen cars on the whole 110-mile journey. Monkeys scampered about on the side of the road. Vultures flew overhead. We passed herds of donkeys and goats. Hump-backed Indian cows grazed drowsily in the fields which amounted to no more than fibrous stalks of dried up hay.

It was a land of contrasts, of large Government buildings and modern electricity pylons abutting on tiny primitive hovels of crudely plastered brick and ancient thatch of hay and reeds. Yet everywhere was colour – in the blue vault of the sky, in the lovely red soil, in the mountains of the background, in the brick of the village hovels, on the horns of the oxen (painted for festivals), in the ever-flowering bougainvillea, in the gay *saris* of the village girls, walking with such poise and dignity, balancing baskets on their heads.

Here we felt the spirit of rural India, its soul and character, and we fell in love with it. As we drove along, in a state of near-meditation, it was slowly borne in upon me that India, with its fertile soil and its eternal sunshine, was potentially a land of 'milk and honey'. She would rise again. Swami's students coming out of the universities would prove the leaven to raise India from her present degradation. Once again this ancient land of *Bharat* would become the *guru* of the world. Her influence would convert Soviet Russia to God, and the world would be saved. It seemed like a mystical vision.

On the outskirts of Puttaparthi we saw a huge Sai University in course of construction on one side of the road, and a hostel of equal dimension on the other. And in the background we could just see the *ashram gokulam* (cowshed) where, in the distance, we caught a glimpse of Sai Gita. We turned down a side street which was still quite primitive. Drowsy oxen stood in the middle of the road and showed no inclination to move despite our driver's frantic honking. Nor did the inhabitants who milled about in the street show any urgency in getting out of the way; they seemed to think they had a prior right over a mere mechanical vehicle!

Slowly the driver manoeuvred his way down the crowded street, although it would have been quicker to walk. And then, suddenly, we came to a halt on the edge of a vast expanse of sand. This was the River Chitravati which had virtually dried up owing to the construction of dams for reservoir water higher up its course. Only a small lake remained, and this I suspect was spring-fed as there was scarcely a trickle of water in the riverbed. Villagers were washing their clothing on the far bank.

Here, as a boy, Swami had played and swum in the river and, a little later, walking along the sandy shore with his early devotees, had performed miracle after miracle. The range of terracotta mountains which encircled and protected the village looked clear and vivid in the pure air and mistless sunshine.

We got out of the car and decided to paddle in the lake. The sand was almost too hot for our bare feet. An ugly but engaging urchin stood by, happily grinning at us and repeating, "Sai Ram, Sai Ram." I watched the villagers wringing the water out of their clothing by flogging the items against great boulders which abutted on the water's edge. I could not understand the vehemence with which they did this — they seemed to be literally beating the living daylights out of their own vestments!

Suddenly I heard Vemu's voice in the background. I only heard the words, "Tamarind tree." "What?" I said. "The tamarind tree," he repeated. "You've read about the tamarind tree, havn't you?"

"Yes, of course I have," I said. When I first read about Swami's miracles on the tamarind tree it had made a very strong impact on me.

"Well, there it is," he said. He pointed to a nearby craggy knoll, about 200 feet high. This was the little hill where Swami had run races to the top with his school chums, often levitating himself to the summit and standing in a halo of light. There was a tiny red flag, not much bigger than the size of a man's hand, to mark the spot at the top. And next to it, the tamarind, a small round evergreen.

I just stared and stared. I simply could not take it in. In fact I could not fully grasp the fact that only a few days before I had been in Tunbridge Wells in England, living through a cold, murky winter, and now here I was, 6,000 miles away, at the birthplace of the *Avatar* of the New Age, paddling in the river where he had swum, standing on sands where his feet had trod a thousand times, and gazing up at the tree on the branches of which, by a mere wave of his hand, he had rewarded his exhausted colleagues after a so called race by materialising fruit. It seemed totally unbelievable. And yet there I was . . .

Tears began to roll down my cheeks. The urchin kept grinning up at me and saying, "Sai Ram." He must have wondered why a tall, strongly built Westerner was weeping at the sight of a tree. Slowly I felt transported back 2,000 years in history. The country-side through which I had passed, with its peasants toiling in the sun, the thronged little street of Puttaparthi with its drowsy oxen and its slow, unchanging tenor, and the vast tracts of sand along the holy Chitravati became for me the ancient land of Palestine, the little village of Nazareth, and the shores of Lake Galilee. In those ecstatic, transcendental moments it seemed to me that Sathyanarayana Raju of Puttaparthi, and Jesus, the Christ, of Nazareth, were one and the same person. I felt an overwhelming sense of joy and, somehow, of relief.

Vemu had seen it all many times before. He hurried us on. I could have stood there all day, and the next day as well.

I will not describe our visit to the *ashram* and the remainder of the day, for my wife has written of it very adequately in her section of this book. I had just two regrets. We went in search of Swami's birthplace, but the house had been recently demolished and a shrine erected in its place. And how I longed, just for once, to chant the AUM at sunrise with perhaps 35,000 devotees. It must be a sound that truly rises to the highest celestial spheres.

On our return to Bangalore we learned that Swami had arrived back from Bombay to Brindavan. We had two days to go before our departure. Secretly we longed for a final interview, to say farewell and receive his blessing, although we accepted that our cup was already filled to overflowing and that we had been blessed immeasurably beyond our desserts.

We attended *darshan* the following day, and twice the day after that, morning and evening, but nothing special occurred. In fact at one of these *darshans* I started to ask him if we might have one final interview to say goodbye, but he ignored this and passed on. He has an extraordinary manner of ignoring a remark without causing the slightest offence; one gets to realise there is a hidden meaning in every gesture and action.

However, on the evening of our last day we were invited to the students singing *bhajans* in his private quarters. This was a great honour. I cannot sing, and Swami has said that if one cannot sing one's best contribution during *bhajans* is to remain silent. So I did; I simply clapped my hands to the rhythms. But it was marvellous to hear the students sing with such gusto and fervour; if only our church choirs could sing like this!

At the end of the *bhajans*, as Swami ascended a spiral staircase to his private quarters, a great wave of compassion came over me. Here was a man who worked seven days and nights a week for mankind, yet surely an *avatar* could not have, among mere mortals, a single completely trustworthy friend, and even less one who could completely understand him. He must at times be lonely, I thought. But I suppose it was the human side of me that saw it like this. Swami has said: "I am always full of bliss."

As we motored back to Bangalore, Vemu could see we were disappointed at not receiving a final word. Our 'plane was due to leave at noon next day. Suddenly he said, "Swami is playing a trick. You see! We will dash over in the morning for *darshan*; there will be time to get you to the airport by noon."

We packed that night and paid the hotel bill. With little hope in our hearts, we agreed. We had accepted with good grace that we would not have a final interview, but we wanted on this occasion just to catch a last glimpse of Swami giving *darshan*. We sat under the banyan tree in a spirit of happy acceptance.

And then the miracle happened. Just before Swami emerged from his residence Vemu came rushing across the sand, beckoning frantically to Peggy and me to come forward. I hurried across the sand with my strained tendon, converging on Peggy hastening from the women's section. Through the residential archway and past the 'guards', up the path lined by students on either side who stood like a spiritual guard of honour. And all in the gaze of perhaps a thousand devotees under the banyan tree who must have watched breathlessly and perhaps, bless them, a little enviously.

At the private entrance to Swami's residence we hesitated. We could not believe we were intended to enter the front verandah entrance. But Vemu turned and said, "Come on, come on, Swami is waiting!" So we gathered our courage in both hands and proceeded. And there, standing on the threshold, holding up *darshan* for our arrival and undoubtedly aware that we had a 'plane to catch, was Swami, smiling hugely!

I fell to my knees and wept for sheer joy. "No, no, you mustn't," he said. So I pulled myself together and stood up. He materialised *vibhuti* for us both. An aide came forward with a piece of paper. I ate mine, but Peggy ate half and placed the remainder in the proffered paper, to keep. Then, turning to a circle of elite around him, and pointing to my wife, he said, "She's a great writer. She writes from the heart!" She will, of course, cherish the remark for the rest of her life, and it has certainly given her a second lease of life.

Finally he took us into his private interview room and gave us his blessing. He answered a personal question which had worried me for 7½ years. (He had certainly looked into my past.) And when we asked if we might form a Sai Centre in England, mainly for English people, he replied, "Very happy, very happy."

139

The solution of my personal question was one of the twin motivators of my visit to India, and just as he had left his 'coup de grace' of a compliment to my wife till the eleventh hour, so, too, he had left his final appraisal of my own enigma to the very last minute. It was so typical of Swami and the way he works.

We left in a daze. I suppose we had passed the final test of acceptance, and Swami had given us this final incomparable blessing. Vemu rushed us to the airport. I think his joy was almost as great as ours. He turned from the front of the car and said with a grin, "007 calling. Mission completed." It certainly had been!

The journey home was a bit of an anti-climax. There was a go-slow on at Bombay Airport and we had a sleepless night awaiting the take-off of a 'plane delayed by seven hours. We arrived home late on the night of February 1st. It seemed like coming from the Summerlands of Heaven to a plane in the semi-lower astral. For seventeen days we had lived through a story from the Arabian Nights, except that it was real. We had met the *Avatar* of the New Aquarian Age; indeed, as we believe, we had met something much more, the *Avatar* of all *Avatars*; and we carried in our hearts a secret which, if believed, would shake the Christian churches to their very foundations, that Jesus of Nazareth had not died on the Cross!

# 3

# THE SECOND COMING HAS COME

I had studied the life and teachings of Sathya Sai Baba for two years prior to my visit to India, and I had come to the firm conclusion that once again "the Word had been made flesh", that the Divine Principle had incarnated – indeed, that an *avatar* had come to save the world from destruction and to usher in a new Golden Age. As a matter of fact, I sensed it with a kind of soul-sight after reading no more than ten pages of the first book I read, and I have been increasingly overwhelmed by the impact since that first magic moment.

But what has impacted me equally is the extraordinary similarity in the life, teachings and personality of Sai Baba and the Christ, not only in the basic but in the specific detail in which both express themselves in words and phraseology which are virtually identical. This is simply not so if you study the sayings of the Buddha, Mohammed, or other founders of a world religion. Of course it is true that all world religions basically assert the same truths, but there is an extraordinary identity between Sai Baba and the Christ which is unique.

In 1968 Albert Eckhart wrote: "The difference between Sai Baba and Jesus Christ is the fact that the first is living and his miracles are confirmed by men, whereas the miracles of Jesus Christ are reported in the Bible only. Nevertheless the behaviour and the deeds of both are nearly and often the same."

Of course when I refer to Jesus Christ I am not referring to the man, Jesus of Nazareth, but to the High Celestial Being, the Christ (from the Greek word 'Christos', meaning the anointed one) who overshadowed and guided him, probably from the time of his baptism in the Jordan. Some believe the Christ to be a Cosmic Being, responsible not only for our solar system, which may be the origin of orthodox Christianity's insistence on the 'only begotten Son'.

The Christ said through Jesus of Nazareth: "I am the Way, the Truth, and the Life. The Father and I are one; no one comes to the Father except by me." On the face of it this incredible statement must, in essence, either be true, or the hallucination of the biggest megalomaniac of his time. Now the teachings of a megalomaniac do not survive for two thousand years. Falsity can deceive for a time, but it cannot survive the centuries unless it has at least the basis of truth in it. As the poet, William Platt, put it: "That which has life shall surely live forever; only that dies which was forever dead." The fact remains that the Christ's teachings and life have inspired saints and martyrs throughout history to follow his teachings and example.

Sai Baba has made even more incredible statements: "My power is immeasurable, my truth is inexplicable, unfathomable. I am beyond the reach of the most intensive enquiry and the most meticulous measurement. There is nothing I do not see, nowhere I do not know the way, no problem I cannot solve. My sufficiency is unconditional. I am the totality — all of it."

Megalomania? Yet in a mere forty years since his mission started this man has gathered round him fifty million devotees in India, has well over three thousand centres in that country, and has built six universities. His fame is now worldwide, despite shunning publicity; there are centres in virtually every country in the Western world and in the Far East. He is probably better known in India, in the real sense, than the Pope is in Europe.

On his fiftieth birthday, Dr Diwaker, an Indian scholar and statesman, said, "Once Swami was a village urchin. Now we assemble from the four quarters of the globe and what do we find — a township at Puttaparthi (the seat of the *ashram* but once a poverty-stricken village) with housing for thousands — philosophers, legislators, educationalists, scientists, technologists, the ignorant as well as the learned, the rich as well as the poor, and from all religions and from all nations. If this is not a marvel and a living miracle I would like to know what is."

"By their fruits ye shall know them." Jesus the Christ went

about loving people and healing the sick. Sathya Sai Baba, too, does just that — he works tirelessly twenty-four hours a day in the service of mankind; he is said not to sleep, and he does not eat enough to keep a normal man alive. He has showered his love on millions, he has healed thousands. As he says, "I am the Embodiment of Love; love is my instrument." And like the Christ it is love in action. Christ, by his crucifixion, founded a religion that spread across half the globe. Sai Baba, in his lifetime, is well on the way to doing the same, by re-animating the soul of all religion, which, although shrouded by dogma and theology is, in essence, Love. It seems to me, therefore, that when one says, "I am the Way, the Truth, and the Life," and the other, "My sufficiency is unconditional. I am the totality — all of it," they are speaking the truth, that they are both God-men, divine, no mere prophets or *gurus*, but the type of Beings who walked the earth millenia ago.

Both interpret the purpose of human life on earth in exactly the same way. The symbolic meaning of the Christian Cross is the eradication of the lower ego — the vertical stroke representing the 'I', or lower self, with which we are born, and the horizontal stroke the erasure of this lower ego. Baba's interpretation is identical: "Your birth has been undertaken for one purpose, the eradication of the lower ego on the Cross of Compassion." Both proclaim the Brotherhood of Man and the universality of the Message. "Go, teach all nations," said the Christ. "My mission is for all mankind," says Baba. "All men are of one lineage, of divine origin. All are cells in one Divine Organism. Therefore, recognise in each being a brother, and banish all limiting thoughts and prejudices. There is only one religion, the religion of Love, only one caste, that of humanity, only one language, that of the heart."

The teaching of both is exoteric and esoteric. Christ taught the masses in simple parables, yet astounded the scholars and theologians in the Temple with the range of his knowledge and the depth of his perception. Baba also teaches the masses in parables, yet he can explain the most abstruse mysteries of the *Vedas* to erudite *Brahmin* pundits.

Both come over as Men of the People, intensely human and lovable, albeit divine, rather than as cloistered holy men. One feels this about the Christ, at one and the same time a friend and a God-man. So, too, with Baba — at one time helping a devotee in distress, or borrowing a razor from his trusted aide Dr Gokak, or stopping the car to give money to a wayside vagrant, and then suddenly performing the most astonishing miracle.

Christ commanded an audience, no doubt of thousands, during his Sermon on the Mount and elsewhere, and was acclaimed by virtually the entire city on his entry into Jerusalem. Baba commands an audience of tens of thousands (up to a quarter of a million) during festivals when he gives *darshan*, or on a whirlwind visit to a big city.

Both started their missions when children. Christ taught in the Temple at Jerusalem at the age of twelve. Baba was performing miracles at the age of eight and started his mission at the age of thirteen.

The one major dissimilarity I detect is in the degree to which Christ practised exorcism. He is continually referred to as 'casting out devils'. Baba exorcises but not to the same extent. On one occasion he is reported as giving detailed instructions to a devotee on how to counter the effects of a black magic rite which had been perpetrated against him, including a description of the exact spot where a sacrificial goat had been buried after the black ritual.

But the basic aims and tenets of faith of both are the same. The Christ did not intend to start a new religion. He came to fulfil the Law of One, and proclaim new revelation, to build on the old, to stop malpractices such as animal sacrifice, to end corruption, to point out the errors in the Scriptures, to amend the old law of an eye for an eye and a tooth for a tooth and substitute the precept to love one's enemies and to turn the other cheek.

Neither is Sai Baba founding a new religion. On his letterhead he has the symbols of what he considers to be the five major faiths — Hindu, Buddhist, Christian, Islamic and Zoroastrian (the teachings of Zoroaster). He is continually re-energising old shrines, and pointing out the interpolations, excisions and misinterpretations of the *Vedas* to *Vedic* scholars. As he says, "I have come to repair the ancient highway to God." One might say that there is nothing new under the spiritual sun.

The belief in the Law of *Karma* and Reincarnation is common to both, although almost all the Christ's teachings on these truths were expunged after five centuries at the Council of Constantinople in 553 A.D. They are, however, still intact in the Aquarian Gospel. "A man reaps what he sows," says the Christ. "Whatsoever acts a man does, good or bad, follow him," says Baba. And he asserts that our personalities and our inter-relationships are so often confused and warped by the moral consequences of numerous past lives, that we are not 'all in one piece', as it were. Quite often he declines to heal, for he knows a person's past *karma* and gauges what degree of suffering is necessary for his ultimate salvation. But he always declines with a loving smile and an encouraging pat on the shoulder. (To one sufferer he explained, "If I heal you now, you will only have to come back again.")

"The Kingdom of Heaven is within you," said the Christ. "We

make our worlds ourselves," says Baba. The teaching of the *atma* (God immanent) indwelling in every human being is almost Sai Baba's first priority. He reiterates it again and again. "The best *guru* is God in you," he declares. "God is in the heart of every human being; derive courage and inspiration from Him. He is the *Guru* most interested in your progress." To a devotee who once asked him if he was God he replied, "You are God; the only difference between us is that I know I am, but you do not."

Christ upheld the role of women and tried to raise their status above the level of mere chattels at a time when men doubted if women had souls. He was often surrounded by women, not only his mother, but Mary and Martha and Mary Magdalene to whom he was clearly devoted. Sai Baba declares: "Woman is equally equipped with man to tread the spiritual path." He elevates women in their vital role of motherhood as being the custodians of future generations. ("The mother is the child's first *guru*.") His first university was built solely for the education of women.

Christ preached Joy and the Life Abundant: "I have come that you may have life, and have it more abundantly." What an ironic travesty the average church-going Christian has made of this sublime saying! Joy is the very essence of Sai Baba's personality and teaching. Listen to those who know him intimately — Howard Murphet, author of two books on Baba: "We who struggle on through sorrow and passing joy, see (in Sai Baba) the embodiment of perfect joy." Or to Dr Sandweiss, author of *Sai Baba, the Holy Man and the Psychiatrist*: "He appears to be in a state of constant bliss. His face and body are lit with an aura of energy which I have never observed in another human being." Or to Baba himself: "I am always full of bliss. Whatever may happen, nothing can come in the way of my smile."

But of course the cornerstone of the teaching of these two God-men can be summed up in the one word, Love. No newcomer to the Gospels, unconditioned by theology, could possibly read them without gaining the overwhelming impression that the paramount message contained therein is that of Love. "Love God, and thy neighbour as thyself, and on these two commandments hang all the Law and the Prophets." It is the golden rule to live by, the criterion to apply to every decision and to every judgement. Sai Baba, too, is the embodiment of Love. It is the essence of all his teaching. "Start the day with love, fill the day with love, end the day with love — this is the quickest and most direct way to God. Most routes are circuitous, but the direct path is Love. Other paths develop conceit, separate man from man, separate man from beast. They contract, they do not reach out; they shrink your awareness of the Divine. My teaching is *Prema* (love), my activity is *Prema*, my instrument is *Prema*, my way of life is *Prema*. There is nothing more precious within human grasp than love."

There is the same similarity in the detailed teachings. "Avoid killing, theft, adultery, greed, addiction to sensuality, anger, impatience, hatred, egotism, pride." Are not these exhortations an appeal to the Christian virtues? In the nine volumes of Sai Baba's discourses can be found virtually every precept of the Sermon on the Mount. I give here some of the sayings of both.

Jesus:    "Blessed are the pure in heart, for they shall see God."
Swami:   "The pure heart sees beyond the intellect; it becomes inspired."
Jesus:    "Know thyself and unto thyself be true."
Swami:   "Be true to your innermost nature."
Jesus:    "Search not for the mote in your neighbour's eye but look to the beam in your own."
Swami:   "Instead of seeing faults in others, search for those in yourself."
Jesus:    "Judge not that ye be not judged."
Swami:   "Do not judge others, for when another is judged you are yourself condemned."
Jesus:    "Cast not pearls before swine."
Swami:   "Do not discuss devotion with those who have none; it will lessen your own."
Jesus:    "Love your enemies."
Swami:   "Carry on even if you are hated, for it is your nature to love and forgive."
Jesus:    "Not everyone who sayeth Lord, Lord, shall enter into the kingdom of heaven, but he that doeth the will of my Father."
Swami:   "The secret of liberation lies not in mystic formulas and rosaries but in stepping out into action."
Jesus:    "Lo, I am with you always, even unto the consummation of the Age."
Swami:   "My grace is ever available to those who have steady love and faith".
Jesus:    "Ye shall know the Truth, and the Truth shall set you free."

Here, Swami relates the story of a monkey which puts its paw through a small hole in a container of food, grabs more than it requires, and therefore cannot extricate its paw; it cannot bring itself to let go of what is surplus to its needs! It is a parable, with wide implications, to illustrate the liberating effect of ridding oneself of ego, pride and self-esteem, of surplus material possessions, of becoming self-aware and self-honest in motivation – in a word, of serving God's will instead of self-will.

Jesus:    (admonishing the procrastinators): "<u>Now</u> is the moment of salvation."

Swami:    "Spirituality cannot wait, now is the right time."

Jesus:    "Arise, thy faith hath made thee whole."

Swami:    "Have unwavering faith and your burden I shall carry."

Jesus:    "For as much as you do injury to these you do it unto me."

Swami:    "I am in the least of you as much as in the best. Do not slander or injure anyone, for you are slandering Me who is in him."

Jesus:    (in the Lord's prayer): "For thine is the power and the glory."

Swami:    "No man can claim achievement, for all are but instruments in the hands of the Lord."

Jesus:    "Come unto me all ye who are weary and heavyladen, and I will give you rest."

Swami:    "Bring me the depths of your minds, no matter how grotesque, no matter how cruelly ravaged by doubts and disappointments. I will not reject you. I am your Mother."

As with the teachings, so with the personalities and miracles. It is clear that Christ had a radiant transparency, a divine charisma, with no trace of affectation, of pride and ego, and that he was motivated solely by Love, with love literally radiating from him. The impact of meeting him must have been soul-shattering. How else could a man walk up to a small group of illiterate fishermen, chat to them for an hour, and then say, "Follow me", and have them do just that, abandoning all?

Sai Baba has a similar effect. The sight of him changes men. Often souls are transformed instantly. It is true that it is not always so. Dr Bhagavantham, one of India's most noted nuclear physicists, took five years of investigation before becoming a devotee and proclaiming him divine, beyond the laws of physics and chemistry!

Baba explains this discrepancy in people's reaction to him thus: "Old souls are like a piece of rock that is already nearly split; it just needs a gentle touch. Young souls are like a piece of concrete that needs twenty blows with a sledge-hammer!"

Dr Sandweiss was an example of the former. On catching his first glimpse of Swami he writes: "What was communicated in that brief moment? The world. Something broke inside me. Some of Baba's love and joy penetrated my soul and I felt myself laughing like a child. Puffed-up self-pride and egotistical attachment to my own set of values and beliefs seemed to shatter in the dust . . . I felt somehow transformed in one dazzling, incredible minute. I was left with my mouth hanging open."

The Christ is said to have had an aura that reached out literally for a mile, and 'sensitives' who came within this radius were psychically aware of his presence and experienced a sense of uplift-ment. Sai Baba's aura has been described by Dr Baranowski, a clairvoyant and Kirlian photography expert from the University of Arizona, as almost limitless. The white (energy) filled the entire room, the pink (intense, universal love) reached literally to the horizon.

The Christ had X-ray eyes that could look into a person and instantly read thought and character. To the woman at the well who was prating about the niceties of religious worship he suggested that she should get her priorities right and sort out the relationships with the various men in her life. Baba, when asked why he gave some people interviews and declined others, has said: "I see into the mind and heart. I see who has an urgent problem and needs the help of an interview." Indeed, his claims go further, and these claims have been proved – he can see the past, present and future of everyone.

Both have proved themselves to be forgiving and merciful Beings. Christ forgave the woman taken in adultery, and showed great com-passion and gentleness towards her. Swami can be harsh at times but only to be kind in the long run. He has what is called a 'Repair Shop' where devotees are put to be corrected of faults (it amounts to no more than a lack of his attention for a time), but once they have repented and mended their ways they are taken lovingly back into the fold. He is the essence of forgiveness and mercy. The austere look of some so called holy men is alien to his nature.

One gets the impression that Christ preferred simple people and the simple life; in the main he chose simple men as his disciples. Baba often rails at the scholars and pedants, with their 'desire of disputation and the laurels of victory over those preening them-selves as learned'. "Be simple and sincere," he tells his devotees. Both show a dislike of the Pharisee type. Christ called them 'whited sepulchres'. Swami calls them 'dry as dust scholars exulting in their casuistry and argumentative skills'.

In contrast both have clearly shown their love of children. Christ upbraided his disciples, "Suffer little children to come to me." Baba shares a similar love. The daughter of a devotee at the Sai Centre in Wellingborough escorted a group of children to Putta-parthi in the summer of 1978. The children took with them seven sacks of 'presents' for Swami, containing everything from a large

148

Teddy bear to a packet of Weetabix! Baba insisted on personally inspecting every single item, expressing his delight according to the degree of love with which he was able to sense the gift was made. He adored them, and spent hours with them while important functionaries awaited an audience.

During the first night the children were too excited to sleep, so Baba lay down on the floor and pretended to sleep with them. The effect was immediate – in no time at all the children were in blissful slumber, and Baba was able to sneak out and return to his quarters.

Both demonstrate a capacity for deeply inspired anger, in the sense of vehement righteous indignation, which is hardly possible in ordinary people since we are liable to let an element of personal anger into even our justifiable tirades. Christ drove the money-changers from the Temple with a leather lash. There is an anecdote about Baba's occasional bursts of 'anger' from a friend of mine who is a devotee and who witnessed such an event. A man who had a very wealthy father who was dying came to him for financial advice. Swami could see that the man was thinking only of his likely inheritance. He thundered at him with an emotion which astonished my friend, for thinking of money when his sick father needed his care, and then dismissed him peremptorily, only to revert to his normal loving self within seconds. The anger was just a necessary 'act'. I suspect that this was true of the Christ, too, with the money-changers. Thus both demonstrate how to 'hate the sin, but never the sinner'.

Both also show in their personalities a combination of deep humility and commanding authority. The Christ was often referred to in the Gospels as 'one who spoke with authority'. One envisages a tall, commanding figure. Yet he knelt down and washed the feet of his own disciples. Swami will often play and joke and behave like a child but, if anyone takes advantage of it, in the twinkling of an eye, he resumes his authority and his divine nature. Once, when a devotee enquired if he might ask a favour, Baba replied, "Of course, I am yours. I have no rights." At one time the servant of mankind, at another the Lord of the World.

Of course both have been maligned and persecuted. "Calumny is the lot of all great souls everywhere, at any time. It would be unnatural if it were not so," says Baba. He is oblivious to praise or blame. Christ was accused of being a wine bibber, and of mixing with publicans and sinners. Baba has been criticised for allowing sinners to use the *ashram* at Puttaparthi. Their replies were similar: "I am come to call sinners, not the righteous, to repentance." Baba replied: "Sinners have more need of me than you have." Christ was accused of healing by the powers of Satan (Beelzebub). Baba has been denounced as a black magician. He has been accused of having a luxurious taste in dress. (He actually wears plain cotton robes.) His reply: "Would I be holier in rags?" It would not surprise me if Christ had been accused in his time of having a physical relationship with Mary Magdalen, an ex-prostitute.

There is also a remarkable similarity in the miracles and in the divine power demonstrated. Christ healed the sick. Baba heals the sick daily — there are thousands of well documented cases. Christ raised Lazarus from the dead when his body is said to have been in a state of decomposition. He was clinically dead. Baba has raised the dead on at least two occasions. The body of Mr V. Radhakrishna was also in a state of decomposition.

Both materialised food — Christ at the feeding of the five thousand, and Baba on more than one occasion when the food has run out during a festival. I have also seen film of Sai Baba materialising *vibhuti*, the sacred ash, literally by the hundredweight from an upturned empty urn which would not have held half a gallon of water. Christ changed water into wine. Baba has changed water into petrol and fuel oil — and a piece of granite into a statue of Krishna for a Dr Rao, a geologist at a university in Hyderabad, and then told the astonished professor to eat it, which he proceeded to do, for it had turned into candy!

Christ could control the elements and calm the seas; likewise Baba has made a rainbow appear in the sky, and sent back floods. Christ could levitate and walk on the waters. Baba was levitating at the age of eight.

In fact, Baba has exceeded what little we know of the miracles of Christ in the paltry accounts we have in the Gospels which no doubt are but a hundredth part of what did occur. Baba has manifested himself as a midwife to deliver a child; as a surgeon to perform a critical operation; 'projected' himself and lived for two days with a family of devotees while his physical body was elsewhere.

Yet he claims that his miracles are the least important part of his mission, merely 'visiting cards'. "I give you what you want in order that you may want what I have come to give," he says. He has not had to learn like a *yogi*, nor does he exert any particular act of will. He claims that to perform miracles is within the orbit of his divine nature; it is as easy for him as it is for you and I to sit in an armchair.

But the most significant thing about the miracles of Sai Baba is when he has identified himself with the Christ. He has given a detailed account of the life and journeyings of Christ from the age of twelve to thirty to fill the gap in the Gospels. Christmas itself is regarded as a festival at the Sai *Ashrams* and celebrated with great fervour — in fact more so than in the West where it has become so grossly commercialised. Baba often gives talks to small groups of Christians and points out the excisions and interpolations in the Gospels. To those who feel a sense of disloyalty to Christianity he has on more than one occasion manifested a figure of Christ above his head, thus identifying the two. There are also accounts of people praying before a statue of Christ and seeing it transform into an image of Sai Baba.

Dr John Hislop recounts how, when he was walking one day with Baba, he took two small twigs from a tree, placed them into a cross, blew on them three times, and transformed them into a wooden cross with a silver figure of Jesus on it, explaining that the likeness was an exact replica of Jesus as he was on the Cross! There was a small hole at the top of the upright and, when questioned about this, Baba said that the Cross on which Jesus was crucified was hung on a pole, and not put into the ground. The magnified photograph shows a face not unlike Baba's, strong in character, but gnarled with sweat, blood, and the hallmark of agony. The ribs are bare from lack of food. Blood can be seen flowing from the forehead, and black, dustcaked saliva at the corner of the mouth. There is a haunting expression of agony in the eyes.

One day when some people were looking at this crucifix in Dr Hislop's home in California a strong wind suddenly blew up and there was a crash of thunder from skies which were perfectly clear. This 'mystery' was reported in the local *San Diego Tribune* the following day, confirming that the skies had been clear. It happened at 5 p.m. which scholars believe was the approximate time of Christ's 'giving up the ghost', when similar thunder is said to have broken out and the Temple veil was riven.

Finally, on Christmas Day 1972, Baba referred to Jesus's statement: "He who sent me will come again," and then made the astonishing claim that Jesus was referring to himself, Baba. Although expunged from the Bible, Baba claims that Jesus's words were: "His name will be Truth. He will wear a red robe. He will be short, with a crown of hair." Sathya means truth. Baba wears a red robe, is short, and has a crown of hair.

Is Sathya Sai Baba the Second Coming? Or, even more incredible, since he claims he is not overshadowed, and that he came into incarnation with the divine nature intact, has the Great Celestial Being known as the Christ this time incarnated as Himself, in human form?

Thus far I had written by December 1979. A month later, in January 1980, my wife and I flew to India. On the 19th of January we were taken into Swami's inner sanctum and sat with him entirely alone. After clarifying for us certain questions about unidentified

151

flying objects (UFO's), mediumship, spiritual healing, man's negative *karma* for his cruelty to the animal kingdom, and the physical 'resurrection' of Jesus, I plucked up every vestige of courage that was in me, and referred to Baba's statement on Christmas Day 1972. I said, "Swami, does this omission in the Bible mean that it was You who sent Jesus of Nazareth into incarnation?"

"Yes," he replied. My wife said I gasped, although I have no recollection of this. Followed my final question which lay at the very core of my soul:

"In that case, are You what Western Christians call the Cosmic Christ?"

"Yes," he said again.

It is impossible to convey in words the tone, the quiet assurance, in which he affirmed these two questions. Gently, lovingly, with total conviction, with a sort of ineffable simplicity and, perhaps most important of all, with a total lack of self-consciousness impossible in a mere human. He looked straight into my eyes, which were no more than twelve inches from his, and just said, "Yes." I only know that it was impossible not to believe him.

As the reader can imagine, my wife and I came out of that interview feeling stunned. So Sathya Sai Baba was the One whom Jesus called the Father, the Christ, indeed the Cosmic Christ, the Logos! The Second Coming had come, had lived for fifty-four years, and perhaps only a handful of Christians were aware of the fact . . . At first it was too stupendous to grasp. Yet I only know that I came to believe it, and that I am reporting precisely what occurred.

## 4

# A MODERN RAISING OF LAZARUS

There must be many people who find it difficult to believe in miracles. Man has a well nigh infinite capacity for doubt. So encased in physical form have we become in our involutionary descent into matter that many of us can only believe in what we can apprehend with our five physical senses. Even some modern clergymen have become so materially-minded that they explain away the miracles of Christ as 'symbolic'. Yet miracles, in the sense that they are understood generally, simply do not happen. They are only the functioning of laws, both physical and spiritual, which man has not yet discovered. In centuries to come, as we ascend the arc of evolution and return to something approaching our original 'coat of skin', our children's children will be aghast when they read medical history and learn that 20th century surgeons actually healed the body by cutting out parts of it with a knife; they will seem almost as barbaric to those then incarnate as New Guinea headhunters seem to us!

A hundred years ago the fact that sound and light waves can penetrate the seemingly solid walls of our houses and project themselves on to our television screens would have seemed miraculous. Now we know that it is just a matter of applied physics. So, too, with spiritual law. The time will no doubt come when we shall be

153

able to converse with our friends and relatives in spirit by the use of psychic telephones instead of through mediums.

Personally I have had no difficulty in believing in 'miracles' for many years – not, in fact, since my wife and I were blessed with our own Home Circle, with our housekeeper as the gifted medium. For six years apports occurred almost daily. We also communicated daily with our friends and relatives in spirit. In time the physical phenomena seemed as natural as night following day, and the reality of our friendships in spirit warmer and closer than our friendships on earth. In fact earth life became a sort of *maya* or illusion.

But to those who are not 'sensitives', or who have not been blessed with such personal and convincing experiences, it must be difficult to believe. I would commend to them the words of Professor MacNeile Dixon: "I find it easy to believe in miracles. They are to be expected. The starry world in time and space, the pageant of life, the processes of growth and reproduction, the instincts of animals, the inventiveness of Nature – they are all utterly unbelievable, miracles piled upon miracles . . . " I would add my own words: just think of the structure of a snowflake, the birth of a kitten, the act of falling 'in love' when a very ordinary person becomes magically transformed into someone very precious and very beautiful, or the tiny atom, magnified a thousand million times, appearing as a universe in miniature. To me the whole of life is a miracle.

To many it will no doubt come as a surprise to learn that there is a man incarnate in India, Sathya Sai Baba, an *avatar*, who has on two well documented occasions, actually raised the dead and, in one instance, like the raising of Lazarus by the Christ, done so when the body was in a state of decomposition.

This latter case occurred in 1953. Mr V. Radhakrishna, aged sixty, a factory owner and respected citizen of Kuppam in the State of Andhra Pradesh, was seriously ill with gastric ulcers, with complications. He was a devotee of Sai Baba. He decided to go to the *ashram* at Puttaparthi in the hope that the 'Man of Miracles' would heal him. He was accompanied by his wife and daughter. On arrival at the *ashram* he was put straight to bed. Baba visited him, but made no attempt to heal him. Mr Radhakrishna complained that he would rather die than continue to suffer the extreme pain he was in. Baba smiled but made no promise.

A few days later the patient went into a coma and the wife and daughter, who were at the bedside, heard the 'death rattle' in his throat. Baba examined him, but still did nothing. An hour later Mr Radhakrishna's breathing stopped. He turned blue, and then went cold and stiff. A male nurse pronounced him dead. Swami examined him again. "Don't worry," he said, "everything will be all right." But he still made no attempt to revive him. The faith of the wife and daughter were sorely tested.

The following day they sat loyally by the bedside anxiously awaiting any signs of returning life. But there were no signs. The day passed. Somehow the two women managed to cling on to a vestige of faith that in his own way and in his own time Swami would save the husband. On the morning of the third day the body was dark, quite stiff, and beginning to smell. It was suggested to Mrs Radhakrishna that the corpse should be removed from the *ashram*, but she refused adamantly to countenance such action without the authority of Baba. His aides asked for instructions as to whether the body should be returned to Kuppam or be cremated at Puttaparthi. Baba replied enigmatically, "We'll see."

At this point the two women were in despair. They went to see Baba and pleaded with him. He simply said, "Have no fear. I am here." He did, however, promise to come and examine the corpse later. An hour went by, then two, and there was no sign of Baba. Mrs Radhakrishna and her daughter gave up all hope. Then, suddenly, Swami appeared in the doorway of the bedroom, calm and smiling. The two women burst into tears, like Mary and Martha, the sisters of Lazarus, weeping before their Lord who, they thought, had come too late.

Gently he asked them to leave the room, and as they left he closed the door behind them. They did not know − no one knows − what happened in the next few minutes in that room where there were only Sai Baba and the dead man, but in just a few minutes Baba opened the door and beckoned the women in − there to see their loved one sitting up in bed and smiling! The stiffness of death had vanished and his natural colour was returning. Baba said to him, "Talk to them, they are worried." Mr Radhakrishna, with a puzzled look, said, "Why are you worried? I am all right!" He was aware that he had been in a coma but of no more. Swami then said to the wife, "I have given your husband back to you. Now give him a hot drink." Thereupon he blessed the whole family and left.

The next day the patient was strong enough to walk. On the third day he wrote a seven-page letter to a relative in Italy. A few days after that the whole family returned to their home in Kuppam. Not only was Mr Radhakrishna raised from the dead, but the gastric ulcers and the complications were completely healed. It was a repetition of the raising of Lazarus. In both cases the two women nearest to the dead man had despaired.

Lazarus was probably suffering from a Temple Sleep which had gone badly wrong. This was a practice (handed down to the Jews from the ancient Egyptians) whereby a priest put an initiate into a state of deep hypnosis, akin to physical rather than spiritual death, in order that he should have the experience of dying and gain proof of the after-life, prior to being revived before the silver cord snapped. This is probably why, on being told of the death of Lazarus, Jesus said, "He is not dead, but sleepeth." And why he is reported to have called out in a 'loud voice' when raising him, "Lazarus, come forth!" It was probably necessary to shout to rouse one who was in such a deep hypnotic state that he was very close to actual death.

And what of the cells of the body which had started to decompose? I do not know. I imagine that once the blood begins to flow again the natural healing powers inherent in the body resume their animating functions, like the healing of a sceptic wound.

# 5

# ARMAGEDDON IS NOW

There can be few people who doubt that the world has reached a crisis point in its history. Man is at the end of his tether. It is certain that he cannot pull himself up by his own bootstraps. A moral decline has set in, particularly in the Western world, which he is powerless to reverse. Some form of divine intervention is necessary to save our planet.

Let us take our own country where things are perhaps worse than most, possibly because we have lost an empire and failed to find a renewed sense of mission in the world. Materialism is rampant. The aim of our politicians is always a higher material standard of living, but never a higher quality of life. Yet Sai Baba says, "The ideal of a higher material standard of living has played havoc with society." Indeed it has.

I do not think it is negative to point out the facts. Just as self-awareness and self-honesty are a *sine qua non* for spiritual growth in an individual, so too with a nation. One has to know the enemy, to be fully aware of what is happening. What is negative is to <u>dwell</u> on the evils of the world. One should try to transmute them by prayer, positive thinking, and the evoking of light. Transmute is the key word.

The fact is that all most people want is a better house, a better car, a better kitchen, a better holiday, more money for less work. Hard work has become almost a dirty word. Karl Marx referred to religion as the opium of the people; the modern opium of the people is shopping!

In the Trades Union movement the new commandment is: Crucify the innocent; it pays. And so in a recent winter of discontent we have N.U.P.E. pickets denying cancer patients essential drugs. (And even picketing graveyards so people could not bury their dead.) One such wretch, picketing a Cheshire Home, announced to the Press that his aim was "to make the name of Leonard Cheshire stink." Group Captain Leonard Cheshire, V.C.! Without men such as he that picket would either be dead or facing a thousand years of a renewal of the Dark Ages under the Nazis.

Then there are the Wreckers, the communists, whose aim is not just to destroy the capitalist system (which admittedly has its pros and cons), but to destroy democracy and valued institutions which have been assiduously built up over eight hundred years since Magna Carta, and which have made us perhaps the most politically mature nation on earth. They have infiltrated every sphere of our national life – the Trades Unions, the Universities, the teaching profession, the welfare services, Parliament, the Foreign Office, radio and television.

And let no one think that they work solely by overt means. There are secret cells in high places which cast dark shadows over the whole national mores, for moral decline is a prerequisite of overthrow.

We have pornography and perversion in the hearts of our cities, and spreading to provincial towns. And not just adult pornography, but child pornography. Unbelievable as it may seem there are Mafia-like syndicates in America who are now trying to introduce 'baby' pornography – that is, with toddlers of two or three years of age. It is known that the K.G.B. regard it as part of their work to exploit any possible avenue of moral degradation in order to sap the strength of their enemies.

Crime has increased 1000% since the War. There are now 12,000 burglaries a day in the United Kingdom, with less than 10% of the culprits apprehended. With thousands of work-shy people theft has become a way of life. It is estimated that one adult person in three now goes in for shop-lifting. We have the mugging of elderly women, unknown twenty years ago, occurring daily. There are probably a million old souls who are afraid to leave their homes at night. Hi-jacking and kidnapping, also virtually unknown twenty years ago, is now a grimly regular occurrence, particularly in Italy. Vandalism is costing our country a hundred million pounds a year.

158

On television we have an almost uninterrupted stream of violence and brutality so that many young people grow up in the mistaken belief that violence is in the natural order of things. Accordingly groups of youths go in search of it. Almost worse, adults who should know better, become to an extent de-sensitised and de-humanised by it. This is particularly sad because television could and should be an uplifting medium.

Noise has become an almost national addiction. We have 'punk' music with its terrible vibrations. I suspect that the criterion by which some pop music is judged is the amount of noise the band makes and the frenzied antics its performers get up to rather than the merit of the music.

In the quiet, tree lined avenue in which my wife and I live, the comparative silence is sometimes violated by youths on motor-cycles roaring by at 60, 70, 80 miles an hour, jarring the nerves like a sudden thunderclap, as if perversely intent on making the maximum din possible, just for 'kicks'. And job-gardeners go out to work with transistor sets, as if afraid of the harmonious sounds of nature.

I remember, when I worked for the Samaritans, I was expected to discuss the issues of life and death with a would-be suicide to the background accompaniment of a blaring television set, and when I asked for it to be switched off, the reciprocation I received was that it was turned down slightly.

Silence, that invaluable thing without which one cannot commune with one's God, has become something which we have almost come to fear.

There are half a million alcoholics in the country. And something even more startling — one household in five throughout the length and breadth of the land can now expect a member of the family to be incarcerated in a mental hospital at some time in the lifetime of the household.

Women are increasingly forsaking their sacred role of mother-hood. Half of all mothers now go out to work with young children in the home. And 50% of married couples now admit that they regard their own material pleasure as more important than the rearing and welfare of their children. One child in eight comes from a broken home. There are three-quarters of a million one-parent families in the land.

On a world scale, by the most conservative estimate, a hundred million animals are tortured and killed every year in animal experi-mentation, and often for trivial or meaningless purposes. For example, to manufacture more hair dyes and cosmetics, or to test the stamina of an animal by making it swim until it drowns. And remember, it is not just rats and mice and guinea-pigs which are experimented on, but cats, horses, monkeys and dogs. The dog, known for centuries as man's best friend!

What kind of a monster scientist is it who cuts off the head of a dog in order to transplant it onto another? Or takes a new-born monkey away from its mother and keeps it in a dark box for five or eight years to test the appalling effects of 'deprivation of love'? Or deliberately blinds monkeys to see how they fend for themselves in the jungle?

At the present time the world is spending 30 million pounds a minute on armaments. It is estimated that one large megaton bomb dropped on New York would kill ten million people. I suppose a dozen or so dropped on the United Kingdom would put large tracts of our island under the sea. Yet there are 16,000 megaton bombs in existence, enough to kill every man, woman and child on the planet several times over.

There are those who say that a nuclear holocaust has happened before in the universe, that the asteroid belt was once the planet Maldek (the Russians call it Vulcan) which blew itself to pieces through nuclear fission, and is now giant chunks of matter orbiting endlessly in space.

I am reminded of the remark Dr Robert Oppenheimer made as he watched the first experimental atomic bomb explode in America. He was silent and pensive for a while, and then, quoting the *Bhagavad-Gita*, he said, "I am become the Destroyer of the Worlds!" I watched his last television appearance before he died. Poor man, he looked half monk, half madman which, I dare say, was about what he had become.

There is a true story of two American criminals who were serving life sentences. After ten years in prison they became introspective and began to look into themselves. One was a Negro and the other a white. The Negro said to the white man, "You know, Joe, if there is a God He must be Love, otherwise He wouldn't let the likes of you and me continue to live!"

Can one say assertively, with any degree of confidence, that the same criterion does not apply to mankind as a whole, in its present state? I know my wife and I find it increasingly difficult to sustain the burden of continuing to live on this planet. There are times when we go into a quiet corner and weep. We are really weeping for God. In our tiny way we know what the Nazarene felt when, standing on a knoll overlooking the city of Jerusalem, it is reported that "He looked on the City and wept".

Of course, as individuals, the average person feels helpless in the sway of world events. But we should remember that every reformer starts as a minority of one. And there are things that we can do something about. For example, crime and pornography. If enough pressure was brought to bear on the Government more stringent measures would be taken.

I think we should all ask ourselves the question whether the past virtues of the British people – tolerance, slowness to anger, and a genius for compromise – have not become our vices, and whether we have not allowed freedom to drift into licence? Have we forgotten the axiom: "For evil to triumph all that is necessary is for good men and women to do nothing"? How silent will the silent majority be?

Have not our values turned a somersault when a convicted train robber who has escaped from prison is treated by the popular press as a hero; and a true hero, the Police Constable in the Iranian Embassy siege, is hounded from his home because his children are insulted at school, and the paintwork on his car is scratched with obscene words, as if he were either a fool, a villain, or a living affront to a warped conscience? Or when we read with indifference that major film companies now admit to administering 'slush funds', paying upto £200,000 in addition to inflated salaries, with which to enable their stars to purchase supplies of cocaine and heroin?

The United Kingdom is no exception. India, the country that was once the *guru* of the world, is just as bad and, in some respects, worse. I will quote Sai Baba:

"The greed and selfishness which are affecting this country are tragedies for humanity, for India has the role of guiding and leading mankind to the goal of self-realisation. Youth is growing up in India in the hothouse of faction and passion, not as in the past, in the cool bowers of reverence and humility. Elders indulge in fights, vengeful litigation, corrupt means of earning money and cut-throat competition. Their low behaviour, in the home, the village, in clubs, in the civic bodies, in the legislature, in all walks, sets the standard for youth."

In Calcutta it is no uncommon occurrence for Mother Teresa to find a live baby thrown away in a refuse bin as if it was a cockroach. And if you walk down the main shopping street of any major Indian city you will find pathetic, whimpering souls who have been intentionally maimed at birth, either by blinding or by having their arms lopped off, leaving ugly stumps, in order to work as beggars for evil-minded syndicates. It almost passes belief that man should sink to this degree of degradation and inhumanity.

Of course there is a credit side, a positive fight-back by a minority of evolved souls. It may be that the world is in a spiritual vacuum between two ages, the Piscean and the Aquarian, that one set of values is dying and a new set has not yet crystallised and found its feet. It may be that we are suffering the birth pangs, and

161

that there has to be an upheaval on a world scale before a new and better dispensation can be ushered in. It is ironic that good so often comes out of evil.

On the positive side there is a greater sense of internationalism. The world has become a smaller place. One could argue that this has come about through the great advance in modern communications, but let us give the moral conscience of the world the credit. If there is famine or epidemic or earthquake in some part of the globe, even a remote part, relief is usually at hand by organisations like the U.N.O. or Oxfam or the Red Cross, and many others, albeit sometimes belatedly and not on a large enough scale. Half a century ago, I imagine, the Vietnamese 'Boat People' would have been left to their fate. At about that time, as a young man travelling in China, I learned that it was a common occurrence, attributable to 'Fate', for several million Chinese to die from famine, epidemic, or flood, and the news did not even receive the attention of the world's press.

There are tentative experiments in multi-racial societies, as for example in Zimbabwe and the United Kingdom, and on a wider scale of co-operation in the economic and political fields through the E.E.C. After fighting three wars (two on a major and horrific scale) in less than a century, France and Germany have at last come together and formed the nucleus of a group of European nations that are co-operating by consent rather than by the compulsion of conquest or power politics. Could it be the first embryonic step towards future World Government?

Despite the materialism in the world one senses a spiritual hunger among its peoples, or at least among a minority of spiritually orientated souls. One even senses this behind the Iron Curtain. It is as if there is a great dividing taking place, a sifting of the wheat from the chaff. A small minority is approaching closer to God, while the majority is becoming increasingly materialistic.

In our own country, spiritual centres of light have sprung up in the past few decades. Examples are Findhorn, the Wrekin Trust, the White Eagle Lodges, and of course the Theosophists. And there are many, many smaller groups, unknown and unpublicised – sometimes no more than a dozen people who gather together in each other's houses to pray and meditate and invoke the Light. We are told from spirit that the beneficial effect is out of all proportion to the seeming paucity of effort.

On balance, too, I have confidence in youth. They are more matured for their age, and more integrated in character than my generation was. Their boy—girl relationships are more natural. Yet they are far less promiscuous than most people assume; it is not youth but the middle-aged who haunt the strip clubs of Soho.

They are growing up with the integrity to question, to drop ancient shibboleths and to go in search of truth for themselves. In America, there is an increasing trek to the East in search of a better way of life. The concept of the 'Grand Society' has let them down. In our country, we have voluntary drop-outs who are not necessarily irresponsible, work-shy young people, but many, I believe, are old souls who have incarnated into a sick society and have lost their way.

The Flower People of the Sixties, endearing but tragically naive, had the right idea — to revolt and to try to make Love the central theme of their lives. The play *Jesus Christ Superstar* was an heroic attempt by youth to re-discover the pristine as opposed to the theological Christ.

In many spiritual and allied fields there has been progress. Fifty years ago the Spiritualist movement was illegal. Now there is a Spiritualist church in virtually every town in the U.K. and a weekly newspaper with a circulation of over 100,000. There is more concern for animal welfare — anti-vivisection societies have expanded, and many other organisations such as 'Compassion in World Farming' and 'Beauty without Cruelty'. There is similar concern over pollution. Ecology groups have sprung up.

There have been advances in spiritually orientated education. The Rudolf Steiner schools, a mere handful before the War, have grown in number to over four hundred in the non-Communist world.

Politically we have created in this country a welfare state and a national health service. There is no longer any real poverty in the U.K. The poorest of our citizens are rich by Asian and African standards.

And yet the sum total on the credit side (and, of course, there is much else in addition to what I have briefly referred to) seems a puny contribution towards combatting the evils of the world. It seems like a fight between David and Goliath. The world rumbles on like the Gadarene swine towards the cliff. There is an impending sense of doom, almost of inevitability. Things get worse rather than better, year by year. Violence increases, unrest increases, hijacking increases, assassinations increase, and attempted assassinations. This year the Pope, the President of the United States. Next year, the Royal Family? It was unthinkable a decade ago . . .

Obviously there are many contributory causes. The decline of orthodox religion has had an effect. Church-going used to be a regular feature of life, and although for many it was a social custom rather than a true act of worship, the Church did exercise a considerable moral authority over the whole fabric of society. That has gone.

The Industrial Revolution and the growth of large towns have had an influence. When man abandons nature, he is abandoning his natural environment of which he is a related part, and he is thus losing an ingredient essential to his spiritual well-being. The scientific age, too, that God is somehow out of date, and that science will one day explain everything. Nothing could be further from the truth since science only explores the physical world. Science has been unduly enthroned.

I believe Freudian psychiatrists have done immense damage to our society. In the Fifties and Sixties there was scarcely a serious television programme which did not have its consultant psychiatrist on the panel. They were the High Priests of Society. Fortunately they have now been debunked, but the damage has been done; licentiousness posing as progressive liberalism has a strong appeal to those who are inherently immoral or aggressive, and is therefore difficult to rectify.

After all, if you develop a science on the assumption that man is a body without a spirit rather than a spirit with a body, your whole edifice of thinking is based on a false premise. You are encouraging the development of the lower ego rather than its sublimation and eventual eradication. "Let everything hang out" in the interests of "self-expression" is to encourage man to revert to his animal nature, to deny his dual personality which is divine as well as animal. It is in fact a denial of the whole purpose of life which is to realise our higher or divine selves. Think of the damage such a doctrine can do in the upbringing of children; it virtually discourages all morality and self-discipline. It is manifesting itself in the disrespect, and even violence, which is now shown in the classroom.

I believe these pseudo-scientists have influenced the whole climate of opinion in our country since the War. They have indoctrinated the thinking of the teaching profession, the welfare services, even the judiciary; it is possible in our present circumstances for a man to commit a serious crime like rape and receive no more than a suspended sentence.

There is also a theory that our planet is receiving cosmic energies from outer space which are intended to have a stimulating and uplifting effect. On the more evolved, these energies probably are encouraging us to higher purposes, but on the less evolved they appear to be having the reverse effect, particularly on the young, which may in part be the cause of such recent phenomena as soccer hooliganism, vandalism, and the almost maniacal behaviour of students in the Middle East.

It is my belief that by far the major cause of the world's plight is a cosmic one — a last desperate throw of the dice by the Powers of of Darkness to separate man from God and keep him in the trough of materialism to which he has descended. It is said that the 'War in Heaven' has already been waged and won, but that on the principle of 'as above, so below' it has to be won down here as well.

I believe that millenia ago, long before recorded history, man was an almost exclusively psychic being with what esotericists refer to as a 'coat of skin'. In this condition he was fully aware of his spirit origin and spirit destiny — in fact, in touch with the Godhead. But he did not evolve. He tended to regard his sojourn on the semi-physical plane of Earth as a waiting time before returning to his natural home in spirit.

Accordingly, the Hierarchy decreed that he should descend further into matter, to become increasingly incarnate and identified with the physical form and sense, in order to develop his intellect and the resources of the Earth. I believe this descent into ever denser matter on the arc of involution has been taking place for millions of years, and that during this time man, increasingly encased in physical form, has lost his psychic faculties and his awareness of God. He has thus come to regard the physical world and his physical body as the sole reality instead of the *maya* which it is. He has also come to regard intellect and logic as the only criteria of truth.

It may be that the Aborigines of Australia, supposedly the oldest existing continent, are a hangover from those ancient days. They are highly developed psychically and under-developed intellectually. They do very little with their lives except hunt for food.

Man's destiny is to pass through the trough of materialism into which he has descended and to ascend the arc of evolution in full consciousness, that is, with his intellect developed and his psychic faculties re-awakened, and in this state eventually to re-merge with the Godhead.

But while he is in the trough, in the *Kali Yuga* Age of Darkness, what better time for the Powers of Darkness to attack and attempt to keep him there, permanently separated from God?

Rudolf Steiner, in his time regarded as Europe's greatest mystic, claimed there was a Trinity of Evil, just as religion tells us there is a Trinity of Good. In Christian terms this is the Father, Son, and Holy Spirit; in Hindu terminology it is Brahma, Vishnu, and Shiva.

The first aspect of the Trinity of Evil is usually referred to as Lucifer. His task is to find an instrument to utilise for conquest. The second aspect Steiner refers to as Ahriman, whose work is to soften up the populace, prior to conquest by the tool of Lucifer, by encouraging a material way of life and by fostering moral decline by an over-incitement of the physical senses.

It is my belief that Lucifer has chosen atheistic communism as his instrument, and that Ahriman has been preparing the way with remarkable success. Who can deny that we in the West have become increasingly material and increasingly pleasure-seeking and sybaritic? We seek jungle rhythms while we work, strip-clubs while we relax and, judging by the bookstalls, many of us choose girlie magazines, if not downright pornography for our reading. Probably seven advertisements out of ten on commercial television are for food and drink, and almost invariably with a sensuous connotation. Tight-fitting jeans are symptomatic of a closer identification with the pelvic aspect of the physical body. We seek 'instant' remedies for the slightest degree of pain.

Our moral fibre has been sapped to the point where we lack the will to defend ourselves. Our N.A.T.O. commanders do not consider that we could resist a Soviet onslaught by conventional weapons for more than four days. We should collapse as rapidly as France did in 1940. We are relying for our defence on the American nuclear shield.

Of course the majority of communists are not aware of the role they are playing – they are innocent dupes. But the steel-hardened cadre in the Kremlin, versed in the doctrines of Karl Marx (who some say was a secret Satanist), are very well aware of it. I do not think they would shrink from committing any crime to conquer the world.

The portents are indeed ominous. Has an empire ever expanded with such rapidity? In a little over half a century the Soviets have subjugated half of Asia, half of Europe, and are well on the way to conquering the soul of Africa. Has a weapon ever been invented, manufactured, and stockpiled which has not subsequently been used? Mustard gas was used in the First World War, and the atom bomb in the Second. No wonder the world stands in fear and dread . . .

Armageddon is at hand. It is a battle for the soul and mind of man, a final confrontation between the Powers of Darkness and the Powers of Light. On the one side stand the Kremlin atheists, implacable, ruthless, cunning, power drunk with success, and de-humanised in character; and on the other the decadent West which, with all its faults and weaknesses, still stands for freedom and, haltingly, for God. As President Kennedy said in Berlin, "At least we do not have to build a wall to keep our people in."

By every test of logic and historical experience a holocaust must come. And yet I do not believe that it will. I believe that a planetary miracle will occur. The *Avatar* of the Age is incarnate on earth whose avowed aim is to avert it. He has said: "I have come to repair the ancient highway to God . . . *Avatars* do not succeed or fail; what they will must occur, what they plan must take place."

His triple Incarnation, spanning perhaps 250 years, was forecast in the *Upanishads* 5,600 years ago. It was prophesied that there would be a Machine Age, and out of it would come the possibility of total destruction. His task is to restore *Dharma* among mankind, and he has promised that he will not fail. He has said: "I have come to inscribe a golden chapter in the history of humanity, wherein falsehood will fail, truth will triumph, and virtue will reign. Character will confer power then, not knowledge, or inventive skill, or wealth. Wisdom will be enthroned in the councils of nations."

How can he possibly succeed in the face of such overwhelming odds? It is difficult to conjecture on the ways of an *avatar* with our human consciousness. He might stimulate the minds of Russia's scientists, increasingly researching the new field of parapsychology, to prove the existence of God to the satisfaction of their political masters so that the whole communist ideology might crumble. He might also bring about the collapse of the capitalist system in America. He might allow a minor catastrophe to occur to aid the inauguration of a new order and a new Golden Age. This could be in the Middle East in accordance with the Pyramid Prophecies. He has recently materialised a map of the world as it is to be. He has said there will be adjustments to the surface of the planet and a certain clear-out of the population. He might invoke the aid of the Space People. If there is enough prayer and goodwill he might transcend, or partly transcend, man's accumulated past *karma* by the use of his *sankalpa.* The ways of an *avatar* are simply not comprehensible to the minds of men.

In the meantime, in the following chapters, I will try to outline some of the ways Sai Baba is setting about his task of transforming mankind by the only way that is possible, by "lighting the Lamp of Love in our hearts". The irony of the world's impasse is that ordinary people, the world over, including those behind the Iron Curtain, want only peace, but they are not yet willing to pay the price of adopting the simple panacea of <u>enthroning love in their hearts</u>. It is as simple as that.

# 6

# THE MIRACLES OF SATHYA SAI BABA

I have no doubt that the miracles of Sathya Sai Baba would require many volumes of a book to record. It is my belief, and also that of Howard Murphet (author of *Sai Baba, Man of Miracles*), that only a small proportion of his miracles has been set down on paper, or is even known except to the recipients of his grace. The vast majority of India's teeming millions are humble, semi-literate peasants. They would have no access to publicity. And the majority of Baba's miracles are not done in public; they are done through mental prompting, a manipulation of circumstances, by giving a person a dream with a strong symbolic meaning, or by a visitation, either in his etheric body or by projecting his actual physical form, to heal, to rescue from danger, or to give comfort to one who is dying and whose span on this earth is nearing its end.

Yet despite this, Dr Bhagavantham (formerly scientific advisor to the Indian Ministry of Defence and President of the All India Science Institute) has this to say about the miracles of Sai Baba: "No living man of miracles has been witnessed and attested to by such an army of professional people as Sai Baba."

In this chapter I am giving a small sample of what I believe to be a tiny fraction of his miracles. The question might well be asked: how many miracles does Baba perform a day? I think the true answer is that his entire life is a continuous succession of miracles. He very seldom engages in small talk, he is said not to sleep (and has confirmed this). He virtually works in the service of mankind twenty-four hours a day. Even seemingly casual words or actions to devotees or would-be devotees have a meaning, and sometimes long-term significance.

I suppose he must have periods of repose, but they are very few and far between. Never a day goes by when he does not materialise *vibhuti.* Never a day goes by when he does not touch the soul of a newcomer to *darshan* by his mere presence. Never a night goes by when he does not read through hundreds of letters, or rather touch the envelopes, diagnose psychically the contents, and decide what action to take. And never a day or night passes when he does not go out of his body (and probably many times) to the aid of a devotee, or even a non-devotee who is calling on God by a different name.

When Dr Gokak made a lecture tour of America at Swami's behest, he was re-energised spiritually and, as he put it, "made aware of Baba's true glory" by constantly witnessing *vibhuti* and *amruta* (a sticky, sweet-tasting liquid referred to as the nectar of immortality) materialising on his pictures in the shrine rooms of devotees in this far-off land. He had become a little dulled and insensitive to Baba's divinity by living day by day with one who had taken human form and sometimes behaved in a very human way.

I myself have witnessed this miraculous phenomenon in the shrine room of a friend of mine in London. After a particularly fervent and joyous period of *bhajan* singing a group of us suddenly noticed two parallel lines of this opaque liquid trickling like rain-drops on a window from Swami's mouth, on the large picture of him, to a point approximately adjacent to his heart, where the flow stopped. We watched in absolute amazement. No doubt this gift of his 'visiting card', as he refers to such phenomena, was his way of showing us his omnipresence, and indicating to us his approval of the devotion expressed in the singing.

Few of us realise that when talking of Sai Baba we are talking, in the secular sense, of the 20th century's greatest phenomenon and, in the spiritual sense, of the first major *Avatar* for five thousand years, since Krishna. He has said that the Buddha, Mohammed and Jesus of Nazareth had some degree of divine vision, but only he and Krishna the fully divine vision.

When Swami was a tiny tot his old grandfather, Kondamma Raju (who lived to be 110), was calling him 'the Little Master'. At four he started feeding beggars by raiding the family larder, and as punishment had to forego food for up to four or five days. He appeared to suffer not one iota. At five, to the astonishment of his parents, he was seen riding on a flower-decked bullock cart during a festival procession, and when enquiries were made by the parents why their child was given this place of honour they were told by the village elders and holy men following on foot that he was their *guru*!

At six, he started materialising food for his schoolmates from an empty basket, telling them that he had an angel friend who brought things for him. Also pencils, rubbers, notebooks, etc. so that when the educational authorities responsible for the supply of these materials came to replace them and found there were still ample stocks they suspected the village teachers of not doing their jobs properly!

If anything was lost Swami was always sent for, and he invariably knew where the missing article was.

Accounts vary as to when Baba started materialising fruits on the tamarind tree which still grows on the top of the hill abutting on Puttaparthi, but he was still a child. Often the fruits were out of season or not known in the vicinity.

At the age of ten, Swami seems to have gone through a different period which lasted about six months. He would disappear into the mountains for days on end. Sometimes he was silent, even a little morose, at other times he would laugh or weep for no apparent reason. He would be found reciting long verses in Sanskrit which he had never read. One wonders if an *avatar*, when taking human form, has to go through a test, an initiation to perfect himself before commencing his mission. There are references in the Gospels to Christ being taken up 'to an exceeding high mountain' and being 'tempted of the devil'.

Baba's parents were worried and wondered if the boy was possessed. A local exorcist from a nearby village was called in. He appears to have been a sadistic fake – Professor Kasturi describes him as a "gigantic man, with blood-stained eyes and untamed manners". He shaved Swami's head, buried him in the sand up to the neck, and applied a redhot poker to score marks from the scalp to the forehead, pouring acid juices into the holes. The boy just smiled and appeared to feel no pain.

Then this brute of a man beat him on the joints with a heavy stick. Finally he applied a mixture to his eyes which made his head swell beyond recognition. Swami simply directed his parents to obtain a remedy he knew of, and immediately his eyes opened wide and the swelling subsided. Years later he told his parents and devotees that he had 'willed' all this to happen. "I wanted to make known that I am divine, impervious to suffering and pain," he said.

At twelve, he graduated to High School at Uravakonda where his elder brother was a teacher in Telegu. There he gained a reputation as a fine writer, a good musician, a genius in dance, a student wiser than any teacher, and one able to see into the past and future. Teachers vied with one another to teach him. The headmaster bowed to him in reverence. He became the leader of the prayer group, inspiring both students and teachers, the life and soul of the school dramatics – writing, directing and acting in the plays – and the backbone of the athletics team, for he was a very fast runner.

Yet his brother, Seshama, was still sceptical of his powers. His final conversion came when he took his young brother to the Temple of Virupaksha, near Hospet. A service took place. Seshama attended, but Swami insisted on staying outside. When the priest lit the flame on the altar to illumine the interior of the shrine, there was Sathya Sai, standing erect and smiling. In utter amazement, Seshama rushed outside, and found Swami standing against a wall where he had left him!

The conversion of the family came about at approximately the same time. The father, Pedda Raju, admitted to Kasturi years later that at this time he believed his son was guilty of performing tricks by sleight of hand. He sometimes became very angry at his son's continual claims that he was a reincarnation of Sai Baba of Shirdi.

One day when the family were all gathered together the father requested his son to offer them proof. Baba materialised *vibhuti* and scattered the ash in all directions around where they stood. Then, taking up a bunch of flowers, he casually threw them on the ground and, to the astonishment of the family, they fell in a pattern which spelt 'Sai Baba' in Telegu, as if some divine magnet had arranged them! The father concluded that no amount of trickery or dexterity could perform such a feat as this.

A year later, at the age of thirteen, Baba threw his books away and left school. He said to his brother, "I am going. I don't belong to you. *Maya* has gone. My devotees are calling me. I have my work." Like Christ at the Temple in Jerusalem, he was denying his own family, and he was almost exactly the same age. He was given a tremendous send-off from the school, with a procession of the townsfolk. At thirteen, just before his birthday in November 1940, he was virtually proclaimed an *avatar*.

He returned to Puttaparthi, but not to live with his family. He set up a sort of camp in the garden of the village accountant who built him a shed as a prayer hall. This soon had to be extended as the pilgrims began to flow in. It was at this time that he first mass-materialised food. He broke two coconuts, poured the juice into some empty food containers, and there was then food for all present.

The accountant's wife, Subbamma, became a devoted devotee. She virtually made the house over to Baba and his rapidly expanding following. Sometimes she cooked for eight hours a day. When, years later, she lay dying, Swami journeyed from a far distant place to be by her bedside, but he arrived too late: she was already dead and about to be cremated.

He sat beside her and miraculously brought her back to life by twice calling her name gently. Whereupon she opened her eyes and clutched his hand in joy. Then, speaking gently and lovingly, and materialising drops of Ganges water from his fingers into her lips, he let her pass on in a state of bliss. To this day Swami speaks of Subbamma with great affection.

The time came when the accountant's home and garden (in which tents had been pitched on every available yard of ground) became too small to accommodate Baba's growing band of devotees, and a small *ashram* was built. His bedroom in this original *ashram* was just eight feet by six. Now, some forty years later, the *ashram* at Puttaparthi has accommodation for ten thousand visitors!

While still a teenager, Baba was so full of fun that he sometimes performed miracles that were really practical jokes. He was never a man of sorrows! The first occasion was when he was still a child at school. For lack of attention he had been ordered to stand on a chair. At the end of the lesson a new teacher entered the classroom to take the next lesson but, to his surprise, his colleague remained seated. There was a whispered conversation during which the first teacher explained that when he tried to rise the chair remained glued to his behind. The second teacher, an enlightened soul who was well aware of Swami's magical powers, suggested that the child be released from his penance. As soon as this was done the embarrassed teacher was able to withdraw from the classroom without the chair sticking to his posterior!

On another occasion, during a bullock cart journey with several vehicles in convoy, he projected himself as a girl in distress pleading for a lift, materialising feminine clothes, etc. The party gave the girl a lift, but then, to their dismay, they discovered that Swami was missing. After a hectic search he was found, but the girl had simply disappeared. The devotees gently reprimanded their leader for causing them so much concern, but Swami only laughed. All his life he has been at pains to see that no barrier exists between the *Avatar* and the mere human, with his sense of humour and his sense of fun. He is, as it were, divinely human.

In his late teens, Baba started his mission in great earnestness. He performed his first operation in Bangalore for a duodenal ulcer, materialising his own instruments out of the air. He started casting out evil spirits, and he commenced his healing and counselling mission.

It seems that for healing miracles, *vibhuti* remains the foremost cure for many ailments. It is my belief that he does not always materialise this ash but that sometimes it emanates from his body, from a point about one inch from the tips of his fingers. He three times materialised *vibhuti* for me during my visit in January 1980, and it seemed to trickle from his fingers as he poured it into my palm. I have also studied close-up photographs.

Kasturi has calculated that by 1970 he must have produced five tons of *vibhuti* in his lifetime. The figure could well be double by now. It varies in form, taste, smell and colour. It is hard cube or fine powder, sweet or tasteless, fragrant or pungent, and white, grey or darkish. But the vast majority is a fine grey powder, sweet in taste and smell. It sometimes forms on his brow, eyes and cheeks and, when he leaves his body, on his mouth, thumbs, toes and forehead.

Here is a small sample of cures by the use of *vibhuti* alone. The father of a devotee at Puttaparthi had a stroke. Baba gave the son a packet of *vibhuti* and told him to go home and place it on his father's forehead. But after the son had departed, Swami realised that the train service was too slow and that the son would arrive too late, so he went out of his body and placed the ash on the father's brow himself. When his son returned he was overjoyed at the recovery of his father but perplexed that, when he had opened the box of *vibhuti*, he found the contents missing. Baba had teleported the ash to himself during his out-of-the-body visitation.

Dr D.S. Chander, a dental surgeon of Bangalore, suffered from gallstones in the bladder. He was cured by daily drinks of *vibhuti*. So, too, a man with a blockage in the urinary passage who was about to have an operation. The blockage was removed by drinking the ash in water. A parachute-jumper who was sterile and could not have children was told by Baba to take *vibhuti* internally. He did so, was cured, and had a family.

Dr Bannerjee, a professor of chemistry at the Indian Institute of Science at Bangalore, had a niece with a virulent cancer. She was cured by the sole use of *vibhuti*. One, Siva Kumar, was suffering from cerebro-spinal meningitis, causing paralysis of one side and loss of sight and speech. He became semi-conscious and turned blue, but was able to make feeble signs that he wished to have a bath in *vibhuti*. To his amazement he found he was able to get out of bed and walk unaided to the family *puja* room (sanctuary) where he meditated for two hours, after which his speech and eyesight returned. In this case the mere wish for, rather than an application of *vibhuti*, appears to have effected a cure.

Sometimes Baba uses *vibhuti* as an anaesthetic. The son of the Maharaja of Venkatagiri was operated on by Swami for appendicitis

173

in this way. The boy felt no pain and the wound healed immediately to a very small scar.

But possibly the most remarkable cure by *vibhuti* was a man of thirty-six who had polio at the age of twelve and had suffered paralysis for twenty-four years. His mother brought him to *darshan* at Dharmakshetra in Bombay, actually carrying him in her arms, and placed him in the care of Mr S.A. Pather of Durban in South Africa since it is the custom for men and women to sit in different sections at *darshan*. Swami noticed the cripple, materialised *vibhuti* and rubbed it on the man's right hand. He then took the left hand and rubbed it on the right, and walked on. Almost immediately the man felt sensation returning to his limbs, arms and legs. Then, very apprehensively, he stood up, moving one leg at a time. Soon he was actually dancing up and down for joy, with tears streaming down his face. He had recovered the full use of his arms, hands and legs after twenty-four years of immobility. Apart from Mr Pather, this of course was witnessed by hundreds at that *darshan*.

Baba by no means always uses *vibhuti* for healing. At the hospital in Puttaparthi he materialises pills, powders, ointments, syrups, oils and fruits. Mr P. Parathasarathy, a Madras businessman, was healed of arthritis by eating an apple which Swami materialised for him. The same man's mother was healed of total blindness with jasmine leaves.

The cousin of a close Indian friend of mine who suffered from extreme nymphomania was completely healed of his obsession by rubbing on his genitals a special oil which Swami materialised. He now leads a moral, happily married life.

The doctor in charge of the hospital at Puttaparthi, Dr Sitaramiah, was reluctant to take on the job until Swami assured him that he would do the healing! Baba often operates himself, materialising any extra instruments he may require and, when he doesn't, he supervises the operation, guiding the surgeon's hand.

There is a Dr Rao, a surgeon in Bangalore, who is so conscious of being overshadowed by Swami during operations that his white coat has been known to turn saffron, only to revert to white when the operation was over . . .

The files at the *ashram* hospitals are full of cases of cures totally inexplicable to science, and often cases which prove so difficult to cure in the West, such as cancer, rheumatoid arthritis, etc.

Of course numerous cures have taken place in the interview rooms at the two *ashrams*. Even if a physical cure does not take place immediately there is a strong likelihood of the seed of a future cure being sown through the transformation of character, leading to the all important curing of the soul.

174

As Professor Kasturi says, "Seldom does a person leave the interview room with a dry eye." Swami gives everyone hope and courage, assurance and solace. Here his omniscience and omnipresence reveal themselves. He tells the visitor what he has said, done, or felt, to whom he has spoken and on what, what he fears, has planned, or suffered, or what dreams he has had.

To quote a devotee: "Baba's words do not only console, but open up new levels of consciousness and reveal hidden strengths and goodness in one's nature. The seeker is enabled by his grace to know himself, to realise more keenly his duties, responsibilities and shortcomings. All this he does in the most natural way, patting one affectionately on the back, his eyes alight with a merry twinkle. One is left speechless at his miraculous perception of one's individual problems and needs."

Baba often heals, rescues, or consoles by leaving his body, either in the etheric form or by projecting his physical presence. A businessman devotee was seriously ill in a hospital in Hong Kong. He was being given blood transfusions in both arms. Suddenly he saw Swami appear through the wall and he spoke to him. Incredulous and feeling he might be hallucinating, he said, "Swami, is it really you? Will you touch me?" Baba took his hand: it seemed solid enough. Still not entirely reassured he asked Baba to lift him and carry him to another bed, which Baba proceeded to do, including all the equipment. After sprinkling the patient's bed with *vibhuti*, Baba disappeared again through the wall. When the hospital staff came in they were completely mystified; there was no way such a sick patient could move himself in this fashion. When the devotee told his story they simply did not believe him, until an Indian doctor arrived on the scene — he was working at the hospital. He believed him.

The man recovered and travelled back to India to thank Baba. Seated at *darshan* and awaiting his opportunity, Swami recognised him, smiled and said, "Hello, Hong Kong!" There was no normal way Baba could have known he had been ill and was in Hong Kong on business.

Mr Radhakrishna, an elderly devotee, fell down a deep wide well. A non-swimmer, he was astonished to find himself suspended waist high in the water. Eventually, after much panic, a rope and basket operation was mounted and the old man was hauled to safety, none the worse for his ordeal. He, too, travelled next morning to Puttaparthi to thank Baba but, like the businessman in Hong Kong, he was forestalled. Seated on the sand, awaiting *darshan*, Swami came out onto the balcony of his residence, saw him, leaned over, and shouted, "My shoulders are still aching from holding you up so long last night!"

In June 1949, Baba's temperature shot up to 104 degrees and then quickly dropped to normal. At dinner that night he told a young devotee to warn his mother to be more careful about fire. A telephone call was put through to Madras, to his mother, Mrs Venkatamuni, who confirmed that her *sari* had caught fire in her shrine room. She was put through to Baba who, when asked if his hands were burnt, laughingly said, "No, but my temperature just rose for a while."

In the early days, devotees testify that when Baba went out of his body, his limp form would make gestures such as dragging, pulling, lifting, bandaging, etc., which later he explained was saving someone from being drowned, or burnt, run over or crushed. Once, while talking to a group of people at Muthukur, he went out of his body to drag someone from a Jeep which had overturned on him. On another occasion, his unconscious body started to beat his own devotees who stood around him. He explained later that he had had to do this to save a devotee's life during bad rioting in Hyderabad.

They also testify that he has appeared to them in all manner of guises — as a beggar, a *sadhu*, a workman, a cobra, even as a dog. (Sai Baba of Shirdi, too, was alleged to be able to take the forms of animals.)

One appearance, as an electrician, is particularly remarkable. Dr Ramakrishna Rao, at the time Governor of two Indian States, was travelling with his wife in a train without a corridor, at night. Suddenly the electric fan caught fire. There was clearly a danger that the whole carriage would catch light. Dr Rao sent out an S.O.S. to Baba. To his absolute astonishment an electrician entered the carriage from the running board while the train was in transit, extinguished the fire, mended the fan, and finally stepped out onto the running board and disappeared into the night, asking Dr Rao to close the door behind him.

Next day Dr Rao and his wife boarded a 'plane, and again catastrophe struck. As the 'plane was about to land, the under-carriage wheels stuck and the pilot prepared to make a crash landing. But a devotee on board, wearing a ring Swami had materi-alised for him, was prompted to go into the cockpit and pull a lever which miraculously released the wheels. At the airport Dr Rao telephoned Baba and, while he was relating the story of their escape in the aeroplane, Swami interrupted him and said, "But you havn't mentioned the electric fan in the train!"

A method of healing Swami sometimes practises is to actually take on the disease, or the negative past *karma* of a devotee. Probably the best known case was when a devotee suffered a very serious heart attack (from which, Swami said later, he would not have recovered.) It was just prior to a festival. The whole of the left side of Baba's body became paralysed, including his left eye, and his speech was also badly affected. He managed to indicate that he would be all right in five days when the festival was to take place at which he was due to deliver a discourse. But as the days went by he seemed to get worse. At times he lost consciousness and groaned, his mouth became terribly mishapen, and he had to drag himself across the floor to the lavatory. It was a severe test of faith for even those closest to him. Some clearly doubted if he would ever recover and pleaded with him to see a doctor, but he adamantly refused.

On the morning of the festival, with a large crowd assembled, he insisted on being carried out to the rostrum and placed in a chair. A sort of mass emanation of groans, wailings, and tears rose up as the crowd saw their beloved Master in this piteous state. It was made worse when he made a feeble attempt to speak through a microphone and could not manage it. It seemed the ultimate disaster.

Then, motioning for a bowl of water, he dipped his right hand in it and sprinkled a few drops over the left leg. After a few moments he straightened this leg, gave a kick, stood up, placed the microphone in position, and gave a perfectly normal discourse. The crowd went absolutely hysterical. For once, the festival became something of a riot, and people who had almost taken leave of their senses had to be restrained.

Apart from strokes and heart attacks Baba has been known to take on mumps, typhoid, childbirth pains, and severe burns of his devotees. There are one or two cases of rather strange, eccentric healings. Once a devotee had a high fever. Swami noticed a bumble bee and caught it in his hand. He gave it to the devotee, and when it flew off the fever had also vanished. Was it a miracle? Or, unknown to science, does the bumble bee carry within itself some curative properties?

On another occasion a devotee was short of black beads which he needed to embellish a shrine idol, and came to Swami. There happened to be a black ant crawling on his bare foot. Swami picked it up and placed it gently in the man's hand, whereupon the ant suddenly became a palmful of black beads!

There have been two attempts to poison him. Each time, as one would expect, he knew beforehand. On the first occasion he simply smiled, deliberately ate a double portion of the poisoned food, and then went out and simply vomited, and thereafter suffered no ill effects. A sample of the food was analysed in a laboratory and found to contain a virulent poison.

On the second occasion, he decided to digest the food in order to prove to the would-be assassin that he could cure himself. After a day or two of experiencing the symptoms of severe food poisoning, he did cure himself.

It does not appear to be necessary to be a devotee of Sai Baba to be healed or rescued. There is a case of a *yogi* who had no interest in Baba who was saved from drowning while floating down the Ganges. Swami heard his call of distress while resident at Rishikesh.

Professor Kasturi says there are two essential requisites – either to carry a materialised article (which seems to act as a kind of transmitting set) or to call on God, by whatever name, with all one's heart and soul.

Nor does distance make any difference. Apart from *vibhuti* materialising on Baba's pictures all over the world, there was the case of Mr and Mrs Venkatamuni who lost all their traveller's cheques in Paris. They were desperate and sent out a *'cri de coeur'* to Swami. The next day Mrs Venkatamuni found the cheques in her handbag which she had emptied a dozen times during the search.

As an example of how the time factor can be completely irrelevant, and how patience can be rewarded, an old sage, aged eighty-seven, came to Swami. As a child of seven he had had a great longing to see a vision of the elephant-headed god, Ganesha. For forty-one consecutive days, the boy had recited a particular *mantra* which was said to give this vision, but nothing had happened. Swami reminded him of his persistence and praiseworthy *sadhana*, and proceeded to reward him by giving him a vision of his beloved god, Ganesha. Thus, an old man had had to wait eighty years for an answer to his prayers . . .

Baba has been known to enter the secular scene to influence court decisions. He once went out of his body for twelve hours to save an innocent pilot from wrongful prosecution for embezzlement of funds. I imagine the length of time was due to the lengthy court proceedings, for the evidence was said to be damning, and although it is not recorded whether he was visible or invisible, I imagine the latter – that is to say, he was manipulating the minds of the judge and lawyers. A verdict of not guilty was brought in.

I can personally testify to a similar case where Swami appears to have influenced a court decision, although absolute proof is impossible. During a group interview at which I was present at Brindavan a friend of mine, an American musician, asked Swami to help him over a pending legal action in which he was being sued for a very large sum of money for defamation of character. He had 'insulted' the plaintiff during a live television show. Baba instantly diagnosed the case and said, "Yes, I will help you. This man is not defending his honour, he is out for the money." Later in the interview Baba asked my friend for the plaintiff's name.

Some months went by during which my friend and his wife were under great stress. To lose the case would have broken them financially. On the eve of the action the plaintiff offered an out of court settlement for a fraction of what he was suing for. My friend was sorely tempted to accept. It was a great test of faith in Swami's promise. He stood loyal, and in the event the judge dismissed the case — the plaintiff received not a single cent!

There is a mass of what I would term miscellaneous miracles and healings. Once a car ahead of Swami's, in which devotees were travelling, ran over a small boy who was badly injured. Swami got out of his car, touched the boy, and he was immediately healed.

On another occasion, his car ran out of petrol during a night journey. He told the driver to fetch some water in a can from a nearby pond. Stirring it with his fingers, he changed it into petrol.

Similarly, during a festival when the lights failed due to the generating plant running out of fuel oil. He took some water and this time changed it into diesel oil.

At Trichinopoly, while addressing a meeting, he diagnosed a man in the audience who was deaf and dumb. He called up the deaf mute, healed him, and then made him speak over the microphone!

Dr Bannerjee records how Swami caused him to be 'possessed', as he believed, by Krishna, in order to correct him of his wrong impression of that *Avatar*. Apparently he had a total misconception of Krishna, believing him to have been a rake and a libertine. Suddenly he experienced the sensation of feeling exceptionally holy and pure. After a little while Baba placed his hands on his head and 'dispossessed' him — that is, he cast out an *avatar* instead of a devil, and Dr Bannerjee felt normal once again.

Once, the same doctor touched Swami's robe at *darshan* and to his astonishment found that his damaged finger which had been exceedingly painful, was immediately healed. This seems analogous to the story in the Gospels when a woman was healed by touching the robe of Jesus who, 'sensing that power had gone out of him', turned and said, "Woman, thy faith hath made thee whole."

On rare occasions it seems that Baba uses his *sankalpa* (will) for healing or directly influencing events. He has said that, sometimes in cases of dire need, he overlooks the Law of *Karma* and directly intervenes with nature, since he has said that natural catastrophes such as floods, earthquakes, etc. are due to man's inhumanity to man. There was a time when the River Chitravati was flooding so badly that the village was in danger. He simply 'ordered' the floods to subside, and despite the fact that the rains continued, the water level immediately began to recede. Similarly he has ordered a storm

179

· during a festival, and it has done so.

an lady, crippled for years with arthritis, arrived at the
ɪheelchair. She had the effrontery to say, "I don't
Baba, I don't believe you can heal me." He replied,
ɪhether you believe in me or not – get up and walk."
.ᴗɪ was such authority in his voice that she felt compelled to try.
She stood up and walked, was completely cured after years of
immobility, and left her wheelchair behind in India.

And on a more mundane level, a young student was suffering
from continuous dysentry which would not clear up. He
commanded the body to "Stop purging!" – and it did.

Apart from the raising of the dead, possibly the most significant
phenomenon about Sai Baba is the formation of *lingams* in his
stomach which he delivers from his mouth at the annual Shivaratri
Festival. I understand he has discontinued this practice in recent
times, but for years it was an event which caused tremendous
excitement and spiritual exaltation among his devotees, particularly
the more evolved.

The *lingam* is about an inch and a half in length and an ellipsoid.
The mineral is quartz crystal, gold or silver. The number produced
varies from one to as many as nine. It symbolises the primary
polarity principle of positive and negative forces, the principle of
opposites on which the whole cosmos is founded.

To quote Sai Baba himself: "The *lingam* is a symbol of begin-
ningless and endlessness, or the Infinite . . . That in which all
names and forms merge . . . and That towards which all forms
proceed. It is the fittest symbol of the omnipotent, omniscient and
omnipresent Lord. Everything starts from it and everything is
subsumed in it." (*Vision of the Divine* by Dr Fanibunda, page 55).

This seems to me to give an explanation of the origin of opposites, of positive and negative forces, of 'good' and 'evil' which
perhaps, one day, will be re-harmonised into a whole and no longer
be what they seem.

As the *lingam* represents the basic principle and power of
creation, it is considered by the Hindus to be the highest object of
worship on the physical plane. It is also claimed that its elliptical
shape creates a channel between God and the worshippers which
is the reason why its annual delivery by Sai Baba at the Shivaratri
Festival has caused such spiritual exaltation among his followers.

The materialised objects of all descriptions which Baba has
produced during his lifetime are legion, and probably now run into
tens of thousands. Sandalwood images, silver icons, silver sandals,
ivory figures, emblems of Shiva in topaz and sapphire have all from
time to time been materialised and given to people. Also rings,
lockets and rosaries galore. These latter are not, as some critics

imply, cheap trinkets. The elements of which they are composed are said to have curative properties, and they are also said to ward off evil spirits.

As can be imagined, they also establish a closer link between the wearer and Baba, both physical and spiritual. As he says, "I give you what you want in order that you may want what I have come to give." I can personally witness that to wear a materialised object establishes this link.

In the summer of 1980, I was saved from a serious accident. I was working on some scaffolding when the ladder on which I stood suddenly reared over backwards like a bucking horse. It seemed inevitable that I should be hurled to the ground, which was concrete, and suffer serious injuries. In a panic I cried out to Swami and kissed his ring. For a second, perhaps two, I was unaware of what happened, although I did not lose consciousness. I only knew that I found myself with my two feet firmly planted on a pair of tall steps a few feet below the bottom of the ladder, and holding the ladder with both hands about a foot from the ground.

As I surveyed the scene from ground level there was no way, by the ordinary laws of gravity, that this could have occurred. I am sure it was Swami who saved me.

There appears to be something about sand which makes it particularly easy for Swami to materialise objects from it, or to perform miracles of alchemy. Many, many miracles have been performed on the sandy reaches of the River Chitravati at Puttaparthi, or by the seashore. In fact, his disciples sometimes try to entice him onto the sands, for they know that miracles will occur. He will take a handful of sand and give it to a devotee as a handful of sweets or a lump of sugar candy. He might materialise a picture of himself, or of Sai Baba of Shirdi. Once when walking along the sands, 108 beads (symbolising the 108 attributes of God Incarnate) fell at each step and were picked up by the devotees in attendance, and made into a rosary. He has produced copies of the *Bhagavad-Gita* on the sands, and in different languages, and once in especially large print for a devotee who had impaired eyesight.

On the birthdays of Rama and Krishna, he invariably sits down on the sand with a group of devotees around him and digs out an image of these two *Avatars* which he gives to someone present to place in his or her shrine room. I personally know one lady who was given a two-foot gold statue of Krishna in this way, and has it in her *puja*.

Professor Kasturi gives a long list of rivers and seashores where Swami has performed similar miracles. Once at Masulipatam he walked straight into the sea and was seen riding on the back of a sea serpent, and when he returned to the shore his clothes were completely dry!

As an example of how Baba has never in his whole lifetime materialised anything for himself, he once was returning to Puttaparthi at dusk from a country trek with a small group of devotees when a cobra slithered across the track and bit him on the leg. Baba fell down and foamed at the mouth. He managed to convey to the devotee in closest attendance that he wished him to circle his hand three or four times, and when the devotee did this he suddenly felt, to his utter amazement, what Kasturi describes as a 'sort of talisman' in the palm of his hand. This was applied to the snake bite, and Swami was up and perfectly well in five minutes. Thus even when confronted with the venom of a lethal snake Baba insisted on transferring the power to materialise to another rather than produce a remedy for himself.

Often in his life he has had some difficulty in persuading former disciples of Sai Baba of Shirdi that he is a reincarnation of the old Muslim saint. To counter this he sometimes raises both palms, where there appears a vision of himself in one and of Sai Baba of Shirdi in the other. He has materialised numerous photographs of the previous Sai Baba, sometimes to correct wrong impressions.

Once, as a child, he took his own sister into a room at the family house and gave her a vision not only of Sai Baba of Shirdi, but of the whole locale in which he lived. He has given full details of the first sixteen years of the old saint, of which there is no record.

Once, as a teenager, he was invited to the palace of the Rani of Chincholi whose husband, the Raja, had died. They had both been devout followers of the Saint of Shirdi, and the Rani was interested to see this boy who claimed to be his reincarnation. On arrival at the palace, Baba pointed out the changes which had taken place since his incarnation at Shirdi — of a tree which had been felled, a well which had been filled in, a new row of shops which had been built. Then he enquired of the Rani where a certain picture of Krishna was, which Sai Baba of Shirdi had given to her husband. She had no knowledge of such a gift, so Baba suggested that a thorough search of the palace be made. To the astonishment of the Rani the picture was finally found. She became convinced.

Once, Baba went out of his body to Delhi to convince one, Chidambara Iyer, who was vacillating between the two. He projected himself physically as a fellow cyclist and engaged this man in conversation as he was bicycling home from work. Together they stopped off for a few moments at a shrine where Baba adopted his usual custom of raising his two hands and giving the man a vision of Sai Baba of Shirdi and himself on either palm. Then he cycled off and, to the amazement of this man who was watching him, he suddenly disappeared into thin air!

Baba has often recognised old devotees of his former body and, to their astonishment, given them accounts of his association with them in his former life. Some who have known both say there is an unmistakable identity of mission and message. One such is Yogi Suddananda Bharathiar of Madras. Kasturi, too, says there is an extraordinary similarity in speech, style, attitude, outlook and teachings.

Although in the vast majority of cases Sai Baba materialises objects, he does sometimes teleport them. On Howard Murphet's first visit he did both – he changed a flower into a diamond; but on Murphet's birthday he teleported an old American coin to him with the year of Murphet's birth on it.

When a devotee dies and there is no one in the family to cherish the treasured object Swami has said that it returns to him. When a materialised object is lost or stolen he teleports it back. C.M. Padma was once given a second rosary by Baba, and when he enquired why, Swami said, "Yours was stolen last night. This is it." He found this to be true when he returned home. His house had been broken into and the silver box in which he kept his rosary had been taken.

A devotee once inadvertently spent a favourite rupee note with the signature of his best friend on it. Swami teleported it back to him.

A lady coffee plantation owner lost a diamond ring which had great sentimental value. Months later, while visiting her home, Swami noticed that she was still grieving for the loss of the ring, so he teleported it back to her from wherever it was and, to her delight and amazement, she found it was the selfsame ring.

There have been cases when Baba has teleported an object back to himself when the recipient has not proved worthy of the gift. A hard-up musician once contemplated selling a rosary Swami had materialised for him. It immediately disappeared. Chastened, he returned to the *ashram*, and Swami relented and gave him back the necklace which he recognised as the same.

Perhaps the most remarkable case was when a lady had lost her *japamala* for no less than four years. One day, when she was walking along the river bank at Puttaparthi with Swami, he suddenly dug out this selfsame necklace, which she immediately recognised, from the sand and handed it to her, saying, "You lost this in Bangalore four years ago."

Other examples of actual materialisations are when a lady broke her spectacles at *darshan* and Swami materialised a new pair which the lady found to be of the same prescription.

Once, in his private quarters with a group of devotees, he

materialised a photograph of the room, and when the devotees complained that the background was a bit dim, that his hair was awry, and that he had not shaved, he replied, "My dear fellows, this is a photograph of myself, and things in this room, exactly as they are at this moment!"

During a discussion on the various theories of the origin of man Baba once said that humans were more closely related to tree-dwelling apes than to the ground-dwelling varieties. A professor of anthropology was present and enquired further. Swami then materialised a tail-less, hairless, tree-dwelling ape in miniature. This work of art and of scientific accuracy is now in the Natural History Museum at Brindavan. Could it be a miniature of the 'missing link'?

Finally, I would like to describe what, apart from raising the dead, are perhaps two of Baba's most remarkable miracles. The first took place between 1948 and 1950 when the *ashram* at Puttaparthi was being enlarged. The Purnachandra Auditorium has a width span of 140 feet and there are no central columns. The roof is supported by giant girders. These proved impossible to transport by lorry because at that time the last section of the road to Puttaparthi was little more than a bullock-cart track — there were broken down culverts, boggy stretches of sand, and so on. The lorries sank down to their axles and stuck.

The chief engineer heard of a mobile crane at a nearby dam construction site which had been set aside as being in need of repair. He consulted Baba. Swami gave him several packets of *vibhuti* and told him to sprinkle it over the engine. He did as he was told and, to his amazement, the engine sputtered and then started!

Thus the last part of the transportation of the girders was negotiated by the use of a rusty old crane, started up by *vibhuti*, and driven like a tank (for I understand it had caterpillar wheels) over streams, bogs, and the half fallen in culverts to the outskirts of Puttaparthi where Swami himself took over the steering wheel and dumped the steel monsters at the precise point they were needed for erection.

Even the engineer grumbled because he had no adequate equipment to raise them into position. Undeterred, Swami instructed him to rig up a primitive arrangement of ropes and pulleys which seemed totally inadequate, meanwhile gathering around him about five hundred devotees and training them to shout the words "JAI SAI RAM" in a very special way.

As the tugging and pulling started a loud shout of "JAI SAI RAM" rose up and, to everyone's astonishment, the girders also rose up and were hauled into position as if they were as light as aluminium. Thus, as possibly occurred at Stonehenge and the building of the pyramids, the power of sound was utilised. (Swami has averred that at the time of Krishna, small flying machines existed which were 'fuelled' by the sound of *mantra*.) It must have been like Joshua's army at the siege of Jericho, only this time the power of sound was used for construction instead of destruction.

In 1957, the sage, Satchidananda, witnessed Baba in an out-of-the-body state. Just before going into a trance he cried out in a loud voice, "Don't shoot!" in Telegu. A government official had lost his job when the reorganisation of India's States was taking place and was about to shoot himself with a pistol, when there was a loud knock on the door. He quickly hid the gun under the sheets of his bed and opened the door, there to see an old college friend with his wife and a bearer. They talked for about two hours, during which time the friend and his wife managed to cheer up the civil servant so that he no longer had any thoughts of suicide. Not for one moment did he notice anything strange about the visitors, who had talked of old times they had shared together.

He invited them to stay overnight but, to his disappointment, they made their excuses and departed. He then went into his bedroom to recover the gun with the intention of putting it away in a safe place, only to discover that it had vanished. On coming out of trance Baba immediately had a telegram sent to him: "Don't worry, the instrument is with me."

Meanwhile the civil servant, suspecting that some extraordinary miracle had occurred, checked with his real friends at their home, which was a long way away, to find that they had been nowhere near the vicinity at the time of their seeming visit!

Thus Baba had not only teleported the gun to himself, but had materialised himself as three people at the same time, enacting roles in the minutest detail of correctness of appearance, voice, gait, gesture, and idiom, and even in the recitation of events when the official and his friend were at college together . . .

Swami Satchidananda maintains there is nothing in the whole of India's scriptures to match this incredible phenomenon.

Yet Sathya Sai Baba tells us that his miracles are the least important part of his mission, and indeed this is so. His mission is to save mankind by a spiritual transformation of the world.

# 7

# THE WELFARE WORK OF SATHYA SAI BABA

*"By their fruits ye shall know them."*

I have written of the vast scale of materialisations and healing miracles of Sathya Sai Baba. Much less is known of his educational and welfare work which he regards as far more important than the miracles. I am writing of these aspects of his mission, partly because they should be known, and partly to disarm those critics who question why he does not materialise food rather than *vibhuti* in a world where there is so much hunger, and why, if he is an *avatar*, does he allow earthquakes, famine and epidemics to occur.

The answer is that he does, on occasion, materialise food for the hungry, and there have been times when by the direct use of his *sankalpa* (will) he has transcended man's negative *karma* and alleviated the consequences of seemingly natural catastrophes which have in fact been caused by· man's selfishness and greed.

But to do so generally would be to break the sacred Law of *Karma* on which the whole of creation is based. Baba's task is to spiritually transform mankind so that these calamities do not occur; were he to create a kind of artificial Garden of Eden before we are ready to sustain it we should revert within a century to the sort of conditions that are prevalent in the world today.

In the meantime he has embarked on a programme of education and welfare the like of which, for sheer scope and imagination, has never before been attempted by any *avatar*. Its scale is truly gigantic. "My life is my message," he says. Let no man think that when Baba claims to be the Embodiment of Love, with love as his instrument, that he does not practise what he preaches. He is no cloistered holy man or *ashram* guardian.

It is in the field of welfare that the mind almost boggles when one grasps what Sai Baba is doing all over India. Most of this work is done by the Seva Dal organisation which Swami has set up, of which there are now 20,000 trained members. Training is given to the volunteers in the organisation of field hospitals, blood donor camps, dental camps, opthalmic camps, etc. On the vocational side a wide variety of skills is taught. Apart from the elementary crafts of plumbing, carpentry and bricklaying, such diverse skills as motor rewinding, scooter and automobile servicing, projector operation, refrigerator servicing, and agro-industrial equipment servicing (that is, farm machinery for the land, and bulldozers, cranes and the like, at dam and road construction sites).

The women are taught knitting, soap-powder making, tailoring and embroidery, cooking and jam making, interior decoration and similar home crafts.

In fact, these volunteers can turn their hand to almost anything. They are full of initiative and ingenuity. Wherever there is a need they think up a scheme, however homespun. And in a country like India, with its vast population, its backwardness by Western standards and its absence of a national health service, the needs must sometimes seem like a bottomless well. The Seva Dal volunteers may be seen doing almost anything, from removing large boulders for making a bullock cart track from a remote village to its primitive crematorium in order to give the deceased some semblance of dignity on their last journey, to organising a field hospital where up to a hundred doctors may be in attendance.

They collect secondhand classbooks for children whose parents cannot afford them, and re-bind them. They teach blind pupils Braille, and they act as 'scribes' for them during examinations. They make crutches for the crippled which are called 'Sai supports'. They offer their services as blood donors to the hospitals and donate their eyes in their wills. One opthalmic hospital in Madras has received 400 eyes from Seva Dal volunteers.

They run, and exclusively staff, an Old Folks Home in Monegar Choultry.

There is a 'Medical Service Day' each year in December when

gifts such as oxygen cylinders, wheelchairs, Braille books, and other equipment are donated to the less well equipped institutions.

Let us take one State, that of Tamil Nadu, in which the city of Madras lies. In Madras alone, 50,000 patients a year benefit from the First Aid Centres which have been set up. Free medical check-ups and X-ray screenings are done, and there are free dispensaries for drugs. The drugs are collected from the well-to-do residents of the city who have supplies surplus to their needs (and over-prescription is common to all countries), or from pharmaceutical firms whose top executives are Sai devotees and who donate free supplies, as well as doctors who donate their free samples. At the dispensaries in Madurai, Ramanathapuram, Coimbatore and Kallamadi there is an average of a hundred patients a day at each centre.

Of course co-operation is sought and willingly given to the existing services. For example, befriending of elderly and lonely patients who have no relatives is undertaken in hospitals. It is called 'adopting'. Film shows of Sai Baba are given in the wards and cassettes of *bhajan* singing are loaned. Blood supplies from the donor camps are sent to hospitals, and sometimes much needed supplies of rare blood groups are obtained. Foster parents are found who are willing to take children who are orphaned or mentally retarded, from the existing institutions. Sai Baba adopted hundreds of children orphaned in a disaster.

But the bulk of Sai Baba's work is undertaken in a spirit of private enterprise. It has the grateful and enthusiastic support of the Indian Government. In areas where there are large groups of Seva Dal volunteers, whole villages are 'adopted' and the most pressing social needs attended to. Recently villagers were astounded to see educated girls from one of Sai Baba's universities for women digging a long drainage canal, working in the hot sun with spade and pick-axe, and gladly joined in the task. Also removing silt from dried up wells and deepening them until they yield water again.

There is a voluntary scheme for a medical check-up in all the schools and orphanages in the State. About 50,000 children have been screened in this way, with a follow-up service administering drugs, tonics and vitamins. Also spectacles and hearing aids.

The field hospitals are usually set up in remote areas of the countryside where doctors and hospitals are not readily available. In 1979, over 30,000 patients, mostly villagers, were treated in eleven such camps in isolated parts of the State. They were staffed by an average of fifty to eighty doctors and two hundred para-medical helpers who gave their services free, and were equip-ped to deal with tuberculosis, eye surgery, gynaecology and other specific conditions.    Severely sick patients were transported to Madras for specialist hospital care, and in due course taken home again to outlying districts in the State.

Perhaps it is invidious to mention any one doctor, but Dr Modi, an eye surgeon, has given his services free to Swami for the past twenty-five years.  He travels to field hospitals all over India, and in that time is estimated to have performed 100,000 cataract operations, with a success rate of over 90%.

Great efforts are made to feed the hungry. (Every volunteer in Sai Seva is asked to put aside a handful of rice daily which is then collected monthly.)   In the remote areas a register is compiled of the old and destitute who are fed daily.  Eighty such centres exist in the State of Tamil Nadu alone.  Food packets are also provided for the poorer children in Madras who cannot afford a midday meal at school.

In 1976 there was a severe drought in the Coimbatore District. A thousand peasants in the villages were provided with daily food and drinking water for six weeks until Government relief arrived.

And in the following year a truly gigantic rescue operation was mounted by the Seva Dal.  A terrible cyclone hit the coast of Andhra Pradesh. A twenty-foot tidal wave swept inland for up to forty miles, causing enormous devastation.  Thousands died, whole villages were literally washed away, and hundreds of cattle and stock were drowned. Disease quickly spread.

It so happened that it was at the time of Swami's birthday celebrations when an All India Conference of the Seva Dal and 3,400 Sai Centres was also taking place.  Swami cancelled everything and sent the Seva Dal into action.

The first job was to wade through slush and mire, through fumes and stench, to collect the rotting corpses which lay in huddled heaps and carry them to a place of cremation or burial.  Some were found entwined in the branches of fallen trees they had climbed in a vain attempt to escape the rising waters.  Corpses of cattle also had to be dealt with.

Nearly a million rupees flowed in for relief from Sai devotees within a matter of days.  Four relief camps were set up with a full complement of doctors and Seva Dal volunteers.  Truckloads of food, clothing, blankets, tents, and medical supplies were rushed in as near to the camps as possible in the sodden ground, and then carried as headloads by the devotees.

Thus five thousand forlorn men and women rendered destitute, who had somehow managed to escape, were cared for and saved. Other small groups who had found refuge elsewhere were reached by wading through mud and water and provided with food. But for the presence, courage, and resourcefulness of the Seva Dal it is doubtful if Government relief, when it did come, would have arrived in time.

They worked literally day and night in the most appalling conditions for four weeks, and when the floods had subsided they even erected primitive hutments which they equipped as best they could with cooking utensils, reed mats and rugs and, singing *bhajans* to lighten the gloom, managed to persuade the stunned and grieving remnants of the populace to take up their lives again as fishermen and farmers.

It was a truly heroic operation which tested the Seva Dal to the limit and brought out the best in them. Many fainted temporarily from the nauseating stench and were near collapse at the end of four weeks from lack of sleep and food. I do not think it could have taken place except for the inspiration of Sai Baba.

In more normal times, at the *ashrams* at Puttaparthi and Brindavan, where beggars tend to congregate, Swami sees they are all adequately fed. At the recent World Conference in November 1980 he urged every devotee family to set themselves the target of saving enough food to feed one beggar every day of the year.

When funds are available Swami builds whole rows of small cottages in a particularly poverty stricken area. He especially favours the *Harijans* (God's people), the so called 'untouchables', in order to play his part in ridding the country of caste prejudice.

One can say that almost every conceivable need is catered for, albeit on a still limited scale in a country which is so over-populated and so poor. Even group weddings are arranged for those too poor to afford one, with special food and clothing provided free for the bridal couple and up to twenty friends and relatives of each.

I can honestly say that I have not covered more than half the scope of the welfare and humanitarian work which is being undertaken in this one State of Tamil Nadu — and repeated elsewhere, for I do not think it is an exception. As far as I am aware the same thing is taking place in every other State of India. In total, it makes a truly prodigious effort.

No doubt the needs of one State vary from those of another. In the two States in which the *ashrams* are sited, for example, there are courses for villagers in modern dairy farming at the *ashram* model farms. In Bombay, where there is considerable unemployment, I inspected a well equipped workshop at Swami's Dharmakshetra to teach unemployed youngsters various trades. No doubt this is emulated at the main Sai Centres in all the big cities. Dharmakshetra also has a large lending library and a class-room for coaching the backward. Swami also has an Agricultural

Polytechnic in Bombay, and Schools of Technology in Puttaparthi, Bombay, Calcutta, etc.

It is safe to say that the two priorities of hunger and sickness are attended to all over India by the Seva Dal volunteers. Swami, too, does his personal share, apart from inspiring and setting in motion the whole organisation. He loves to feed the needy. He was doing it at the age of three! At the Dassehra Festival, on the day given over to feeding of the poor, he insists on personally doling out food to anything up to 15,000 people, with the help of the volunteers, and each year a *sari* is given to the women and a *dhoti* to each man.

He frequently visits prisons and remand homes. His presence and his stirring words have a miraculous effect. Many a prison cell has become a shrine room, and many a delinquent a devotee. Friend of ambassadors, cabinet ministers, scientists and philosophers, he is even more a friend to the wrongdoer, the lame and the blind, the crippled and the sick. As he himself says, "I am happiest when I am with those who are most in need." Sai Baba gives comfort, hope and spiritual uplift wherever he goes, but he does not forget our physical needs. As the wise man from the East said, "Even God hesitates to offer the starving anything but bread."

# 8

# EDUCATIONAL WORK OF SATHYA SAI BABA

*"I am not so concerned about the 'marks' a student gains at college as the 'remarks' made about his character."*

Sai Baba

The *avataric* vision of repairing the ancient highway to God is at present through education. The era of miracles to prove Sai Baba's miracles is said to be diminishing, and a new era with the main emphasis on education is receiving more and more of his attention.

He says, "Discipline which should illumine our path to learning is now a remote lamp. Virtues like renunciation, integrity, justice and truthfulness should be the natural attributes of man, but these are not to be found in our schools. Two noble ideals which should inspire our students, a spontaneous love of duty, and a passionate desire to rate social good above everything else, are lacking. Instead they are obsessed with a blind imitation of unscrupulous leaders, exhibitionism, love of excessive pleasure, and a sickening longing for ever-increasing comfort."

In the past decade Sai Baba has initiated hundreds of schools throughout India, with the emphasis on character-building and universal spirituality. First come the *Bal Vikases* (primary education in human values) which are weekend courses for the very young to supplement orthodox education. Then there are full-time schools, the *Vidya Viharas* (elementary education through the joy of learning) which children enter in their early teens. Here *sadhana, yoga*, social service, meditation, and hymn-singing are practised. Swami also has Elementary and High Schools in many places which specialise in character-building, *sadhana*, and social service. Finally come the Colleges, which have now attained the status of Universities.

At Puttaparthi there is an elementary school, a secondary school, a high school and a college or university, so that children can start and end their entire education, with complete continuity, according to the Sai principles. This even surpasses the Rudolf Steiner system in the West where students complete their education at eighteen, and if they wish to go on to a university have to choose an orthodox one where they may become addicted at a vulnerable age to undesirable practices.

There are 2,000 *Bal Vikas* schools in India, catering for 40,000 children, and increasing at the rate of 6,000 children a year. At the 1980 World Conference Swami decreed that every affiliated Sai Centre, including those abroad, should initiate a *Bal Vikas* within two years of its inception.

At these kindergarten schools the rudiments of all religions are taught, and a sense of morality is not cultivated by didactic lecturing, but through story-telling, the performing of plays, and singing. This is a far better way of instilling nobility of purpose, self-sacrifice and heroism into a child's mind than by pedantic homily.

The method has much in common with the Rudolf Steiner system. When my own son, who was educated at a Steiner school, was about ten a visitor inspecting the school enquired of his class which was their favourite subject and, to his consternation, there was an enthusiastic and unanimous shout of "Religion!" This was because religion was not taught as 'Religion' but by graphic and detailed story-telling of the world's heroes in all fields of life. Children love listening to inspiring stories which appeal to their imagination and fantasy.

On one occasion my son's form master was finding it difficult to curb the antics of a small group of bullies, of which there is always an element in any school, though very much less so in Steiner schools. No amount of persuasion, reprimand or punishment had the desired effect, and so one day he hit upon the idea of telling the whole class a story with a moral which he actually invented. It was the story of a cabin boy at sea whose life was made such a misery by the bullying of his shipmates that he finally threw himself overboard and was drowned. The story was told very graphically and in great detail so that the children were all ears to hear the ending.

At the end there was a hushed silence. The master was careful not to point to the moral, nor to hint that the story was intended for the benefit of the class bullies, but from that day on, all bullying ceased! The culprits were made to feel ashamed by an appeal to their imagination rather than to their undeveloped sense of morality. There is an analogy in the acquisition of wisdom – one acquires wisdom through life experience rather than through intellectuality and academic erudition.

And so it is with the *Bal Vikas* – there is no didactic teaching. As Swami says: the preaching of morality does not teach or show a child what kind of man he ought to become and why. It is only concerned with imposing a set of rules on him – arbitrary, bewildering, contradictory and, more often than not, incomprehensible. The child grows up with nothing but resentment and fear for any concept of morality. Ethics appear to him only as a phantom scarecrow, demanding the drab performance of dry duty.

Sai Baba has already established five colleges in India, at Puttaparthi (which has recently received university status), Brindavan, Bhopal, Jaipur and Anantapur, with a sixth in Jamnagar, completed but not at the moment of writing, staffed. There are about a thousand students in each. He himself acts as a kind of guardian angel/headmaster to all of them. He knows most of the students personally. There is a master plan to build two universities in every State in India, which has the enthusiastic support and gratitude of the present Government of India.

They are not, strictly speaking, theological colleges. They are called the Sri Sathya Sai Arts, Science and Commerce Colleges. He has said: "Education without character, science without humanity, commerce without morality are useless and dangerous." He is trying to rectify this current state of affairs in India, and ultimately the world, by training generations of young men and women who will become India's future leaders in all fields, and thus inject spirituality into the whole secular scene. Moreover he has said that these students will provide the physical vehicles for the incarnation of 'old souls', so that the propagation of the right type will snowball.

I have seen a sample of the Brindavan students, and I have never seen a finer cadre of young men in my life. They were tidy, well mannered, respectful, happy and integrated, brisk and intelligent, devout and inspired – indeed, the elite of the elite. And yet they were not the sons of the rich; more than half came from the rural areas.

On taking our leave of Swami after our last private interview in January 1980, in the emotion of the moment, my wife forgot her handbag, and a young student standing by as an aide, picked it up and handed it to her. On his face was an expression of compassionate understanding of her ecstatic state which befitted a man of fifty rather than a young man in his late teens.

Although character building and spirtuality take precedence over academic distinction in these colleges, it is an ironic fact that Swami's students are second to none in degree qualifications, and perhaps just because of the emphasis on these qualities.

Women play a very important part in Sai Baba's order of priorities. He regards the sacred role of motherhood as almost the most important role in life. Women are the custodians of the future of civilisation. Three of the first five colleges established are for women only.

It is a sad reflection on our society in the United Kingdom that recent statistics show that 50% of married couples now regard their own material pleasures as more important than the rearing of their children. I was uplifted recently by talking to the wife of a friend of mine who was coping with the upkeep of a large house and the rearing of a family, ranging from one month to fifteen years, unaided. I remarked that she had a load on her hands. She replied cheerfully, "Oh, but the children give you back so much." If you put your heart and soul into a job in a dedicated way it brings its own reward. I suspect it is the women who do not do this who find child-rearing unfulfilling.

In order to eradicate any hangover of the former curse of India, caste prejudice, the students do manual work. They milk the cows at the *ashram* farms. They do the labouring jobs when new buildings are erected. They were almost entirely responsible for the building of the hospital at the Puttaparthi *ashram*, and Swami has said that the love and care with which each brick was laid has to a large extent created the right vibrations for healing to take place within the precincts.

In a sense he is resurrecting the heritage and atmosphere of India's ancient universities and adapting them to modern needs. He tells us that millenia ago the universities of ancient Bharat were sited in sylvan settings, in quiet woodland and alongside a river, where peace, harmony and equality reigned. The *atma* in all men was recognised, and the son of a peasant sat next to the son of a king. In those days agriculture was a consecrated profession.

An experiment has recently been made with a full-time boarding school in Ootacamund (Ooty) in the former residence of the 19th century Governor-General, Lord Dalhousie. India's schools, as opposed to colleges, are non-boarding. Founded in 1978 with a small group of thirty children there are now a hundred and twenty pupils from all over the world.  The ancient walls of the school, which at the peak of the British Raj, witnessed pomp and ceremony and merrymaking, now resound to the chant of the AUM and the sound of *bhajans.*  The experiment is undoubtedly a success, and there is a long waiting list.

Swami recognises the superiority of Western education in certain aspects.  For example, some Indian parents tend to implant unnecessary fears into their children by telling them of ghosts, and pointing out the dangers of such harmless and happy pursuits as swimming and climbing trees.  He is trying to rectify these faults in parents through parent—teacher associations.

Summer Courses are held each year, at Brindavan, during the College vacation.  These are primarily designed to implant into young and sensitive minds a world view of things and a comprehensive outlook on religion, as well as to inspire a determination to lead noble lives in a world which has run amok, to act as the leaven in however small a minority they find themselves.  Yet the course attracts headmasters, university professors, psychologists, and educationalists from all over the world.

The subject matter might be straight forward education, or a course on the *Bhagavad-Gita* or the *Ramayana* with Baba's true and enlightening interpretations.  He discourses daily and sometimes twice daily, and holds question and answer sessions.  The message is always of the essential universality of India's spiritual heritage.

The courses have proved a huge success, and more and more eminent people – even judges, scientists and politicians, are attending them.  I will quote from one Western lady who attended a Summer Course: "It was packed, awesome, hot, thrilling, uncomfortable, pure essence, inspiring, stretching, blissful, catalytic, revitalising, transforming, beautiful.  I found every question I'd ever had completely answered."

In 1978, the State of Andhra Pradesh completely recast its elementary schools system, with more emphasis on prayer, music, dance, painting, modelling, and parent—teacher associations.  Six hundred and sixty-five teachers were given a crash course over six weeks on Sai education at Brindavan.  In this short time, Professor Kasturi records, many had their lives completely transformed and were in tears when they had to leave.  They had found a true vocation instead of a mere job.  Thus the whole elementary school system of an entire State has incorporated the Sai ideals.

Further, in 1979, the Minister of Education set up a study group in Bangalore to consider extending the system to the whole of India.

How, you may well ask, does Sai education affect a raw pupil who goes to a college for his first term?  How does life in a Sai

College differ from that in an orthodox college? There is a very interesting chapter in a book by Mr V. Balu, *The Glory of Putta-parthi*, in which he questioned a group of students on these two points.

A few had come from opulent families in westernised towns. Previously, they had lived for pleasure and self-indulgence in large houses with many servants. Brindavan had brought about a steady change in their character and a whole set of new values. Living in dormitories they had learned to share, to become concerned for others, to shed ego, and even to enjoy menial chores like making beds, peeling potatoes, etc. The strict regimen, with reveille at 4:45 a.m. followed by a quick shower, *bhajan* singing, a brisk run, and an hour and a half of study, all before breakfast, although an effort at first, had instilled into them discipline and growing self-respect. New students said they caught the spirit of the place like a glorious infection from the older ones.

Others who had previously been to orthodox colleges, where leisure time was spent smoking and drinking, gambling and reading pornography, found that at Brindavan the whole atmosphere of character-building, spirituality and creative leisure squeezed out such impulses and helped to sublimate them. One said he had given up smoking and drinking because he found spirituality far more intoxicating and satisfying.

They spoke of the untidy, even filthy, conditions of other hostels where nobody cared, but because the Brindavan Hostel gave them the personal feeling that it belonged to them, they took a pride in keeping it spotless.

When this sample of students was asked how they had come to be at Sai Baba's College it seemed clear that Swami was 'drawing' or, in effect, hand-picking them. Some said they had had a sudden urge, others had had a vivid dream, and others had felt a very strong 'attraction' (which they could not analyse) when first catching a glimpse of Swami at *darshan*. No one seemed to be there by 'chance'.

The overwhelming influence at the College is, of course, Swami himself. Not because of his miracles — miracles are much more taken for granted in India than in the West — but because of his divine charisma and his power to change the students for the better. They spoke of the way he totally practised what he preached. He was a leader to whom youth could look up. There was no genera-tion gap — he was able to establish an extraordinary degree of rapport with them and make each feel he was all-important. When he spoke his words went straight to their hearts. He also generated an inner power, soul power.

They said there was no difference in the functioning of the

College whether Swami was absent or present. It seemed his authority derived from love rather than from the ways of orthodox headmastership. They felt his spiritual presence when he was absent. One said, "Even when he is away his spiritual dimension works wonders on us." I would hazard the guess that it does more than in his physical presence.

In Sai Baba's Colleges there is a very close teacher–pupil relationship based on a real sense of caring. The teachers live with the students in the Hostels and set high standards of conduct – they have no expensive tastes, they do not smoke or drink. If a student is backward they give extra coaching in their leisure time, without fee. They share the students' problems like loving parents. In social work they do the dirtiest jobs themselves, like unblocking drains in the villages. They create the atmosphere of a family. There is an invisible string of love which binds everyone together. As a result, the students' respect for the teachers is genuine rather than formal, and there is no student unrest.

The social work undertaken in leisure time does a great deal to eradicate ego, to eliminate any remnants of caste prejudice, and to inculcate a spirit of service in the students. Some who go to Brindavan thinking of social work as menial, even degrading, come to love it. One said he would feel like an unemployed youth if he did not keep it up; another, that fraternising with the peasants had taught him the reality of the *atma* in all human beings; and another, who had previously adopted a rather patronising attitude to helping the poor and the humble, had come to regard service as a privilege. One student who had come from a very wealthy family liked nothing better than to milk the cows on the *ashram* farm.

They spoke of many ways in which they had changed. Some had even arrived as agnostics, but had come to God through Swami. Not as a rule through overnight conversion, but slowly, as a result of the impact of his personality, and life generally at the College. Some had come as meat-eaters but had turned vegetarian out of respect for animals. Many spoke of the way they had learned to control anger and jealousy. The student vice of too much talk and arrogant discussion was absent. They had learned the value of silence. There was an almost complete absence of fights and heated arguments. Boredom was something they could scarcely comprehend; there was too much creative and exciting activity. They had learned to live frugally and simply without accessories. And, perhaps most important of all, they had come to respect each other's faiths and to realise there is only one God.

At the Dassehra Festival in 1979, the Brindavan College students attired themselves in ceremonial robes and discoursed on their particular faith. There was a Sikh from Delhi, a Zoroastrian from

Bombay, a Christian from Hawaii, a Muslim from Libya, a Buddhist from Sikkim, and a Hindu from Afghanistan. Afterwards, they stood in a group with Baba in the centre.

Perhaps the most significant fact that emerged from Mr Balu's survey was when he asked each student if he felt he might be corrupted when he returned to the world, and the reply was a unanimous 'No!' They had taken the 'path of the soul' and the ways of the world no longer held any attraction for them. They felt that Swami had implanted himself firmly in their hearts, and would guide them for the rest of their lives.

It may be they were being a little optimistic; a few, no doubt, will stray from the fold. But it is believed in India that even those who do so will eventually be drawn back, like prodigal sons.

What, then, are the principles of Sai education? Well, of course, it incorporates the four pillars of his teaching: *Sathya, Dharma, Shanti* and *Prema*. But, in the last analysis, I think Swami, in his marvellously apt and simple way, has summed it up in one immortal quotation:

"Education should be about how to live, not how to make a living."

# 9

# THE LIVING PRINCIPALS OF SATHYA SAI BABA

*"The rich must sacrifice their wants so that the poor may secure their needs."*

Sai Baba

As far as I am aware no *avatar* in man's recorded history has engaged himself so intensely in the welfare field as Sathya Sai Baba has in India. It is true that the Christ said, "It is harder for a rich man to enter the Kingdom of Heaven than for a camel (rope) to pass through the eye of a needle," and that for this reason, I suspect, he is sometimes claimed by falsely optimistic communists and others as the first of their revolutionary leaders. Others would argue back that he showed little interest in the secular field, confining himself to healing and preaching, and that his crucifixion was attributable to the high priests who saw him as a threat to their spiritual authority rather than to any Roman fear of him as an agitator. Indeed, one might go further and point out that his uncle, Joseph of Arimathea, to whom Jesus was very attached, was a wealthy man, the owner of farm estates and a fleet of cargo ships.

The Christian churches of today seldom pronounce upon any important issues touching upon our daily lives; indeed, some would say that they profess a one-day-a-week religion, largely unconcerned with secular matters.

Perhaps because India is today a land of such contrasting poverty and wealth, Sathya Sai Baba is as concerned with material and social uplift as he is with spirituality. His colleges are called the "Sathya Sai Colleges for Arts, Science and Commerce". They are not theological colleges. The aim is to spiritualise the whole secular field. As he says, there must be a fusion of the spiritual and material aspects of life. His aim is to give a spiritual blood transfusion to the whole secular scene.

On a whirlwind visit to India's capital city, Baba not only gives *darshan* to up to a quarter of a million devotees, healing comforting, satisfying the spiritual hunger of the masses, but he is bombarded with requests for interviews by government ministers, ambassadors, heads of colleges, representatives of the arts and sciences, heads of corporations. It is no uncommon occurrence for him to squeeze in a dozen or more interviews with these dignitaries in a single day.

At his *ashram* at Brindavan there is often a group of businessmen, financiers, engineering contractors, etc. who stand patiently by until the completion of *darshan* to obtain his sanction and blessing for a project such as building a new factory or the construction of a dam for a hydro-electric scheme. Often they have to wait for hours until the sick have been attended to and the needy comforted. But such are Baba's reputation and divine charisma that they do so willingly and with a good grace.

The principle which he applies to his contact with people is that of absolute equality of all men under God. All men are equal in the eyes of God: the brotherhood of man under the fatherhood of God. He promotes the understanding of this concept and encourages its practice in all fields of human endeavour. But change must come about voluntarily, through each individual's growth in spirituality, and the understanding of an expanding heart. Dr Gokak has described this process as "the revolution of all revolutions", because it is not based on any man-made ideology, but aims to transform society by transforming the heart of each individual.

Baba says, "No society can find fulfilment until the spirit of man blossoms. The *atma* in man has to be realised. The *atma* is the sustenance, the source of every being, and every organisation of beings. It is the one and only source. The *atma* is God, no less. Therefore recognise in every being a brother, a child of God, and banish all limiting thoughts and prejudices based on colour, status, class. The true function of society is to allow everyone to realise the *atmic* vision." So, in this life, the rich should sacrifice their wants so that the poor can secure their needs.

In relation to wealth he says, "The idea of a high standard of material living has played havoc with society. The desire can never be satisfied. It leads to a multiplication of wants and consequent troubles and frustrations. We need morality, humility, detachment, compassion, so that the greed for luxury and conspicuous consumption is destroyed."

Yet Swami is not against the advance of technology (he travels by car and by aeroplane), nor against the creation of wealth. But wealth, over and above one's reasonably frugal needs, should be held in trust, as it were, for promoting the brotherhood of man, and not regarded as one's own.

Nor can an equitable distribution of wealth be enforced by legislative decrees. "This can only be done by transforming the giver and the recipient. No political system can transform the receiver and thrill the giver, however much it tries to equalise. The appeal isn't there, nor the power to sustain. The equality established will be haunted by a shadow, the shadow of the ego. The change must evolve from the heart. All materialistic attempts to equalise society have failed. Only spiritual transformation can bring about the revolution in human consciousness, from which alone the desired changes can accrue."

Once Baba granted an interview to the Marxist editor of an Indian newspaper. He spent two and a half hours with him and persuaded him of his error. The Marxist questioned him about the methodology of his kind of 'revolution' and Baba replied that he had none in the accepted organisational sense. His method is the simple one of transforming the inner individual through love, and the machinery used is co-operation and brotherhood induced by this kind of love.

The editor then asked why he did not cure the ills of the world by his *sankalpa* to which Swami, as one would expect, replied that this kind of instant solution – without a prior spiritual transformation – would not work: the world would quickly revert to the present chaos. He also explained that the whole drama of creation with its *karmic* law (of cause and effect) would collapse.

Pressed by the editor about the difficulties in persuading the rich of such a life philosophy, Swami replied, "The rich can only come to me on the basis of absolute equality. This is why at the *ashram* rich and poor work together, eat, worship and sleep together, do menial tasks together, and share the common austerities of the *ashram*. There is absolutely no distinction. Yet, despite this, the wealthy come to me in order to secure that peace of mind which physical comfort and power cannot give. I convert their minds and hearts to spiritual values and truths."

The rich cannot secure Swami's grace without surrendering their materialistic outlook and self-serving attachments. He tells them, "Ego lives by getting and forgetting; love lives by giving and forgiving." He changes their mental attitudes. He emphasises the need to live a life without desires, a desirelessness based on high thinking and frugal living, rather than a high material standard. He shows them that riches provide a fatal temptation, which is the source and the cause of human bondage.

"Shed your luggage," he says, using one of his parables, "you will travel lighter." It is not material but spiritual satisfaction that ultimately makes life worth living. And he points to the poor who are often spiritually rich, and to the rich who are often spiritual paupers.

During his short stay at Puttaparthi, the Marxist editor discovered to his amazement that the woman who swept the courtyard was a maharani, his personal attendant was an ex-magistrate, and the patient interpreter during his interview was formerly India's leading scientist, Dr S. Bhagavantham!

In the same way, all the students of Sai Colleges are made to do manual work in addition to their studies. One day during my visit to Brindavan I watched a group of students digging trenches for the concrete footings of an extension to the visitors' lavatory. Under a few inches of sand was solid stone. To dig the necessary depth was a pick-axe and crowbar job. Yet, unused to manual labour as they were, I did not see one of them let up for a moment.

In addition to the very large scale of Swami's work in welfare and education, he expresses his spiritual principles in many small personal ways which endear him to his devotees. Often, when motoring, he tells his chauffeur to stop if he sees some destitute old fellow on the side of the road, gets out and gives him some money, or medicine, or *vibhuti*, or another instantly produced Sai gift. Once, when purchasing some farmland for building, he paid three times the asking price on the grounds that the farmer would have to learn a new trade to earn a livelihood. At the Dassehra Festival, which lasts for ten days, he is always happiest on the day dedicated to feeding the poor.

On other festival days, when he rides a flower-bedecked vehicle, he sometimes leans down, picks up a handful of flower petals and scatters them to the crowds lining his path, materialising them in the air into sweets. On one occasion, when his heart overflowed, he did this so that the petals became coins as they fell. Imagine flower petals drifting on the breeze and, with a wave of a masterful hand, descending on to the earth with the ring of glinting coins! It sounds like the telling of fabulous legends, but it was witnessed by no less a person than Professor Kasturi, and by untold numbers of others.

Baba hates waste, and often reprimands his devotees for embellishing their shrine rooms so ostentatiously. "It is a sheer waste of money," he says. "Be simple and sincere." Similarly to groups of his devotees who claim they need a prayer hall: "Why do you need a hall? Make your houses a shrine, impress others with your humility, speech, love, faith and truthfulness. You will gather more into the fold of believers in that way than in any hall."

In his heart of hearts he deprecates his own lavish birthday celebrations, but his devotees insist − it is their way of love. "Celebrate your own birthday," he tells them, "when you are born into the truth."

These then are the principles for living of Sai Baba − voluntary, gradual and individual means rather than compulsory, instant or collective. It must come from inside a man's deepest being so that he himself is in no doubt of its truth. There are no politics or policies in the world as persuasive as a person's own innermost experience of truth. That is why in the world of Sai, politics of every hue are of no importance whatsoever. The perspective is universal and timeless, and the idea of politics to improve the human condition becomes irrelevant. India is a nominally socialist country, but just as Sai Baba's devotees come from every country in the world, they also come to him from every political spectrum. Once they accept his guidance, their own perspective slowly but surely expands in response to the inner experience. Among Baba's devotees there are staunch communists, highly successful capitalists and innumerable socialists. Whether or not they admit it, it is obvious from their attitude that their mundane beliefs occupy a secondary, and increasingly irrelevant, place in their lives.

There is no methodology, no political philosophy. He says the only way to transform society is to transform the individual, through love, to a realisation of the *atma* in all mankind, and in all the kingdoms of nature. And by this method he has promised that a new Golden Age will recur. Let us, therefore, lift up our hearts and work with him to bring about this Golden Age, and thus gainsay the prophets of doom. We are indeed fortunate to be alive at this time. We ourselves will not see the fruits of his work, but our great-grandchildren will, and perhaps even our grandchildren.

The eventual aim, when through spiritual transformation we have learned to master our senses and to work selflessly and harder than under the spur of competition, must be a society built on love, co-operation rather than competition. He has made this very clear. There is nothing wrong in the communist slogan, "From each according to his capacity, unto each according to his need." The vital ingredient that is missing is God. With God at the core the individual remains more important than the State, and the whole communist concept of society collapses.

The day will come when the words of the Scots poet will find their true meaning:

"All gain is base, the victor's wreath, the poet's crown, if conquest in the giddy race means one poor struggler trampled down."

# 10

# THE TEACHINGS OF SATHYA SAI BABA

*"The quickest and most direct way to God is to fill the day with love."*

Sai Baba

## PART I

The three main tenets of the teachings of Sathya Sai Baba are first, the universality of all religions; secondly, that the *atma*, or divine spark, is indwelling in all human beings, which is the basis of the Brotherhood of Man, and the Fatherhood of God; and last, that God is Love, and that the quickest and most direct way to Him is through love in action, or selfless service.

He says: "Let the different Faiths exist, let them flourish and let the glory of God be sung in all the languages and in a variety of tunes. Respect the differences between the Faiths and recognise them as valid as long as they do not extinguish the flame of unity."

The historical fact, however, is that when one religion has planned to extend its influence it has tended to resort to villification of others and to an exaggeration of its own excellence, which has led to separatism and, in the last resort, to the sort of tragic conditions we have in Northern Ireland.

For this reason Baba has adopted as his emblem the symbols of the five major faiths — Hindu, Christian, Buddhist, Muslim and Zoroastrian, and at the base of the 'One' monument to these faiths, both in Puttaparthi and at Dharmakshetra in Bombay, are inscriptions relevant to each.

Under the Christian Cross are the words: "Cut the 'I' feeling clean across and let your ego die on the Cross to endow on you Eternity."

The Fire symbol of the Zoroastrians (called Parsis in India) is an invitation to cast into fire the lower instincts and impulses. The inscription reads: "Offer all bitterness in the Sacred Fire and emerge Grand, Great and Godly."

The Wheel of the Buddhist Faith is a reminder of the wheel of rebirth to which we are bound, and of the wheel of righteousness that can release us. The inscription reads: "Remember the wheel of cause and effect, of deed and destiny, and the wheel of *Dharma* that rights them all."

For the Star and Crescent of Islam the words read: "Be like the Star that never wavers from the Crescent, but is fixed in steady faith."

And for the *AUM* symbol of the Hindus the inscription is: "Listen to the Primaeval *Pranava* (sound) resounding in your heart, as well as in the heart of the Universe."

These inscriptions are not differences, but degrees of emphasis on the pathway to God. For this reason Swami never asks us to give up our religion; indeed, he encourages us to adhere to our particular faith. He even says that if we dedicate ourselves with steady devotion in an effort to rediscover the pristine form and inner meaning of our religion we shall draw closer to him, for the Sai religion is the essence of all religions and all faiths. "There is only one religion, the Religion of Love; there is only one caste, the caste of humanity; there is only one language, the language of the heart."

Love is the key word. "Blessed are the pure in heart, for they shall see God," said the Christ. "The pure heart becomes inspired, it sees beyond intellect and reason," says Sai Baba. I believe the heart *chakra* is all-important as a centre of cognition, and bears the same relationship to the mind as the sun does to the planets of our solar system. It illumines and brings light.

I have noticed in my life that simple but pure hearted people, like old gardeners, often have a degree of wisdom far in excess of their intellects and learning. At the other end of the scale I have also noticed that some of the world's cleverest men, like Albert Einstein, Carl Jung, Robert Oppenheimer and Bertrand

Russell, after long and circuitous journeyings in intellectuality and philosophising, have reached the same conclusions, for surely truth is both simple and profound. Unless we become as little children we cannot enter into the kingdom of heaven. In their old age these men achieved a degree of humility and simplicity which were entirely absent in their earlier years when they were imbued with the arrogance of youthful intellectuality. In old age their egos had gone and their hearts had expanded.

Sai Baba says, "The motive behind the formation and propagation of all the different faiths was the same. The founders were all persons filled with love and wisdom. Their goal was the same. None had the design to divide, disturb or destroy. They sought to train the passions and the emotions, to educate the impulses and direct the faculty of reason to paths beneficial to the individual and society." It is dogma and theology which have confounded this fundamental truth and brought about separatism and schism.

As an example of this camouflaged unity, Dr Fanibunda, a Parsi scholar and a devout devotee of Sai Baba, points out with great erudition in his book, *Vision of the Divine*, the inner meaning of the original teachings of Zoroaster and shows them to be virtually identical to those of Sai Baba.

And in my own small way, after two years of study in which I became increasingly aware of the similarity of the teachings, miracles and personalities of Sai Baba and Jesus of Nazareth, I attempted to do the same thing in an article which was published in the *Golden Age*, 1980 volume, and which I have included in Chapter 3.

If the reader will forgive a minor digression ... I took that article with me to India in January 1980 and showed it to Swami. As he began to read it I noticed his eyes turn from the centre of the first page to my pen name at the top of the page. A faraway look came over his eyes and he whispered in a sort of pensive undertone, as if he was recollecting, "Laing? ... Ron Laing?"

I pondered about this for several days, and then suddenly a flash of enlightenment came to me. It so happens that my great-grandfather, Samuel Laing, was a politician. In 1860 he was appointed Finance Minister for India and was resident in India for a five-year tenure of office in the difficult aftermath of the Mutiny. He was also a noted writer of books on world religions, with a strong bias against dogma. In 1887 he published *A Modern Zoroastrian* with the same theme as Dr Fanibunda, except that he expounded the similarity of original Christianity to the teachings of Zoroaster.

Could it be, I asked myself, that Swami was recalling his former life as Sai Baba of Shirdi in which form he had possibly met my great-grandfather, or alternatively had read his book, *A Modern*

*Zoroastrian?* Time, location, interest and width of vision would have made it possible. In 1860–65, Sai Baba of Shirdi would have been in his late twenties and, in 1887, at the time of publication of the book, approaching fifty.

To return to my theme, it is also a fact that Sai Baba claims to be a *purna avatar* (fully divine incarnation) with the sixteen *kalas* (attributes) of divinity inherent in his being. There is, therefore, no aspect of any religion in its original form which is not contained in the Sai world religion of Love.

The second tenet of his teaching that the *atma*, the divine spark, is inherent in all human beings is paramount. Baba emphasises it again and again. "Converse with God who is in you," he says. "Derive courage and inspiration from Him. He is the *Guru* most interested in your progress. Each will come in his own good time, at his own pace, through his own inner urge, along the path God will reveal to him as his own."

Yet so many people chase from one *guru* to another, from one movement to another, read one learned tome after another, and rush from one lecture to another, almost as if they are driven by some demon to be "in on everything". But knowledge has no value in itself. There must be a balance between knowing and doing and being.

In the end, such people become so confused that I suspect they are virtually agnostic. I am reminded of Omar Khayyam's verse:

> "I sent my soul through the Invisible,
> The sector of that after-life to spell;
> And by and by my soul returned to me
> And answered: 'I myself am Heaven and Hell'."

Search into your heart and listen to the inner voice. Be still, and know that God dwells within you.

I suspect that the majority of the followers of any orthodox religion tend to think of God rather vaguely in an anthropomorphic sense, that is, as some Super Being who dwells in some undiscovered part of the Universe and is in reality beyond our comprehension. Possibly this is the reason why there is such a gap between the theory and practice of religion, indeed a double standard: if God only smiles on us from a distance when we are in a place of worship there is less urge to lead our daily lives, as opposed to our worshipful lives, according to His precepts. But if we are conscious that the divine spark resides inside us, in our hearts, waking and sleeping, from cradle to grave, then that is another matter.

In truth, there is no thing (nothing) but God. All form, animate and inanimate, is His spirit in manifestation, and therefore inter-related. Hence the need for reverence towards all life, including the vegetable and mineral kingdoms.

Swami teaches that we have evolved from mineral to plant, from plant to animal, and from animal to human, in which state we now have self-consciousness and free will. But we are still half animal, half divine, with a higher and a lower self.

He says that the sole purpose of our incarnation on earth is to crucify our lower ego on the altar of compassion in order to realise our higher self. This, too, is the symbolic meaning of the Christian Cross. If we succeed we become, in Christian terminology, a Christed One or, in Swami's words, "the *atma* (the individual Self) merges with the *Paramatma* (the Supreme Self), or the drop of water with the ocean."

At present the divinity within most of us is like a flickering candle. The more we succeed in ridding ourselves of our lower ego, the more scope there is for the candle to burst into flame.

We are, therefore, potentially as gods. Once, when asked by a devotee if he was God, Swami replied, "You are God, the only difference between us is that I know I am and you do not."

How do we best grow to realise our higher self and attain liberation from the cycle of rebirth? Sai Baba's teaching rests on four pillars – *Sathya* (truth), *Dharma* (right living), *Shanti* (inner peace) and *Prema* (love). All are inter-related, and the golden thread of love runs through all.

*Sathya* – truth. The most important aspect of *Sathya* is self-truth, that is, self-awareness and self-honesty. Yet how many of us are self-aware and self-honest? There is so much more pride and ego in most of us than we care to admit, or are even able to see. And, I am afraid, this sometimes applies to mediums, leaders of various religious or sectarian groups, the allegedly exalted.

In middle age I was poignantly aware of this in myself; I had had an up and down life and made many mistakes. I decided to write a spiritual and psychological autobiography for therapeutic reasons. I have mentioned this in Chapter 1 and I make no apology for referring to it again.

It went to half a million words, and it may be that in my zeal I overdid it. There were times when I wrote ten thousand words a day, and there were other days when I took an hour to write a single sentence as I delved into myself. It was really a protracted and intensive period of meditation, in writing rather than thought, for Baba says that three parts of meditation should be self-enquiry. My aim was to re-indoctrinate myself from childhood conditioning, religious and sociological, in an attempt to become as nearly as possible a God given identity, and to see more clearly the beams in my own eye and the true motivation for my past actions.

It was certainly a therapeutic exercise. At the end I felt liberated, free to believe what I believed rather than what I believed I believed, and there is a difference. But the interesting thing was that when I was half-way through I wanted to start again, for I realised that what I had written at the commencement was not true. It was like a continuing process of unwinding bandages from my eyes.

This, then, is what *Sathya* means to me – self-awareness and self-honesty. Baba says we are three people – the one we think we are, the one others think we are, and the one we really are . . . Until we discover the one we really are I do not think we make much true spiritual progress, for the soul is uniquely individual and we have to have the courage to be true to ourselves, however humble and menial our paths may be. Pride, ego and self-deception, and particularly the degree to which we are unaware of these traits of the lower self, are the stumbling blocks.

*Dharma* – right living and right thinking, positive thinking so that the law of cause and effect works for our own good; God-consciousness, seeing divinity in all things, even in evil men, for it is impossible to extinguish the divine spark. Swami says it is possible to be wholly good, but it is not possible to be wholly bad – even Hitler wept when his canary died.

Right eating (total vegetarianism) for, as Swami says, the animals were not created to be killed and eaten by man, but to follow their own evolution.

A right attitude to work, for "work is worship", all work, including cleaning the streets and washing up. Do these mundane things for God. "The secret of happiness does not lie in doing what one likes but in learning to like what one has to do."

*Shanti* – inner peace through detachment and desirelessness, except of course the desire to serve God. This does not mean renunciation of the world, but to live in the world and not be of it.

Baba has no objection to young people finding their niche in life and stretching themselves, nor in the creation of wealth, provided what is surplus to one's needs is held in trust, as it were, for God and not used for the pursuit of indulgence and material pleasure.

By middle age we must tread the path of the soul in order to prepare the spirit for its release. One must increasingly lose a sense of identification with the physical body and the physical senses. "Let the eye see God's footprints in stars and rose petals, let the ear hear God's voice in the throats of birds and peals of thunder, let the sense of touch be content to clasp the hand of the forlorn and the distressed."

211

*Shanti* means the mastery of the sensuous physical senses. It also means that one becomes oblivious to praise or calumny and, in its sublime form, to pleasure and pain. One is prepared to be done or to be undone for God. *Shanti* means surrender.

Finally *Prema.* This is the cornerstone of all Baba's teaching. "I am the embodiment of love," he says. "Love is my instrument. My message is *prema*, my activity is *prema*, my teaching is *prema*, my way of life is *prema*. There is nothing more precious than love within human grasp."

"Start the day with love, fill the day with love, end the day with love — this is the quickest and most direct way to God. Other paths develop conceit, separate man from man and man from beast. They contract, they do not reach out; they shrink your awareness of the Divine."

This is not to say that Baba decries other paths such as meditation and *yoga* or renunciation of the world, for some, but it takes very much second place in his teaching. His advice is always personal and individual. On rare occasions he will advise a hermit type of person to retire into the forest or mountains and spend his life in meditation. One elderly man was so advised on the grounds that he would spread more light in this way than he would by living in the community. But in the vast majority of cases, particularly of Westerners, he advises us to carry on with our work, but with a changed attitude.

To me the way of meditation is like circumventing a mountain by going round it — it is a long, circuitous journey. The Way of Love is like blasting a tunnel through the centre and arriving at the other side in half the time.

By love, of course, he means love in action, or service. "Only in loving can the embodiment of love be gained" — we have to love in order to become love. It is so simple, really. God is Love, so we can only merge with Him through loving service. He once said that two days of loving service will do us more good than two months of meditation.

He tells us to serve because we shall know no peace until we serve. "It is an inner urge to experience a sense of kinship with all mankind, with all life." But we must serve without a sense of duty. "Duty without love is deplorable; duty with love is good; love without duty is divine." Swami's discourses are, in essence, one continuous exhortation to love and to serve.

And also, alas, a continuous pointing to the stumbling blocks we are prey to — ego and pride, gossip, friction, and jealousy in groups, power seeking and a desire for one-upmanship, too much talking and not enough listening, too much shrine worship and not enough love in action.

One sometimes wonders if he does not have more trouble with his devotees than with those who bear no label but who lend a helping hand wherever they can. But it was ever so with all the Founders. Did not Christ's disciples argue among themselves as to who would sit by his right side in the Kingdom of Heaven?

Finally, for the forlorn, the depressed and the lonely, he has this to say: "Come just one step forward, I shall take a hundred towards you. Shed just one tear, I shall wipe a hundred from your eyes. Bring me the depths of your minds, no matter how grotesque, no matter how ravaged by doubts and disappointments. I will not reject you. I am your Mother."

To those who may one day be blessed with an interview with Baba I would say this: if you are psychic you may well be overwhelmed by the vibrations of love and energy which emanate from this God-man. If you are not psychic, like myself, you may well do as I did, which was to fall at his feet, to break and weep, to put my arm round him and have him put his arm round me. You will know then that he is indeed your mother, and your father, and your best friend — in fact, the only true friend you will ever have, for human friendship is breachable, but the friendship of Sai Baba is not. And you will have, too, the incomparable blessing and comfort that there is one person in this world who knows you to the very depths of your soul and, despite your faults and failings, still loves you. If your loyalty is unwavering his grace will be ever yours.

## PART II

### *The Avatar who exudes total devotion to all mankind*

Sathya Sai Baba came into incarnation with limitless knowledge. He does not read books or meditate, and he has never had a spiritual *guru*. He was inattentive at school. Yet, apart from the countless miracles he has performed, of materialisations galore of everything from a diamond to a deerskin, and of healings of virtually every disease known to man, he is also Wisdom Incarnate — poet, pundit, linguist, educationist, artist, mystic.

He quotes from the Bible, the *Koran*, Socrates, Johnson, Herbert Spencer, Kant and Karl Marx, among others. He quotes from all Hindu scriptures and throws new light on ancient utterances. On one occasion, he spoke for fifteen consecutive evenings to five thousand students and scholars at Brindavan on the *Vedas*, with special reference to the cluster of irrelevancies and misconceptions which have arisen through the centuries. Would that he would do the same with the Christian Bible . . .

213

Several years ago, Professor Kasturi, editor of *Sanathana Sarathi*, the monthly *ashram* magazine, published a series of articles by Baba on the ten volumes of the *Upanishads*. When the tenth article was due on the last and most weighty *Upanishad*, the old man went to collect it, only to find that Swami had not done his homework.

The article was due to go to press that day, so Baba sat down then and there and wrote out his contribution, seemingly without effort or thought, and handed it to the astonished professor. It was ten pages, and there was not a single correction or erasure. The time taken was precisely the time it took Baba's pen to move across the pages. Now, Kasturi is certain that Baba has never read the *Upanishads*.

Much the same thing happened to Dr Sandweiss when he took the manuscript of *Sai Baba, the Holy Man and the Psychiatrist* to Swami for his blessing. After chiding Sandweiss for a few passages, and in particular for his references to India's abject poverty (explaining to him that the beloved land of Bharat was as wealthy as the West until it was plundered by the people of the West), Baba gave the book his blessing, and then, with a twinkle in his eye, said that he hadn't even read it!

Whether this God-man has some divine faculty incomprehensible to human consciousness, or whether he has instant access to the *akashic* records or the halls of learning in the world of spirit, I don't know. I only know that when I first watched him at *darshan*, I had the strange feeling that I was watching a man with a thousand minds who worked in a thousand different ways. It is as if he sees the whole contents of a book and the essence of its truth in a flash, as if he is watching a re-run of one's past and a vision of one's future on a television screen.

There is a mountain of evidence of this extraordinary omniscience. His mind is outside time and space. He has said, again and again, that nobody with human consciousness can understand him, and that it is useless to try; one can only experience him. "Everyone has to approach Me and experience Me. It is not enough to be shown a stone and to be told a mountain is a million times bigger than a stone. You have to see the whole mountain."

He has said that if all the scientists in the world got together, with whatever equipment, they could not analyse him. "Science measures the outer form of objects, only *Vedanta* goes to the very core of the being of things which is God." He has smiled sometimes when *Vedic* scholars have approached him as a mere pundit without realising that the very source from which the *Vedas* sprang is living here among them.

Another of Sai Baba's marvellous gifts is his extraordinary facility to transform profundity into simplicity. It is my belief

214

that truth is both simple and profound, as indeed some of the world's cleverest men like Einstein and Jung discovered towards the end of their lives. Baba has a genius for lucid exposition of even the most abstruse theological conundrums. Many of India's pundits have come away from an interview with instant enlightenment and clarification of problems which had perplexed them all their lives.

It was the same with his personal letters which he used to write to his devotees until the numbers grew into millions and he was compelled to adopt other methods of communication, such as giving them symbolic dreams, manipulating the circumstances of their lives by the use of his *sankalpa* (will power), or by etheric or physical visitation. His style is simple, yet magical and poetic, and he writes from the core of his heart in such an intensely personal and touching way. His written words seem to act as a catalyst to uplift the recipient to a state of 'inner vision' or semi-transcendental consciousness in which enlightenment comes in a way which erudite prose could never achieve. It is as if he speaks and writes in the language of the gods.

Much of his teaching is given in simple parable, or pithy, cogent, and even homespun, aphorism. For example, if a person is too attached to material possessions he will say: "Shed your luggage, you will travel lighter," or, "Properties are not proper ties." Or, if he is asked why divinity comes in human form rather than trailing clouds of glory, he will say, "If you want to save someone from drowning you have to jump into the water. If I had come with four arms you would have put me in a museum."

It seems to me, therefore, to be a worthwhile aim to try to present those parts of his teaching most relevant to ordinary people living ordinary lives in a way in which the simplest souls can understand – that is, by quotations of a similar type to the above.

The cornerstone of Baba's teaching is LOVE. It is the key word in everything that he says and does. To be with Swami in interview is to love him instantly. It is a totally unforgettable experience. Here is a being in human form, the like of which one has never seen before, without a vestige of pride or ego, or *karmic* accretion, who exudes total devotion to all mankind, to all life. He is indeed 'love walking on two feet'.

His love is intensely personal, and yet at the same time universal. He has no favourites: the sinner comes within his fold as much as the saint. To a sensitive soul who is 'ready', to meet him is a transformation; one's life becomes divided into two halves: Before Baba and After Baba. Thereafter he completely fills one's life.

"I am the embodiment of love," he proclaims simply, without modesty or pride. "Love is my instrument." Indeed it is. He has said that if he is to be remembered by any one facet of his divinity he would like it to be *Prema* (love). "My message is *prema*, my activity is *prema*, my teaching is *prema*, my way of life is *prema*; there is nothing more precious within human grasp than love."

"There are those who preach short cuts to liberation. But Love alone can give liberation. The grace of God cannot be won through the gymnastics of reason, the contortions of *yoga*, or the denials of asceticism. Love alone can win it; love that needs no requital, love that knows no bargaining, love that is paid gladly, as tribute to the All-loving, love that is unwavering."

"Love alone can overcome obstacles, however many and mighty. There is no strength more effective, no bliss more satisfying, no joy more restoring." And why? Because God is Love – it is as simple as that.

"My life is my message," says Baba. And what is his life? Loving service to mankind twenty-four hours a day, seven days a week, on a scale the magnitude of which in terms of performing miracles, healing the sick, transforming souls, educating youth, and in the field of welfare and humanitarian work, has never been equalled by any *Avatar* of God in man's recorded history. He is said not to sleep, and he has affirmed this. Asked once if he needed rest, he replied, "If I needed rest I would not have incarnated!"

Listen to Dr Diwaker, Indian scholar and statesman, speaking at Sai Baba's fiftieth birthday: "Once Swami was a village urchin, untutored, unloved, uncared for. Now on his fiftieth birthday we assemble from the four quarters of the globe, and what do we find? Politicians and philosophers, educators and legislators, scientists and technologists, the learned as well as the ignorant, the rich as well as the poor, and from all nations and all religions. If this is not a marvel and a living miracle I would like to know what is."

In forty years, from village urchin to the most potent influence, in both the secular as well as the spiritual fields, in the whole of the Indian subcontinent. And all by the power of love . . .

I would hazard a guess that in two or three decades he will be the most potent influence in the entire world. For that is his avowed aim. He has said: "I have come to repair the ancient highway to God . . . I have not come on behalf of any sect or creed or religion. I have come to light the Lamp of Love in the hearts of all humanity."

And regarding a possible nuclear holocaust: "The calamity which has come upon mankind will be averted. A new Golden Age will recur. I shall not fail: it is not in the nature of *Avatars* to fail." There will not be a nuclear holocaust. The One we all yearn for has come.

What of those who are not so deeply impacted by Baba, and then wonder why? Swami explains it thus: "Old souls need a gentle

216

touch with a hammer, young souls need twenty blows with a sledge-hammer!"

Yet old souls are sometimes ordinary, humble people; one does not have to be erudite or have a string of letters after one's name. It is the heart that counts. He often upbraids those who talk about the rich and the poor, when he senses they mean it in a material sense. The rich are often poor in spirit, and the poor rich.

Who, the reader might ask, is this God-man, Sai Baba? Well, it is a matter of faith, and it is up to each to judge and make up his own mind. But I would suggest that there is no man on earth who is doing as much for humanity on such a large scale, and that on this score alone he is worthy of attention.

"By their fruits ye shall know them." And Sai Baba's fruits are truly prodigious.

His seemingly limitless powers are certainly not through *yogic* development. He came into incarnation with his divine will (*daivic sankalpa*) intact. He was performing miracles as a child. One can only say that what he wills just happens. As Dr Bhagavantham says, "He transcends the laws of physics and chemistry. I have therefore to declare this man a transcendental being, divine." And this from India's leading nuclear physicist.

Swami has himself made many announcements about his nature from time to time. I will quote just two of them. "When I am with a man I am a man, when I am with a woman I am a woman, when I am with a child I am a child, and when I am alone I am God."

And again, in his typical homespun way, "When there is a small local disturbance a police constable is enough to put it down. When the trouble is threatening to develop into sizeable proportions a police inspector is sent; when it grows into a riot, the Superintendant of Police himself has to quell it; but when, as now, all mankind is threatened with moral ruin the Inspector General comes down, that is the Lord."

A triple incarnation, spanning two hundred and fifty years or more (first as Sai Baba of Shirdi, now deceased, currently as Sathya Sai Baba, with Prema Sai to come in the 21st century) was forecast in the *Upanishads* over five thousand years ago. It was prophesied that there would be a Machine Age from which would emerge a material way of living and the technological means to destroy the planet, and that this triple incarnation would slowly unfold its influence and save the world from destruction by restoring righteousness among men. It is up to the reader to judge. The life of Prema Sai will not end until the 22nd century, so there is another hundred and twenty years or more for Swami to achieve his goal.

Despite his fifty million devotees, with centres in sixty countries of the Western world alone, he says, "My work has hardly begun."

217

Mercifully Swami's teaching is an open book; there is no abracadabra about it, no initiatory rite for the esotericist only. It is for all humanity, the rich as well as the poor, the learned as well as the ignorant. The only real *sine qua non* is the pure heart.

Sai Baba teaches evolution and the *atmic* reality of man. As he says, we have arrived from 'animalness' to 'human-ness', and the next stage is divinity. Through the indwelling God or *atma* in us, the divine spark, we are potentially as gods. We have to rid ourselves of the 'I' in order to realise our higher natures. "The sole purpose of your incarnation is to crucify the ego on the altar of compassion," he says.

"The purpose of life is to grow in love, expand that love and to merge with God who is Love, and this is best done through service." "There is no discipline like service for the eradication of the ego."

"Man's reality is the *atma*. Everything else is trivial, things one shares with the birds and beasts. This is the unique privilege of man. He has climbed through all the stages of evolution on earth to inherit this high destiny. If his life on earth is frittered away in seeking food and shelter, comfort and pleasure, as animals, man is condemning himself to a further life sentence (another incarnation)!" In point of fact, in our basic nature, most of us abhor a dreary life of eating, sleeping and drinking. In the core of our being we seek liberation from the trivial and the temporary.

"The *atma* is the sustenance, the source of every being, and every organisation of beings. It is the only source. The *atma* is God, no less. Therefore recognise in each being a brother, a child of God, and banish all limiting thoughts and prejudices based on colour, status, class."

In everyday language this means that the same 'bit of God' exists in you as it does in me, which makes all men and women brothers and sisters. It is also true that we are all cells in one vast organism which we call mankind. Consequently, injury to another is injury to oneself. It is a salutary thought.

Sai Baba does not encourage us to give up our particular religion, for all religions have the same goal, and in their pristine form preach the same thing. "Welcome all religions as kith and kin," he says. "The *Vedas* are the grandfather, Buddhism is the son, Christianity is the grandson, and Islam is the great-grandson. If there is any misunderstanding between them it is just a family affair. The ancestral property, of which all are co-sharers, is the same."

All rivers flow into the same ocean, and cows although differing in colour give the same milk. As a matter of fact, if one rediscovers the pristine form of one's religion one will come closer to Baba. "Follow your own God," he says. "You will find you are coming closer to Me, for all Names and all Forms are Mine."

My own favourite quotation on the universality of all religions is this: "There is only one religion, the Religion of Love; there is only one caste, the Caste of Humanity; there is only one language, the Language of the Heart."

I suppose one of the first questions an aspirant, new to the spiritual path, will ask is: How to find God and truth? He is liable to seek out a *guru*. Swami says, "There is no need to go anywhere in search of truth; it is there inside you as the divine spark, but it has to become a flame."

Similarly with books. A friend once said to me, "You don't learn anything from books. You only recognise what you already know." There is an element of truth in this.

Baba says that if we seek worldly *gurus* we will run from one to another. "God is your best *guru*, and He resides in your heart." "Do not seek *gurus* in hermitages and so called holy places. There are many false *gurus* today who preach desirelessness, and yet are riddled with personal desires themselves. They care more for publicity than practice."

Dr Frank Baranowski, the expert on Kirlian photography, discovered this during a research tour of India's holy men, until he came to Puttaparthi and saw Swami's aura which he described as "not that of a human being". Sadly, I have found this to be true in my own experience. Many *gurus* and leaders of pseudo-religious groups are full of ego and spiritual pride, and are often mercenary.

Ironically, Baba says, "Man extols God as omniscient, omnipresent and omnipotent, yet ignores His presence in himself!" "God is in the heart of every human being . . . "

"There is a road for each heart to God. Each will come in his own good time, through his own inner urge, along the path that God will reveal to him as his own." No need to rush it, to become compulsive. Spiritual growth is slow. It should be like an oak tree rather than a Japanese larch. As Swami says, "Start early, drive slowly, arrive safely."

He also exhorts specialisation: "Instead of digging four feet in ten places, dig forty feet in one. Concentrate on one chosen path." In other words, become a specialist rather than a Jack of all trades (albeit with an open mind).

Yet how many people do we know, carping critics and letter-writers, who pride themselves on their all round knowledge and erudition in irrelevant detail, and yet never seem to come off the fence and commit themselves to anything. They are like paddlers in the shallows who lack the courage to dive deep into the ocean where the pearls are. They are more interested in some event that may or may not have happened two thousand years ago than in the fact that we now have a *purna avatar* incarnate who is trying to save the world from a nuclear holocaust!

As for Absolute Truth, can we really hope to find this with our human consciousness? Those who do are, I fear, driven by anxiety; they want truth wrapped up in a neat parcel. All we can do is to love and to serve, and to gradually unfold towards the Light. We must learn to float through life, in faith and trust, always remembering that God dwells in our heart and is our best *guru*. "Our own experience is the best guarantee of truth for us," says Swami.

Nor should we be afraid of change. Change is a quality of life itself. Everything is in a process of growth or decline. Yet most of us resist change. We grow roots and build material security around ourselves, like a fence. There is nothing wrong in building a home and loving it, but if we become too 'attached', we find it difficult to face upheaval and re-orientation. We must have the courage to change, to follow God's destiny wherever it leads. This is the way of growth. As Swami says, "Life is a bridge over the sea of change; pass over it, but do not build a house on it."


## PART III

*"Hands that help are holier than lips that pray."*
Sai Baba


Sai Baba not infrequently pours scorn on formal worship and formal methods, including meditation and *yoga*, by which spiritual aspirants endeavour to improve themselves, unless these methods are accompanied by true devotion. No amount of hymn singing, vows, fasts, offerings of flowers, prayers, will do a scrap of good unless motivated by sincere love. Self-development for the sake of self is self-cancelling.

"It is not he who says 'Lord, Lord!' but the one who does the will of my Father in Heaven," said the Christ. Swami amply confirms this: "Mere formal worship or mumbling of hymns or mechanical routine performances of ritual cannot induce God to reside in your heart," he says. "Liberation lies not in mystic formulas or rosaries, but in stepping out into action."

One cannot help thinking of the number of Hail Mary's purporting to ascend to the heavens each day throughout the world, but which in fact ascend nowhere. He often, too, upbraids the priests for their pomp and pedantry — "dry as dust scholars" as he calls them.

On religion generally he says: "Devotion is not a uniform to wear on worship days and then to be discarded." It should mean the promotion of an attitude that is ever present. Once, when I suspect he was a little weary of what I term churchiness, he said, "The good-hearted fellow who professes no religion at all is the truly religious man."

And again: "It is good to be born in a religion, but it is not good to die in one. Grow, and rescue yourselves from the limits and regulations and doctrines that fence in your freedom of thought, the ceremonies and rites that restrict and direct. Reach the point where churches do not matter, where all roads end from where all roads begin."

This, of course, is to say that children need some spiritual background, but by adhering strictly throughout life to some narrow sect or creed, with its confining beliefs and dogmas, one is preventing the consciousness from expanding.

Alas! Few have the courage not to belong: we feel the tribal need. Yet we should have the faith to regard ourselves as children of the One God who is Love, and to believe what we truly believe instead of permitting 'experts' to do our thinking for us, for experts are notoriously wrong; they cannot see the wood for the trees. And never was this more true than with theologians. In this way, even if we are wrong, we are at least adhering to one of the fundamental tenets of life: unto thyself be true.

On the various forms of *yoga*, Sai Baba has this to say: "They may calm the mind's agitation temporarily, or may improve the health and prolong life for a few more years, but that is all. What do you hope to achieve with that body in those extra years?" Most people, including the medical profession, seem to feel that the object of life is simply to live as long as possible.

I do not say that Swami decries *yoga* and meditation in all circumstances. He has actually written a book on the subject of meditation called *Dhyana Vahini*, but it takes very much second place in his order of priorities. It is an aid, not an end. The first priority is always service, or love in action. I can assure the reader of this — it is overwhelmingly apparent in his teachings, and he confirmed the point to me in private interview.

"No one can train another in meditation," he says (and think of the meditation classes that exist in the world!). It is possible to teach pose, posture and breathing. But meditation is a function of the inner man; it involves deep subjective quiet, the emptying of the mind and filling oneself with the Light that emerges from the divine spark within. No text book or teacher can teach this. "Purify your emotions, clarify your impulses, cultivate love. Then only will you become master of yourself." And if this is best done by lying in the bath and reflecting, then so be it. One might say that the Second World War was won in this way, for it was Winston

Churchill's habitual practice.

I admit that I am a little prejudiced about meditation, probably because I have never been able to make much progress along this path. Baba says that it should increase one's self-awareness and one's self-honesty. I find I do this best by writing a self-examination diary.

He also says that the end product of meditation should be an all day long communion. (Am I being God-conscious, seeing God in everything, for there is no thing but God; all life is God in differing forms . . . ? Am I thinking negative or positive thought? Am I gossiping? Am I talking too much and listening too little? Am I ego-motivated or God-motivated in what I am doing?)

In his marvellously simple way he reminds us that most of us carry a watch. It is spelt W-A-T-C-H. W is for watch your WORDS, A is for watch your ACTIONS, T is for watch your THOUGHTS, C is for watch your CONDUCT, and H is for watch your HEART!

I hope the above observations will be of some comfort to those who find meditation difficult and physical *yoga* impractical. Or even to those like myself who feel a little guilty when they see some bearded aspirant sitting for hours on end in the lotus position, looking very holy, as if one has not achieved the necessary high spiritual status to emulate such conduct.

Swami has averred, again and again, that there is no better discipline than service for the eradication of the ego, and that this aim is the sole purpose of our sojourn on earth. Nothing could be simpler or more categorical than that.

So, take heart, those of you who spend much of your time in the kitchen, or changing nappies, or cleaning the streets, for 'Work is worship' — all work, even the menial chores. If you do these things for God I promise you it will make a difference. And who shall say that one form of service is higher than another in God's overall plan? Remember, it is better to be a good plumber than a bad prime minister.

Many people find it difficult to balance material and spiritual living, to live in the world and yet not be of it. Difficult decisions sometimes have to be made. Swami has no objection to youth stretching itself and finding its potential. "In the early years a desire for worldly achievement might be good; it is only in the later years that it is bad." "Love the things of the world, that is their due, and no more," he says. "Grasp God with the right hand and the world with the left. Gradually the left will lose its grip." (Which, Baba says, is perhaps why it is called left, because it is left behind!)

He is no dour puritan. He is intensely human, and has an unfailing sense of humour. He prefers the word 'error' to 'sin'. "Do not call yourselves the inheritors of sin, you are the children of immortality." Neither is he a spoilsport – he once said to the students at his Anantapur College for Women, "Be centres of love, compassion, service, mutual tolerance, and be happy, very very happy."

Yet on the enigma of pain and suffering he has some seemingly harsh things to say. I say 'seemingly' because we have to face the fact that life in our present stage of evolution is a school, often a hard school, where growth and the paring away of the ego mostly come from making mistakes and from suffering, and also that much suffering is of *karmic* origin.

Swami says that God has ordained sorrow, for without it man will not cling to God. On pain, he says, "Give up; be willing to be a permanent invalid or to recover, as God wills, but suspend all conclusions. Open your heart to pain, for it is God's will, wrought for your own good. It is His plan to dissolve the ego. Welcome it as a challenge. Turn inward and derive the strength to bear it and benefit by it."

I can honestly say that it has been so in my case. At one period I suffered from deep depression for two years. I knew a loneliness that amounted to desolation. I felt I was living in a world where God and human warmth did not exist – a sort of Orwellian existence. My will deserted me – it was a victory to get out of bed in the mornings. During this time I was twice hospitalised, and on both occasions nearly died. I experienced physical agony. The second time I nearly burned to death in a car accident. My face was terribly disfigured. I was blind and lost my voice for a time.

But I recovered, mentally and physically, and with hindsight I am grateful for the suffering. My spirit was strengthened, my faith consolidated, my compassion heightened, and I developed embryonic psychic qualities.

On suffering generally Swami says: "Why worry when God, in order to make a lovely jewel out of you, heats and melts, cuts and carves, and resolves your dross in the crucible of suffering?"

To his devotees: "I stir, I knead, I pound, I bake, I drown you in tears. I have come to reform you, to transmute you."

On the Law of *Karma*: "You may be seeing Me today for the first time, but you are all old acquaintances for Me; I know you all through and through. I know why you suffer, how long you have to suffer, and when your suffering will end." There have been many times at *darshan* when he has had to pass by a pair of supplicating hands, but always with a pause, a deep look of compassion, consoling words, and a gentle pat on the shoulder.

Sometimes his compassion has literally overflowed so that he has set aside a devotee's negative *karma* by taking it upon himself, as a stroke, or a heart attack, suffering the requisite amount of time, and then curing himself. In the last analysis he says: "The greatest joy springs from the greatest sacrifice."

As the poem goes: "A picket frozen on duty, a mother starved for her brood, Socrates drinking the hemlock, and Jesus on the rood. And millions who, humble and nameless, the straight hard pathway trod; some call it Consecration, and others call it God."

Twice in my own small way I have been willing to follow this path. On the second occasion I reached a pitch of devotion for another human being which I believe was as near as I shall get whilst incarnate to a pure love of God. Both times I made the utmost sacrifices which were regarded by my friends as improvident, quixotic, and even mad. Indeed they were, but the deepest impulses of the heart and the most courageous actions are often considered mad by the world's standards.

Both times I lost out in what the world would call total personal disaster. But I survived and rebuilt my life, and in the aftermath I realised the truth of this great saying of Sai Baba's, that "the greatest joy springs from the greatest sacrifice." It is in giving that we receive, or, as the poet put it, "I have that which I have given."

And so I look back on these two episodes with gratitude, for the purgation of ego and for the growth of compassion. I believe, when my earthly span is over, I shall see two little five-pointed stars of aspiration illuminating the darker patches on the canvas of my *akashic* record.

There must be thousands who have made the ultimate sacrifice in battle and, despite the pain, felt a greater sense of joy than mine. I am sure that Rupert Brooke was one such.

With ordinary people death should, of course, be welcomed, when one's span is over; it is an integral part of life, an adventure like birth. Yet, as Swami says, "Man walks about as if death is some distant calamity." More often than not it is a relief for the tired, a refuge for the persecuted, a milestone for the pilgrim, and paradise for the faithful. It can too, of course, be a lesson for the wayward. But it should not be feared; it is a gift, a birthright.

Sai Baba is full of compassion for the underdog, and for those who despair. "I am happiest when someone with a heavy load of misery comes to me, for he is most in need of what I have to give." "I only ask that you turn to me when your mind drags you down with grief and despair." He points out to them that if their prayers are sufficiently anguished, sincere and protracted, it is not within his nature to fail to respond. He once said to a friend of mine, "Even God surrenders to love." It is tantamount to saying that if we nag him enough with the right frame of mind and the right need he will answer our prayers! Some would call this the spiritual law of cause and effect, but it is the same thing.

At the same time he points out that we create our world ourselves, that happiness lies within us, and that the mind is potentially all-powerful. He has sometimes quoted the old English adage: "Where there's a will there's a way."

Success and failure are misleading terms; it is the effort that counts. "I seek the quality of the spiritual effort, not the quantity." It is sometimes better to fail with effort than to succeed with ease.

Swami reveres all life, and preaches that we should do the same: "God is in all that exists. He is intelligence in the insect, faithfulness in the dog, latent energy in the rock." Asked by Dr Hislop if inanimate things can feel, he replied, "There is nothing in the world which has no heart, which is incapable of feeling joy or grief."

Again: "There is no thing which is not ensouled," and that includes the animal, vegetable and even the mineral kingdom. In my former Sussex home there was a natural stream running through the garden. I decided to dam it and make a swimming pool cum lily pond. One day, when the bricklayer was laying the stone for the containing walls, he paused, scratched his head and said, "Funny stuff, stone. It's alive." He had worked with it all his life, and he knew.

So I try to revere all life. I drive my car as if it was human, and my cars have invariably outlasted those of my mechanically-minded friends who tinker with their vehicles every weekend. I talk to the birds. Sometimes, on impulse, I embrace one of the bushy conifers in my tiny garden, and I can almost feel the healing vibrations it is giving back to me.

The one creature I have a fear of is the common toad. I think it stems from babyhood. I was strapped in a cot and deposited in an earth-floored summerhouse which was a favourite haunt of toads. I have vague memories of my elder brother, who hated me, picking them up by the skin of their backs and pointing them in my face. I have a horror of their yellow under-bellies. But in later times I have come to terms with my phobia; if I see a toad in my greenhouse I have learned to live with it.

All life, too, is inter-related. As a countryman I have never had difficulty in accepting this. Even the humble earthworm has a purpose which I believe in some minute way affects our health; the food which sustains us is grown from soil which over the centuries has passed through its body. When man turns his back on nature and dwells in large cities his basic equipoise is disturbed; he needs its sounds, its natural food, and its slow changing tempo.

Sai Baba reveres women, and their role in life. "Woman is

equally equipped with man to tread the spiritual path. No nation can be built strong and stable except on the spiritual culture of its women." He emphasises, again and again, the sacred role of motherhood. "The mother is the child's first *guru*," he says. But he deprecates strongly the tendency in modern woman to try to raise a family and build a career at the same time.

Here are a few miscellaneous examples of Swami's quotations:

"Peace in the home is the first step towards peace in the world." In other words, the first priority is to put our own house in order.

"Faith passes from one mind to another," which is another way of saying that 'religion is caught, not taught'. Therefore, let your light shine. Example is better than argument; in fact, it is sometimes better to lose the argument.

"Converse with God who is in you – He is the *guru* most interested in your progress." Worldly *gurus* are fallible, God is not – He is changeless, immutable. A *guru* may be an aid on the pathway, but he should never become a mentor. The soul is unique, the sum total of many lifetimes; no fellow being can plumb its depths. In the last resort we are on our own, with God.

"The purpose of life is to kill the 'I'." "Welcome trouble, for that alone brings sweetness to the spirit."

"When others shout, reply in whispers: set the level of the tone yourself."

"Wasting things is wasting God." I would hazard the guess that what goes into the dustbins of the West would feed the world's starving.

"Be simple and humble. Do not be proud of your status or class. Always tell yourself: It is He, not I. He is the force, I am but the instrument." The temptation to let ego creep into our achievements is indeed great, even sometimes among mediums and healers.

"Hands that help are holier than lips that pray." Action is better than worship. Again and again he reiterates this. It cannot be too strongly emphasised.

He once said, "Two days of social service will do you more good than two months of meditation".

To the anxiety-ridden or the depressed: "Why fear when I am here?" And: "Keep remembering Me and fight."  .

On our potential divinity: "I am you, you are I. You are the waves; I am the ocean. Know this and be free, be divine."

To encourage: "Follow the Master, face the devil, fight to the end, finish the game!"

I will end where I began, on the recurring theme of Love. It is a word which is understood in too small a context. It covers the whole gamut of human living, from the mundane to the sublime.

From a girl and a boy on a park bench to coping with the difficult lady next door, from cleaning messy beds in a geriatric ward to a dog which drowns itself to save its master, from a brother who sacrificed his artist's hands to enable Albrecht Durer to become a famous painter, to the Polish priest in a concentration camp who volunteered his life for execution to save a fellow patriot.

In the land of the living, as St. Paul said, "Love suffers long, and is kind; love envies not; love vaunts not itself, is not puffed up . . . Love bears all things, believes all things, hopes all things, endures all things."

Wherever love caresses, confusion and disorder vanish; boredom − the great vice − melts, inertia dies, disharmony is swallowed up, old fears fade away, old wounds are healed, leaving no scar tissues, resentments and grudges are impossible, cheap gossip and tawdry fault-finding disappear. Joy and health are established, life becomes gladness, optimism and goodwill, the sufferings of others are shared and released. Love gives freedom to all without in the slightest degree allowing freedom to be twisted into licence.

Love never plucks a soul prematurely. It is content to aid the ripening process and do the plucking in time and season. Love waits for man to come to himself, to weary of his self-willed futility, arrogance and suffering, to tire of the darkness that condemns himself and generations yet unborn. Love waits and recognises the opportunities to act: The creature's failure is love's chance.

Nor does love seek to amend itself with reason, logic, common sense. Love is the supreme reason, the matchless logic, the robust common sense. Love makes the ordinary things extraordinary, the common things uncommon, the weak things strong, the little things huge, the low things high.

Love is Reality, the liberator, the miracle worker.

Sathya Sai Baba is drawing the religions of the world into the one Sai religion of Love. He says that each religion speaks of a part of God, and then asserts that this part is full and total. He claims to have the sixteen *kalas* (attributes) of full divinity. And the following is the essence of his simple message:

"Start the day with love, fill the day with love, end the day with love − this is the quickest and most direct way to God."

"Through love alone can the embodiment of love be gained. Here no scholarship is needed; in fact, scholarship is an impediment, for it caters to egotism, and it breeds doubts and desires for disputation and the laurels of victory over those preening themselves as learned." We have to go out into the world and love until we become LOVE and merge with God who IS Love. It is as simple as that. And if anyone thinks it is too simple I would commend to them the conclusions which some of the world's cleverest men have come to – men like Albert Einstein, Carl Jung, Bertrand Russell, and Dr Robert Oppenheimer – that Love is the fundamental law of the cosmos.

"Come just one step forward, I shall take a hundred towards you. Shed just one tear, I shall wipe a hundred from your eyes." You have only to ask, with a pure heart. You do not have to go to India: Sai Baba is omnipresent. All you need is a small photograph of him on your bedside table, and to ask with a pure heart and genuine anguish in your soul.

Finally, the simplest and most significant, indeed almost cataclysmic, announcement of all:

"If you develop love you do not need to develop anything else."

Think of the ramifications of that! Think of the mothers with large broods of rowdy children who have no time to meditate or practise *yoga*, to read or go to lectures. Think of the simple souls in the world who can scarcely read or write, and the majority of the world's population are simple souls when one envisages the teeming millions in India and China and in the vastness of Africa. I will repeat: "If you develop love you do not need to develop anything else."

Love is the medium through which the creative principle works. It fills all space, and without it nothing could survive. No atoms could hold together, no planet could wheel, no insect flit, nor any plant grow. Nothing could be born and nothing could be reborn. It is the only integrating force in the world. And it is the only hope for the world. That is why Sathya Sai Baba is the only significant phenomenon in the world. No one and nothing else really matters.

# 11

# THE PRACTICE OF LOVE

## THE LITTLE WAYS

Little things lead to bigger things. There is an old Chinese proverb
that if you want to put the world to rights you must first start with
yourself, to put your own house in order. Then your family, then
your neighbours, then your town, then your country, and then the
world. Yet how many leaders of supposedly religious or spiritual
groups and self-appointed *gurus* do we know who pride themselves
on their spiritual status and erudition who are in fact, when we
get to know them intimately, full of ego and spiritual pride.

Even India's so called holy men are not blameless, as Dr
Baranowski, the Kirlian photography expert, discovered on his tour
of India when he photographed the auras of a hundred of that
country's 'holy men'. He found nothing particularly outstanding
in any of them, and in some a good deal of egoism, spiritual pride
and prior concern for their own reputations and the financial
preservation of their *ashrams* rather than for the spiritual welfare
of those they presume to guide and counsel.

I remember a few years ago watching one such alleged holy man
on television. He was holding a bunch of white flowers on his
knees. As he talked he picked off the petals, one by one, and

dropped them on the floor. I suppose it was his method of dood-
ling, but for me it ended his validity as a holy man. He had given
himself away with this 'little' gesture.

Apart from the wisdom of learning to walk before trying to run,
most of us are ordinary people leading very ordinary lives. We are
not going to become saints or heroes. Most of us are not going to
have the time to study philosophy, or to read the *Gita*, the *Koran*,
or the Bible in any sort of depth. What we need is to have our
imaginations opened as to how we can express love in little and
ordinary ways in our somewhat humdrum lives.

First, in work. Swami stresses again and again that work is
worship. If we do our work for God, however menial, it will change
our whole attitude, even towards the most humble and repetitive
jobs. In a remarkable book called *Release* written by a hardened
American criminal who spent thirty years of his adult life in prison,
and who about two-thirds of the way through his last sentence
became converted to non-denominational, pristine Christianity,
the author relates how it changed his whole approach to prison
work. He grew to love the old sewing machine with which he sewed
mail bags. He achieved a high degree of skill with it, and he worked
it like an artist.

Better to do a week's work in this spirit than to spend a lifetime,
once a week, in a church in repetitive un-heartfelt prayer. There is
a right and wrong way of doing everything, even lifting a sack. So
develop skill and pride of work, even if you are a refuse collector.
Do the washing up and changing of nappies for God.

That is not to say that one should not pray. Its power is far
greater than most people realise. Thoughts are things, and often
have a greater effect than physical actions; in fact, it is the mass
thought of the world as much as its selfishness which has brought
it to its present crisis. But do not pray in a stereotyped way, or at
a set time only. Pray when the spirit moves, and from the heart
rather than from the head.

Before visiting a troubled soul, while working for the Samaritans, I always stopped the car and prayed for five minutes. I said
something like this: "Almighty Spirit, our Father-Mother God,
empty me of all that is not Thee, of all ego and pride. Fill me with
a spirit of true humility, within the framework of the courage to
say what has to be said if the occasion demands. Let Thy divine
light shine through me. Not I, Father, but You through me." It
invariably worked.

Often in an interview I would get stuck, at a loss to know how to
proceed. Then suddenly the conversation would take a new turn,
and a fresh rapport would be established on a different topic or
level of consciousness. I would leave, sensing that an unhappy

230

person was uplifted and grateful, and I feeling elated for having been given the opportunity to serve.

If you do not feel up to this kind of work and a friend calls in distress, and the problem seems beyond you, try looking into his or her eyes with pure love. It will probably do more good than hours of talk or an attempt to give advice. It may even do more good than a psychiatrist, for you will be radiating the healing power of love. In any case, if you do give advice make sure when you say, "If I were you I should do so and so," that you mean "If I were you" and not "if you were me!" You have to project yourself into the mentality of your friend.

Learn to <u>listen</u>. Most of us talk far too much and listen far too little. Frank Buchman, the founder of Moral Re-Armament, put it in a very homespun way. He said, "Man has two ears and one mouth — why not listen twice as much as you talk?" The best listener I ever knew was a Jesuit priest. He was a highly intelligent man, but in a social group he would hardly ever speak. Yet nothing escaped his ears. About every half hour, with his eyes on the person to whom he was addressing the remark, he would say something in a quiet, gentle voice. It was always succinct and marvellously apposite to the needs of that person at that particular time. Not a word was wasted.

Try to become God-conscious. See God in everything that is good and beautiful — in the structure of a snowflake, in the grandeur of an oak tree, in the birth of a kitten, and in the miracle that is Spring. Try to recapture the wonder of a child to whom everything is magic and a marvel, and remember that it is only what the poet Shelley called 'the world's slow stain' that makes us inured to the sheer miracle of life. We only value the air we breathe when we are choking to death.

And see God, too, in what is not good, for there is no thing (nothing) that is not God. All form is God in manifestation. As Sir James Jeans said, "The universe is a 'thought' of God." Search and hang on to the redeeming feature, even in the most dire criminal, for there always is one. When Mother Teresa of Calcutta was asked how she saw a flee-ridden and dissolute old beggar, she replied, "I see him as God who has caught a slight cold!"

You may say there are some human beings who are so degraded, so beyond the pale, that it is impossible not to hate them. Well, I am helped by a phrase I read many years ago in a book called *All Glorious Within* by Bruce Marshall. I cannot remember it precisely but it went something like this: "Be we saint or sinner, capitalist or communist, criminal or law-abiding citizen, at the end of the day we all lie down and go to sleep, we all snore, and we all have navels!" It reduces us to a common denominator, and somehow evokes the sheer pathos of being a human being. It is easier then to forgive than to judge.

Cultivate patience. There is no better way than through motherhood, or in welfare work. One of my first cases, when I did welfare work, was a professional burglar. His mother was a Greek Roman Catholic, and his father a Jewish gypsy violinist who was also a communist and an anarchist. At birth, he was allegedly thrown into the docks at Marseilles and fished out of the water by dockside prostitutes. He was currently living with a girl who walked the streets, was a drug-taker and a drug-pusher, and he had about a dozen children scattered about the country by various women, some of whom he had married and some he had not, for whom he felt no responsibility whatever. He was also, at the time, a repulsive looking man.

My first encounter with him lasted for thirteen hours, during which time he never stopped talking. We had two meals during that time but he continued to talk even when his mouth was full. I doubt if I said more than a hundred words during the whole of that time. The session started at 11 a.m. one day and ended at 1 a.m. the following morning. When I returned home I had a fever and a temperature from sheer mental exhaustion.

I stuck to him for five years and, at the end of that time, he was not only rehabilitated but a spiritually oriented man. I must have spent a thousand hours in his presence, and talked to him for another thousand hours on the telephone. It taught me patience.

Growth upward or downward is slow. It takes time to sink to the gutter, and even longer to reach the stars. One has to 'keep on keeping on'. 'Success' and 'failure' are misleading terms. No dedicated effort is ever wasted. One never knows. One sows seeds in the mind which may germinate in ten or twenty years. They may not even germinate until a person reaches the spirit world. One has to think in terms of many lifetimes.

One should try to avoid negative thinking. So many of us are guilty of this without knowing it. It can become a habit of which we are scarcely aware. I suppose deep down it is the reason why the media tell us that news is only news when it is bad news; it is as if we actually prefer to read of disaster, tragedy and scandal. It should not be so. We should do our best to eject bad thoughts, and if we succeed we should go a step further, and transmute them. Ejected bad thoughts merely pass into the stream of consciousness, but transmuted thoughts are converted, as it were. It should be the same when our friends rant and rave; we should not only listen quietly, but we should try to take the poison into ourselves and transmute it. It is the difference between being involved and standing to one side. It can be tiring, but we shall have the satisfaction of having neutralised the bad vibrations.

A saintly man once said, "I am kept in Heaven by the energy of sin. The Lord sends sinners to me. I sit down with them and do nothing but love them and listen to their troubles. They are filled with negative energy, which they pour out to me. My love for them transforms that energy as fast as they release it. Pretty soon they are empty. A peace has come. Because of their trouble we have both found peace on earth. We have served each other; the sinner serving most."

There is an analogy here with exorcism. An evicted spirit entity may well return to plague the victim, or become attached to another poor soul with a weakened psychic aura. This was the great value of Dr Carl Wickland's work at the turn of the century. He worked with his wife who was a trance medium. When he exorcised a possessing spirit from a patient she allowed the obsessor to entrance her. Thus, through her, her husband could speak with the entity. In this way he often persuaded the interloper to abandon his or her injurious action and depart to a rightful place in the world of spirit.

Of course these are very high standards which most of us cannot hope to emulate. For example, my wife and I were burgled of most of our family silver. It was the first time it had happened. We felt a sense of outrage and humiliation, and also a revulsion at the contamination of the atmosphere of our home. However, by nightfall on the same day we did manage to pray for the culprits. It should not have taken us a whole day!

Too much reading and knowledge can be a pitfall rather than an asset. Knowledge is of value only in so far as it enables us to serve and love more intelligently. But there must be a balance between KNOWING and BEING. It is so easy to lose this balance, to know more than one is, and eventually to become a sterile intellectual. A good book, with passages in it that ring a bell, should be absorbed into our being, so that as a result of reading it we become 'changed', even if only very slightly, in our daily conduct.

Yet many of us read book after book, attend lecture after lecture and remain much the same in our daily lives. I am afraid quite a few *gurus* and leaders of cultist groups are guilty of this. They are really, to some extent, on spiritual ego trips. Better the wisdom of an old gardener than the arid knowledge of a pedant who does not practise love.

There are so many small ways of loving in our daily lives. Try to cook lovingly. Food will imbibe your vibrations and be the more readily ingested if cooked with love. It is a known fact that in prisons the main health complaint is indigestion, not from bad food, but from food which has been cooked without caring.

Talk with love to the flowers and vegetables in your garden. It is an established fact that they respond. A friend of mine who lives in a remote village in Wales plays harmonious music from his transistor radio to his vegetables. The local villagers are nonplussed at the size of his crops.

Answer the telephone warmly and courteously rather than with a curt and snappy "Hello", or a recital of your exchange and number in a cold monotone. A friend said to me one day, "You even answer the 'phone with love!" It sets the scene for the conversation, rather as the opening paragraph of a novel can.

Rain or shine, cold or hot, have something positive to say or think about the weather, for there will scarcely be a day in your life when you will not be called upon to reciprocate a remark on it, in our climate! If it is raining and there is the usual moan, say, "But God is feeding His vegetable kingdom." Admittedly, it will be cold comfort to nine people out of ten, but the tenth may well say, "I never thought of it like that . . . " And what have you done? You may have sown a seed of expanded consciousness in that person's mind.

If it is cold and frosty in the winter, think of the joy of feeding the birds, even if it is only on the window sill of your flat. Think of the germs and viruses that are being destroyed. Think of the good it is doing the land, of the injurious insect larvae that will not survive the winter to ravage the farmer's crops.

When the news is bad on television, do not waste time in being too appalled or depressed, or worse still, do not become desensitised by the sheer repetition of it. If it is murder, send out an immediate loving thought for the victim and the relatives, and then a beam of light for the culprit. Cultivate the habit of this; it is not difficult, and it will prevent anger.

If you are expecting guests, say a little prayer before they arrive, to be a source of joy and light to them. Resolve to listen more than you talk. I once knew a host who actually went to the trouble of ascertaining his guests' favourite topics and then "genned himself up" on these in order to be a more interesting conversationalist.

Don't be afraid to demonstrate affection. If you are fond of someone give him or her a hug or a kiss, even if it is a stranger with whom you have struck up a rapport. Drop English reserve. A man once told me he had experienced remorse for years at a friend's suicide because on the night of the tragedy he had felt too inhibited to put his arm around him. He sensed that it might just have tipped the scales.

When saying goodnight to your guests wish them love and light. My wife and I call it L and L for short. It always brings a smile to their faces, and this little custom has spread surprisingly.

Finally, I give you a homespun recipe for happiness from Sai Baba: four cups of love, two cups of loyalty, three cups of forgiveness, one cup of friendship, two spoonfuls of tenderness, four quarts of faith, one barrel of laughter. Take love and loyalty and mix thoroughly with faith. Blend them with kindness, tenderness and understanding. Add friendship and love. Sprinkle abundantly with laughter. Bake with sunshine. Serve daily with generous helpings!

## THE BIGGER WAYS

*"Greater love hath no man than that he lay down his life for another."*

I suppose, Jesus is the supreme example of this in offering himself for crucifixion when he could so easily have avoided it. He put up no resistance; indeed, he seemed to will it. He could have raised his vibrations and made himself invisible; there is evidence that he did this on occasions. But after the agony of Gethsemane he deliberately chose to sacrifice himself.

Sathya Sai Baba has on many occasions taken on the negative *karma* of devotees whom he knew could not bear the physical agony, suffered the requisite amount of time, and then cured himself.

We lesser mortals obviously cannot emulate these examples. Yet some men and women, particularly women, do manifest love with an extraordinary degree of patience and self-sacrifice in their daily lives. For example, those who forego their own happiness in order to care for sick and elderly relatives, or work with maladjusted children, or in geriatric wards or mental hospitals. It is true, too, that some seemingly very ordinary men and women do show the most astonishing heroism when confronted with a sudden emergency, even to the extent of risking their lives. It seems that the spirit of God lies dormant in us until a crisis brings it to the surface.

I make no pretence of being a hero, and I doubt if I could work in a geriatric ward, but I do submit, in all humility, that the following true story of the redemption of a long-time alcoholic and sex pervert was an example of sustained love, and might just qualify as an example of 'loving in the bigger ways'.

I first met Harry in his late fifties. He had been an alcoholic for twenty-five years, since the passing of his much loved wife, Mary. During this time he had been to various organisations such

235

as Alcoholics Anonymous, the Samaritans, etc., but to no avail. When I met up with him he had been incarcerated in a mental hospital for two years where he had become more or less institutionalised. He was not altogether unhappy in the hospital. He had made a few chums, got on pretty well with the staff who permitted him the occasional visit to a pub. He was friendly with the head gardener and worked in the greenhouses, which he enjoyed. And, of course, he had no financial worries.

But the pressure for beds finally left the authorities with no alternative but to release him into the big wide world. It was too much for him after this long period of institutionalisation – he simply could not cope with himself or with life, and he took to heavy drinking again. At this point, the local Social Services asked me to do what I could to help. They had found him a tiny furnished bed-sitter and a job as a porter in a supermarket in a nearby town.

I agreed to do what I could. I was running a welfare group at the time, doing roughly the same work as the Samaritans, except that when circumstances demanded my wife and I had those we were trying to help to live with us rather than merely to visit them. Our principle was to "do a lot for a few rather than a limited amount for the many". It was the only way to help the real down-and-outs.

I contacted Harry's doctor who told me he had lost count of the number of suicide attempts he had made over the years. He thought it was about twenty, although there had never been a serious attempt. It had always been to draw attention to himself and be taken care of for a few days. On one occasion, he was still talking to the Samaritans on the telephone when the ambulance arrived – they had worked fast!

At our first meeting, I took him to our local pub. He drank four pints of beer while I, in order to keep him company, sipped at half a pint of a beverage I do not like. He told me a little about his life. When I bade him good night he said, a little apprehensively, "I hope I see you again . . . " "You will," I replied succinctly and drove off. I did not delude myself into thinking I had made an impression on him. At this stage, I am sure he simply felt he was on to a good thing, finding a welfare worker willing to pay for four pints of beer!

It may seem strange that I should take an alcoholic to a pub. But in ten years of welfare work I never told anyone to pull himself together, or used the word 'ought', or said he was not to do what he was patently trying not to do. Nor did I ever mention religion. My prime motive was not to convert but to help. I simply set an example and manifested as much love and light as possible. And I used the tools of common sense and unrelenting loving-kindness, but the loving-kindness had to be unrelenting. In this way a person's interest in spirituality would sometimes be aroused, and he would ask me what made me 'tick', and I would tell him a little about my faith. Example was much better than 'lecturing'.

Harry was in a bad way. He was finding it increasingly difficult to get through a day's work as a porter, even though he was being 'carried' by a good-hearted mate. In the evenings he sat brooding and drinking in his pub. For food he bought a sandwich or sometimes fish and chips. There were days when he ate literally nothing. His stomach was so heavily lined with alcohol that food made him vomit. Obviously, he could not continue in this fashion.

I persuaded him to let me take him to a mental hospital to be 'dried out'. He knew the ropes, having been through the same procedure many times. He was given a substitute drug to still the craving for alcohol, and put in a closed ward.

About the third day he took a little food. At the end of a week he was eating normally and feeling much better. After a fortnight's stay he was discharged. It was amazing how rapidly he recovered.

I collected him from the hospital. During that fortnight I had done some thinking. I made the acquaintance of two girls who shared a room above Harry's, and sounded them out whether they would be willing to help. They were cheerful, good-hearted girls in their mid-twenties, and they readily agreed.

They gave Harry's room a thorough spring-clean, hung a picture above his mantel piece, installed a small kitchen table next to the unused gas stove, and generally gave the room a new look. When Harry entered it he could hardly believe his eyes.

The three quickly became friends. The girls began to mother him. They cooked him the odd meal, with a green vegetable, and did his washing, and called in most days for a half-hour chat. For my part, I bought him a set of garden tools and urged him to renovate a small plot of ground at the back of the tenement which had once been a garden but was now a rubbish heap.

At first he showed no interest or enthusiasm, although I knew he had once been a keen gardener. But I suppose he felt under some sort of obligation to me for purchasing the tools. One day, when the sun was shining, he summoned up the will and had a go. The first yard of the mile had been taken.

At the end of the month he had cleared the ground and sown the seeds. The girls helped. By midsummer he had as flourishing a little vegetable garden as one could wish to see — there was not a weed in it. He showed it to me with great pride. But the really important thing was that since leaving the hospital he had not touched a drop of alcohol.

His mind cleared, and the embryo of a new lease of life was generated in him. He gave up his job as a supermarket porter and obtained a post in his old trade as a chef-caterer in a nearby Old Folks' Home. His salary was doubled, and he was given a pleasant, modern flat with everything found. There was a large garden attached to the Home which he volunteered to look after in his spare time.

He bought a kitten as a companion. Harry loved animals — it was one of his redeeming features. And, of all things, he began to write short stories about animals. He wrote from the heart, and although simple his stories were moving. That summer, he wrote and had published four short stories about pets he had owned. As a working class lad, brought up in the poverty-stricken North-East in pre-War days, with virtually no education, he was naturally thrilled and proud to see his name in print.

I visited him regularly and got to know him intimately. He came to trust and confide in me completely. Poor fellow, he had many faults and weaknesses. He was bi-sexual; at low moments he had indulged in many squalid little homosexual affairs. And in times of near destitution he had even resorted to male prostitution. But he was guilty of one heinous addiction, indeed crime, which was even worse than this, and for which even one's fellow convicts in prison isolate one: he had from time to time assaulted children.

Harry had been brought up in a coal mining area of extreme poverty. Homosexuality was rife among the miners. It seems that where men work in close comradeship, whether under the earth or on the seas, this is not uncommon. He had been assaulted himself as a child.

His father had deserted his mother who became a prostitute. The family lived in a tiny house. The children went to school without shoes. There was only one room and one bed, for Harry and his three sisters. Can it be wondered at that in these conditions the children indulged in incest and regarded it as natural?

Somehow my wife and I still managed to show him compassion. We felt that a man who loves animals and gardens could not be wholly bad. This made a great difference to him. He still had two friends, even when the last veil had been torn aside.

In his late 'teens he had joined the Army and was trained as a chef. In his early twenties he fell very much in love and married Mary, his first wife. He served during the War in the Tank Corps and took part in the D-Day operations. After the War, in civilian life, he did well enough for himself. In his prime he held a post as a head chef-caterer for an Oxford College, catering for four hundred people.

For fifteen years Harry and Mary were deeply in love and very happy. There was a very strong psychic affinity between them. It may even be that he had found that rare phenomenon on earth, his twin soul. They were inseparable. Mary was the central pivot of his life, his reason for living. They were telepathic as twins.

Then, at thirty-five, she suddenly and tragically died of a heart attack. Harry literally pined his heart out and, metaphorically speaking, died too. The truth was that although it was twenty-five years ago that the poor man's spirit was broken, he had never recovered. Try as he did to rebuild his life and to live again, deep down he had simply felt that he was 'existing'. No one could replace his soul mate.

He took to drink after Mary's passing, although for many years he was able to control his drinking, or rather, Mary controlled it for him, for Harry was psychic, and constantly aware of her spiritual presence. When he had 'had enough', he became aware of a 'tap on the shoulder'. He would obey this spirit admonition and repair from the pub to his home.

You may think that Harry was fortunate to have this spirit link with his beloved Mary and that it should have been a great source of comfort to him. But although he was naturally psychic he was not a very evolved soul. Mary's spiritual presence served only to set in relief her physical absence, and to make his anguish the more intolerable.

He was left with two children, a daughter and a son. For fifteen years, with the aid of a housekeeper, he brought them up until they married and left home. It was during this time that he fell heavily from grace.

At the age of ten his daughter was the image of her mother. Harry developed an incestuous relationship with the child which continued until she married. The details, as he recorded them to me, were ugly, although he never hurt the child physically. Some may question how I was still able to befriend and show compassion for such a man. I can only say that during the five years I cared for Harry, again and again, perhaps a dozen times, I saw him rocking himself to and fro in his chair, his hands clasping his head, tears running down his cheeks, in an agony of remorse and self-condemnation such as I have never witnessed in another soul.

As I watched him, mindful of his childhood, his bereavement, and the dreadful effect that alcohol can have on a man with perverse sexual instincts, I could feel only sorrow and compassion. There were times when I all but wept with him.

When the children left home his housekeeper also departed, and Harry was alone in the world. He felt desperately lonely. In a moment of weakness he remarried, hoping for companionship, to a woman looking for security. There was no love between them. The marriage was a failure. His second wife quickly sensed that she was second best and living with an invisible rival who she could not combat. Harry found little relief from his loneliness. Alas! they had only one thing in common – a predilection for sexual perversion. Harry began to drink more and more heavily, and this time in an uncontrollable manner. Mary had seemingly deserted him. From the day of his second marriage he was no longer able to make spirit contact with her. He regarded this as his betrayal of his one true love.

Of course it was not so. When those we love pass on, they are only too happy if we find another partner. Indeed, they often encourage us to do so. Mary had no doubt withdrawn to give Harry's second marriage a fair chance. But he did not see it like this. He felt a traitor and it made things worse.

It was then that he took to male prostitution. He was incapable of earning a living by any other means. His wife actively encouraged him, laying her hands avidly on his ill-gotten gains. They came to hate one another. Things went from bad to worse until Harry was taken to a mental hospital. While he was in hospital his wife divorced him. He was in no state to contest it, even had he wished to.

Such was his life story. It was not until late in that first summer of my befriending, when he was making progress, that the full force of his love for Mary came home to me. One day I had a 'prompting' to take him to a National Trust garden of great natural beauty. There was a terraced chain of four lakes where shoals of gaily coloured fish meandered among giant crimson water lillies, and wild mallard (in spring, with a flotilla of tiny ducklings in train) swam within feet of you. On the banks were mountains of rhododendrons, twenty feet high, groves of camelias of almost equal height and perhaps two hundred years old and, in the spring, literally acres of daffodils and bluebells. In the background was perhaps the finest landscaping of trees, indigenous and foreign, in the whole of Britain.

It was a truly awe inspiring sight on one's first visit. The peace, when there are not too many visitors, transports you to the summerlands of heaven. I thought it would uplift Harry, but I could not have been more wrong.

The strangest thing happened. Arriving at the first lake, Harry suddenly left me, ran in full flight to the edge of the water and flung himself down on the ground in a frenzy of anguish and tears. His body twisted and his hands padded the grass like one demented. I was dumbfounded, and felt at a total loss. For a moment I thought his mind was deranged.

He recovered, and we proceeded, but he did not vouchsafe any explanation of his conduct. About a hundred yards further on he did the same thing. This time I walked up to him and tried to comfort him. He looked at me with hate.

"You couldn't have done a crueller thing, Ron, than to bring me here," he said in an anguished voice.

He added a few words which gave me the clue. More than thirty years before, at the approach of D-Day, Harry's Tank Corps Division had sheltered under the trees of this park, awaiting Eisenhower's fateful order. On his time off, he and Mary had walked along the banks of these lakes. On the spot where he had flung himself on the grass, they had made love, at night, with the ancient pines and giant Wellingtonias guarding the glistening moonlit water like dark sentinels.

I thought quickly. I got him to his feet and said vehemently, "Face it, Harry, face it!" A trauma is created when we are confronted by an experience which is too painful to face, like the sudden death of a loved one, but if we do face it and live through it, even in the aftermath, the blockage is removed and, although saddened, we experience a certain sense of relief.

But it was no good. I had to give up and take him back to the car. Even the beauty of the place depressed him. He had come to equate beauty with sadness since the death of Mary. A grove of daffodils in the spring saddened his heart unbearably and turned his thoughts to her.

Back in the car we sat in silence. He calmed down a little. Then he said resignedly, "Perhaps you have done the right thing, Ron." Be that as it may, from that day Mary returned to his life. Once again he became psychically aware of her spirit presence. Perhaps I had had the right 'prompting' . . .

His progress during that first year lasted for nine months. During that time he did not take to drink. Then, on Christmas Day, there was a staff party at the Old Folks' Home. The matron naturally invited him to join in the festivities. Unfortunately he had not revealed that he was an ex-alcoholic. He was offered a drink. At first he refused, but then he succumbed. Just one drink — but it was enough to start the syndrome.

By this time I knew about the syndrome from his doctor. It usually lasted six weeks. During this time he refused all help and became very difficult. It was partly the bitter-sweet pleasure of a prolonged drunken orgy which he did not want to be deprived of. But it was also the rebellion of his ego against admitting that he was in need of help. A man does not like to admit that he lacks the will power to conquer his particular vice.

There was nothing to do but wait patiently and befriend h

until he was ready to be dried out. It was a gruelling time. I had to sit in pubs and listen to self-pity and maudlin talk for hours on end. He could be very negative in this state. One day he said to me, "I marvel at your patience. Where do you get it from?"

I reflected for a moment. Then I said, "You learn it through practice, by a determination never to give up, by thinking in terms of eternity rather than in months or years. After all, one life span is only a split second in the pulse beat of eternity." He looked at me uncomprehendingly.

I did, however, have one lapse. He had got it into his head that his span was approaching the end. He had had a hint from his doctor. His liver was in an advanced state of disease. He also had chronic bronchitis and poor blood circulation. He was full of maudlin self-pity about his supposed approaching end.

One day he went on and on about it, for hour after hour. Everything I said was ignored, every vestige of light I tried to throw out was transmuted into darkness in one long wearying and perverse monologue until the vibrations of the room in which we sat seemed as black as the lower astral. I just felt it perverse to let him continue. I <u>had</u> to protest in order to turn the tide.

I stood up and said, "If you are going to die, Harry, I can only say 'thank God'. It is one step nearer to Mary. It is the Great Adventure, and for you the Great Release."

I raised my arms and almost shouted, "Hallelujah!" Then I walked over to where he sat and said, "For crying out loud, let's have something positive from you. Now, stand up! Raise your arms and say 'Hallelujah!' " And to my astonishment he did just that. We were a comical pair, a somewhat beaten up welfare worker and poor dissolute old Harry, standing there, with arms raised, and shouting at the top of our voices, "Hallelujah, hallelujah!" at the prospect of his approaching death. But it did break the sequence, and the negative flow did cease for a half hour or so.

During this protracted orgy of drink he totally confided in me. Many times in this work I have found myself playing the Father Confessor. People want you to know the worst and to feel that they still have a friend. He showed me a copy of his wife's affidavit with which she had obtained the divorce.

We were trained in the Samaritans never to be shocked. But on this occasion I was shocked, although I was careful not to show it. I read it through with a deadpan expression. Then, simulating sincerity, I said, "I have read worse than this, Harry." It was a lie. It was, I think, the most hideous document I have ever read in my life.

Towards the end of this syndrome of drinking there was a serious crisis. Harry announced that he had arranged to visit his married daughter on the Isle of Wight. She was due to go into hospital for a minor operation. He felt it would be a good opportunity to see something of his grandchildren, and particularly his eleven-year-old grand-daughter, and to help take care of them during their mother's absence. Her husband was away from home on a contract job, so Harry would be in sole charge.

I felt very uneasy about the idea. Was there something sinister in the motivation, particularly in his present state of heavy drinking? On the day of the journey he must have been in great conflict. He got out of the train half-way to Southampton and telephoned me from a call box. He prevaricated for a time. Then he said just four words, "You know me, Ron."

I knew instantly that my suspicions were valid. I suppose, I should have got in the car and brought him home, but I was busy that day. I urged him with all the command I could muster to take the next train home. But, as I put the receiver down, I did not hold out much hope.

The next morning at eight o'clock I had a call from his daughter. Her father had arrived and she was desperate. She said, "I must go to hospital. I've waited for this operation for months. Yet I cannot leave the children with my father. I know the danger. What can I do?"

She was crying over the telephone. It was a time for immediate action. She was due to leave for hospital in a couple of hours. I said, "It is your decision, but I think you are left with no alternative but to telephone the Police."

Twenty minutes later the Police called me. I referred them to Harry's doctor. Within an hour he was picked up — he was still in bed — escorted to Southampton and put on a train back to the town where he lived. The Police acted very quickly. Late that night he telephoned me. He just said "Ron" and was silent. I could not get him to speak. Finally he got out the words. He said in an anguished voice, "*Et tu, Brutus*," and put the receiver down. He was crying.

I suppose his emotions were hurt — a self-cancelling mixture of anger, humiliation and gratitude. Hurt at what he saw as a bretrayal by his one and only friend, anger at the deprivation at the eleventh hour of his terrible addiction, humiliation by the Police and, with what little that was left in him of his higher self, gratitude. But it made no difference in our future relations. We simply did not refer to the subject again.

The end of the syndrome was rapidly approaching. He had not eaten for days. Finally, from sheer physical fatigue and general malaise, he agreed to be dried out. I made the arrangements and took him to the mental hospital.

He was interviewed by a psychiatrist and assigned to a ward. As we sat waiting in an ante-room I went to the lavatory. On my return I saw him hastily hide a bottle of whiskey in his overcoat pocket. He had taken a quick swill. I said nothing.

We walked across an asphalt yard to the ward. He was given a cubicle to himself. A young Pakistani male nurse searched his suitcase and belongings. He seemed satisfied and was about to depart when the following conversation took place.

"Come on, old cobber, let's have the medicine," I said.

"What do you mean?"

"The medicine, the bottle of Scotch. I saw you hide it in your overcoat pocket."

He put on a marvellous act, and strenuously denied the accusation.

"Seriously, Ron," he said, "do you really think I would come to a place like this to be cured of alcoholic poisoning and bring some of the ———— stuff with me?"

Gently, and smiling inspite of myself, I said, "Yes, old friend, that's precisely what I think you would do!"

His face almost broke into a smile, too. I think he would have handed the stuff over had he not feared losing face with the Pakistani nurse. As he was adamant, there was nothing else I could do. I had a word with the male charge nurse before departing.

Harry made his usual rapid recovery. With the aid of substitute drugs and a closed ward he was well again and discharged in ten days. He was sacked from the Old Folks' Home, but with the help of a subtle reference from me (which was basically the truth), he obtained a similar post as chef-caterer in another Home, this time within easy reach of my befriending centre.

Once again for nine months he did not touch alcohol. He worked hard, got on well with the staff, and saved money. Apart from alcohol his tastes were frugal. I visited him regularly, usually staying for five or six hours. By this time I knew him well enough to tell him some blunt home truths. It gave him food for thought. He sulked a bit, but by the time of my next visit I was always welcome. I did not pull my punches; if he talked too much, I simply told him to "shut up". He said he took things from me which he would not take from any other man alive.

Sometimes he came to stay with us for a weekend at our home where we had a beautiful garden.

He loved that garden. I had created it from nothing. From a half acre bare patch of ground I planted mature plants and conifers up to twenty feet high with a tractor and hydraulic lift, and dammed a natural stream, which flowed through the plot, to make a curved shaped swimming pool cum lily pond, overhung with weeping willows, and built of sandstone.

I put in about a dozen tiny brown trout which, to my surprise, thrived and grew into large fish; there was an ample supply of insect larvae and natural food. It was indeed an enchanting experience to stand by the pool on a summer's evening, watching the trout rise for fly and the swallows swooping down, dipping their white breasts against the glinting surface of the water.

It seemed that in two years I had created the atmosphere of a century. It was amply blessed by our spirit friends. Everything grew profusely there, and particularly the deep red water lilies in the pool which looked like lotus flowers. Many were the 'apports' of twigs of flowering shrubs which my wife and I received during the twelve years we lived there. Harry always insisted on sleeping on a camp bed in our Sanctuary which overlooked this garden. He felt safe and protected there, and I daresay he was!

At this time he began to take an interest in spirituality. I had never talked to him of religion, but it seemed he 'caught' something from my wife and me. He had a retired clergyman 'pen friend' who he had met only once in his life, who wrote to him regularly, quoting Bible texts. Harry cultivated the friendship because the old man kept him supplied with free tobacco, but the letters he consigned to the dustbin.

Perhaps it was the vibrations of our home and garden, created by our friends in spirit, which uplifted him . . . He found that, as he looked out of the Sanctuary window at the garden, he no longer equated the beauty in nature with sadness. He had become reconciled at last to Mary's death.

He began to take an interest in our tape-recordings of spirit communications. He dubbed one or two of his favourites and re-played them in his bedroom at the Home. We lent him a few books. He read some of my wife's articles in *Two Worlds* magazine. And he no longer felt the same physical anguish when he sensed, psychically, the presence of his beloved soul-mate in spirit. I began, empryonically, to hope that he might pull through and be permanently cured.

Alas, he had one final fall from grace. It happened through no real fault of his own. His ex-wife, hearing of his apparent recovery and sensing that he must have some savings, contacted him. There was talk of reconciliation. I quaked when I heard the news. I knew intuitively that it would end in disaster.

His doctor and I did our utmost to dissuade him. For weeks the issue hung in precarious balance as Harry procrastinated. In the end I had to respect his free will. There was a limit to the pressure

I could justifiably apply. He made his decision. He gave up his job and travelled North to where his ex-wife had a flat. The reunion lasted a month. The wretched woman took most of his savings (some £300) and then evicted him from her flat.

Not unnaturally he felt at the end of the road. He went on one final, desperate orgy. I do not know the details as he had travelled a long way North and I lost track of him at this time. But I do know that he came very close to genuine suicide at this time. When, later, I asked him why he had not committed suicide, he reflected for a long time. Then he said, "In the moment of truth, Ron, I just felt I couldn't let you and my doctor down."

Between us we had trapped him with love.

And that, for a full year, I believed was the end of the story. Harry had grown old – old, that is, for his years. Although he did a bit of job gardening he now lived on social security. He found digs with an elderly communist and, although the old man's ideological rantings got a bit on his nerves, he was a kindly man at heart and Harry grew fond of him and found in him a genuine companion. And he had two life-long friends in the South in my wife and I who wrote to him regularly and sent him tobacco most weeks and, from time to time, a little financial aid.

I knew that he still took the occasional glass of beer, but I also knew that he no longer went on protracted orgies. He had come a lot closer to a belief in an after-life, in the existence of the One who he somewhat irreverently called "the Old Man upstairs", and to an eventual reunion with Mary. He had achieved a measure of inner peace, and he was not afraid of death; in fact, he seemed to be just 'waiting'. His health was poor and I did not imagine he would live much longer.

I could not have been more mistaken in my overall assessment. I had overlooked the Miracle Worker. One day, a year later, he wrote to tell me that he had purchased a derelict terraced house and a lot of marshland for the ridiculously low sum of £1,100, borrowing the money on mortgage from the local council, and obtaining a £500 improvement grant. I could hardly believe it.

There were legal difficulties and bureaucratic delays, and sometimes he despaired and nearly gave up, but my wife and I wrote to him regularly and I think our constant encouragement may just have tipped the scales; he stuck to the project and went through with the deal.

Then, for two years, he worked as hard as he ever had in his life, using do-it-yourself methods and applying all the ingenuity he had learned as a poverty stricken urchin in the North-East, until at the end of that time he had a three-bedroom house passed by the authorities as fit accommodation for local university students. He had also somehow found the time and energy to make a garden out of the marshland. He rented two rooms to students from the university and paid off the mortgage in no time. He was now a capitalist and a landlord! The Miracle Worker had certainly given him a new lease on life.

Moreover, during this time, he resumed normal relations with various relatives, his son, his daughter in the Isle of Wight, and three sisters, all of whom had long since written him off as a lost soul. His daughter even allowed his grand-daughter, now fifteen, to travel North and stay with him unaccompanied, without the slightest degree of apprehension.

He has not so much as taken a glass of beer for three years now. His letters portray an increasing spiritual awareness and orientation, indeed often a deep discernment, which proves to us that his redemption is total and valid. He writes: "At last I can look my fellow human beings in the face."

He stayed with us for a night some months ago. Jokingly I asked him what he had done with that bottle of whiskey in the mental hospital. "Did you hide it in the lavatory cistern?" I enquired. "Good God, no," he replied. "That's the first place they search. I put it on top of the wardrobe, somewhere obvious, where they wouldn't think of looking!"

The old clergyman pen friend is deliriously happy in thinking he has brought about Harry's redemption with his Bible texts. Maybe he has . . . But somehow I do not think so. Yet I would not "break the staff on which he leans, nor rob him of the dreams that harvest joy." He may have helped. I think it was the Miracle Worker, the love in action, in all circumstances, however dire, over a protracted period of five years that brought about the miracle.

# 12

# WHO IS SAI BABA?

Sathya Sai Baba is, by the least measures, a world phenomenon; it is my belief that he is a cosmic phenomenon. It has always seemed strange to me, indeed providential, that his parents, Pedda and Easwaramma Raju, gave him the name of Sathyanarayana. *Sathya* means truth, and Narayana means the God residing in our hearts, for truth and the *atmic* reality of man, or God immanent, are two of the fundamental tenets of his teaching.

As a baby, he has been described as "charming beyond description". At the age of three, his old grandfather, Kondamma Raju, called him "the Little Master". At five, he was nicknamed, in the remote village of Puttaparthi where he was born, *Brahmajnani* (one who has acquired the wisdom that reveals the inner reality). Puttaparthi, incidentally, is known historically as the birthplace of many of India's saints. At this same tender age the village elders referred to him as their *guru*. At six, he was performing miracles, materialising food in an empty basket for his schoolmates. Already he was a genius at dance; his rhythm and timing made it seem to those who watched him that he came from an etherial sphere.

At about this age it was his custom to run races with his village chums up a hill abutting on the village and rising up from the holy River Chitravati (a craggy knoll about 200 feet high and strewn with large boulders). He invariably half levitated himself to the top and won the race. On one occasion, in his 'teens, he appears to have done so almost instantly and, standing at the top almost before his friends had started, he shouted down to them, "Watch, I am giving you the *darshan* of flame," whereupon a large red ball of fire, like a sun, appeared beside him with an effulgence so bright that four of his devotees fainted.

At around ten, he was teaching India's pundits about the *Vedas*, interpreting their abstruse passages and pointing out excisions and interpolations, although he had never read the *Vedas*. At twelve, he confided to a fellow pupil at the High School in Uravakonda to which he had been promoted that he would set the world right and establish Truth in all lands.

There is a charming tale of his life at the Uravakonda school. As the brightest pupil in the class it was his responsibility to administer punishment to his classmates by giving them so many slaps on the cheek according to the whim and instructions of the class master. Swami could not bring himself to do it; instead, he gave them gentle taps with his palm, as a result of which he was given the same number of clouts over the ear by the master as he was supposed to have given slaps to his mates! He never bore the slightest trace of malice.

At thirteen, he threw away his school books and announced that his mission had begun. He actually made the announcement from the dais of the school prayer hall during the morning prayer session. He said that he could no longer 'pretend' to be a student, or even a member of his own family. Then, descending from the dais and followed by the whole school, he walked to the house of the local tax inspector who was devoted to this miracle boy. He did not enter the latter's house but sat on a boulder outside and expanded the theme of his coming *avatarhood*. The site of the boulder is now a community hall for Sai welfare work and is regarded as holy. The inspector said that the trek from the school to the stone was interpreted by him in a vision as the inauguration of a world revolution.

Thus at thirteen, just before his birthday in November 1940, he was virtually proclaimed locally as an *avatar*. The whole town went well nigh berserk. A few years later, in 1947, when his travels began, it was recognised throughout all India that a God-man had been born at Puttaparthi. At this time, one Ganapathi Sastri said, "This is the Incarnation of God."

I am only too well aware that in attempting this explanation I am attempting the impossible — to limit the limitless, to understand divine consciousness with my human consciousness, and that the result must inevitably be a failure. Yet I feel urged to make the attempt. Sai Baba has said, again and again, that to understand his incarnation is beyond human comprehension. Waves of *maya* make recognition of the *Avatar* almost impossible.

How, for example, can one understand the following? "My power is immeasurable, My truth inexplicable, unfathomable . . . I am beyond the most intensive enquiry and the most meticulous measurement . . . There is nothing I do not see, nowhere I do not know the way, My sufficiency is unconditional. I am the Totality, all of it . . . Only those who have recognised My love and experienced that love can assert they have glimpsed My reality." Those who have not met Baba are, indeed, armchair critics.

Many have tried to put into words the effect of meeting him, of the sheer impact of coming face to face with the ONE who is indeed the Embodiment of Love. Dr Sandweiss, the author of *Sai Baba, the Holy Man and the Psychiatrist* says, "He is capable of filling our cup to overflowing until you simply cannot hold more, and still he continues to give." I can honestly say that I found this to be my own experience. His love has been described as surpassing the love of all the mothers in the world. When Baba first looked into Sandweiss's eyes, the doctor described it thus: "What was communicated in that brief moment? The world! Something broke inside me. Some of Baba's love and joy penetrated my soul and I felt myself laughing like a child . . . Puffed up self-worth and egotistical attachments to my own set of values and beliefs seemed to shatter into dust, giving way to a sense of awe and mystery. I felt myself transformed in one dazzling, incredible minute. I was left with my mouth hanging open."

Howard Murphet, author of three books on Baba, writes: 'The stream of affection that flowed from him was like an ocean of love. In that ocean one's physical body seemed to vanish and all the hard lumps of separate self, of anxiety, worry, and deep-lying fear, melted away. For these ecstatic moments one touched the edge of the infinite and felt the joy of it."

Professor Kasturi writes: "Every miracle of Baba is an act of grace. It may be a pinch of sacred ash, a piece of candy, a picture created before us. It may be a shower of ash, or the emergence of *kumkum* or fragrant sandal or nectarine honey on a picture. An *AUM* in ash on the floor (from an invisible visit), a continuous flow of scented oil or *amruta* on a *lingam* or a locket. It may be a series of paper slips (materialised in your house) on which counsel or warnings are written in the language you understand. It may be given to you awake, asleep or dreaming, or come as a book in the post which you have not ordered (and which has never been posted). It may be a vision of himself, etheric, substantial, momentary or lasting, but always it is a sign of his love and majesty. The more you want the more he gives; the more he gives the more you grow; the nearer you approach him the closer do you approximate him."

My own pen cannot match these words. When I met Baba I fell at his feet and broke like a child. I clutched him with my arm and clung to him. I knew then that he was my mother and my father and my best friend — indeed, the only friend I will ever have in this vale of tears. When he looked into my eyes I knew that he knew me through and through, and not only in this life but in all my lives and that, in spite of my weaknesses and faults, he still loved me. I laid my burden at his feet, and he accepted it; I experienced a total sense of liberation. When he spoke to me it was with a 'personalness' that I had never known in a human — it was as if in that moment I was the only person in the world. I knew no fear; indeed, I felt an incredible sense of rapport — it was as if a tiny drop of water had temporarily merged with the ocean.

Finally, from an American lady, Karen Blanc, who witnessed the materialisation by Baba of a *japamala* necklace for Maynard Ferguson, one of America's leading jazz trumpeters, after a concert at Brindavan. Maynard blew his heart out for Swami, and as a reward he got his *japamala*. She writes of the occasion: "Why was it so beautiful? Maybe because we all knew at that moment what we had once known as little children but had since forgotten. There is a part in us all, at the very core of our being, that wants to believe in angels, that 'good' triumphs over 'evil', that Jesus did walk on water and that Moses parted the Red Sea. That is why we wept and that is why it was so beautiful. The necklace was made for us all. It was no magician's trick. It was so we could all know, once and for all, that 'it is so, as it is written'." To me, these are magic words.

Forty years after his historic announcement, at the school in Uravakonda, Sai Baba has collected around him 50 million devotees, with centres in 60 countries of the Western world alone. At the recent World Conference at Puttaparthi, there were 12,500 delegates, with delegations, apart from India, from the following countries: Canada, the United States, Mexico, Peru, Guatemala, Venezuela, Trinidad, Iceland, the U.K., Sweden, Germany, Spain, Italy, Greece, North, East, South and West Africa, most of the Middle Eastern countries, the states bordering on India, Malaysia, the Philippines, Fiji, Hong Kong, Japan, Australia and New Zealand. Even Soviet Russia sent a delegation! At the birthday celebrations which followed, there were 350,000 devotees, accommodated on a campus of no less than a hundred acres.

His recorded miracles, healings, materialisations, projections, etc.,

251

number thousands. There is no question of myth or exaggeration. As Dr Gokak says, "No *avatar* has been attested to by such an army of professional people." Doctors, scientists, philosophers, psychic researchers from all over the world have examined him. His unrecorded miracles probably number millions. For example, in my own case, in my own small part of the globe, in the eighteen months since I visited India, the miracles that have happened to devotee friends, correspondents, and to those to whom I have given *vibhuti*, would fill half a book, yet none of these have been recorded. Professor Kasturi emphasises the point: "In the interview room he deals with our personal and intricate family tangles with intimate sympathy, so most of what happens then — the counsel he bestows, the courage he instils, the factions he reconciles, the despair he destroys, the symbols of grace he gives, the revelations he vouchsafes, and the doubts he dissolves, are unavailable for the records." And, of course, the countless miracles he performs amongst India's peasantry do not see the light of day.

His educational work, in founding kindergarten classes for spiritual instruction (*Bal Vikas*) of which there are now said to be 10,000 in India and the world, in inaugurating elementary and high schools, and in building universities throughout India is such that currently the Indian Minister for Education is considering restructuring and incorporating the Sai principles of education into the national educational system.

His work in the field of welfare, his humanitarian work, is equally prodigious. There are 20,000 trained volunteers (the *Seva Dal*) whose task is to set up field hospitals, blood donor camps, first aid centres in the cities, gruel centres in poverty stricken villages, and engage in cyclone, flood and famine relief work, and much much else.

Apart from the spiritual transformation of mankind which is his avowed and main aim, it is safe to say that no entity on this planet, in the twin fields of education and welfare alone, is doing more for mankind than Sathya Sai Baba.

India's leading figures consult him — the President of India, the Prime Minister, the former Prime Minister, most members of the Indian cabinet. Ambassadors, professors of education, scientists and philosophers from all over the world, too, seek his counsel. Many attend the Summer School courses at Brindavan. India's most respected and revered sages accept him. In forty years Sai Baba has become the most potent influence in the Indian subcontinent. It is my belief that in the early part of the 21st century, he will be the most potent influence in the world.

Perhaps it will help the reader to see Sai Baba in his true perspective if I quote from Dr Diwaker, scholar and Indian statesman, who spoke on Baba's fiftieth birthday in 1975. He said this:

"Once Swami was a village urchin, untutored, uncared for, unloved. Now, on his fiftieth birthday, we assemble from the four quarters of the globe, and what do we find? Philosophers and politicians, educators and legislators, scientists and technologists, the learned as well as the ignorant, the rich as well as the poor, and from all nations and all religions. If this is not a marvel and a living miracle, I would like to know what is!" And this despite the austerities of an alien climate and culture, and the considerable risk of disease.

What is the source of this phenomenal success? Well, there are many facets to Sai Baba's personality which contribute to it. His scholarship is prodigious. Professor Kasturi describes it thus: "Without any formal education he has on the tip of his tongue atomic formulae, *Vedic* hymns, medical recipes, and *Tantric mantras.*" He continues: "One sees him as a paragon, a manufacturer sees him as a superb administrator, a doctor as a master of diagnosis and skill, an engineer as one who humbles his pride with his blue pencil, a musician as the primal of melody and harmony, a poet as the poet of poets, and a philosopher as the one who elucidates simply . . . "

In his flowery, poetic style (which nevertheless contains the essence of truth), the old man goes on: "He is the prime educator of the age. Every word is a *mantra*, every speech an *Upanishad*, every exhortation a *Bhagavad-Gita*, every song he sings Scripture."

Sai Baba has the power to succeed, which is perhaps his *sankalpa* (divine will). I am not aware that he has ever started a project which has failed or had to be abandoned. He sometimes takes a long time to make up his mind (at least, that is how we humans see it although, in reality, it is his sense of timing), but once the time is right, he acts like lightning. Buildings go up with incredible speed. Dharmakshetra, the *mandir* in Bombay, which is an architectural gem and full of cosmic symbolism, was built in 108 days (which is, significantly, the number of attributes which man has ascribed to God).

His patience is literally unlimited. He has said that this attribute is the surest sign of his divinity, more than the miracles, the materialisations, or anything else. It is the quality which fills me with the profoundest awe, perhaps partly because of my lack of it. In private interview he reprimanded me for not "suffering fools gladly". It is a fault I am trying to correct. Now let us say that I can apprehend a thousandth part of Sai Baba's reality and glory. Those who write to me or come to me with questions, albeit decent and sincere people, I quickly divine by their misguided and

253

elementary questions, as knowing perhaps a hundredth part of what I know. How then do I try to begin to answer their questions? I long to give them the answers in a form which can be assimilated by them, but I am frustrated to the point of becoming tongue-tied because I see the long long vista ahead, not only for them but for myself as well. Yet Sai Baba is as gentle and patient with an ignorant peasant as he is with a *Vedic* scholar. At the same time, he once sang a Telegu poem, the last two lines of which go:

"I alone know the agony
Of teaching you each step of the Dance."

It makes his limitless patience all the more sublime.

But the real source of his unbelievable success is, quite simply, his LOVE and his LIGHT. In his cosmic form this light must be the "light of a thousand suns". Even in his mortal form the pink of his aura (for totally ego-less love) is said, by Dr Baranowski, the expert in Kirlian photography, to reach "literally to the horizon". It is his light and his will which attract people from all over the world. He has said that no one arrives at Puttaparthi except by his will. He draws people to him from every country of the world, either because he needs them, or they need him.

There is one attribute of Sai Baba, his linguistic ability, which is still an enigma to me. He speaks three or four Indian languages fluently, and a few more less so. But his English, although not exactly pidgeon English, is spoken with a modicum of words, as if he is sending one a telegram! Yet when his official interpreter, Dr Bhagavantham, is translating his discourses from Telegu into English, he is often interrupted and corrected by Baba with the English *"mot juste"*. It seems that he can, if he wishes, speak any language without learning it, for he has been known to speak a little known Chinese dialect to a group of Chinese visitors, and, while I was at the *ashram*, he spoke their native tongue to a group of Iranian refugees. He has said: "When heart communicates with heart language is an impediment rather than an instrument." Perhaps herein, in some way, lies the answer to my quandary?

Have I written enough to convince the reader that Sai Baba is an *avatar*? It is my belief that he is at least a *purna avatar* (a full or integral incarnation), the first since Krishna, 5,500 years ago, for he has said that only in India do major *avatars* incarnate, and this I can well believe. India was the *guru* of the world millennia ago when we in Britain were painting our faces blue and running wild in the forests. He has also said that the Buddha, Mohammed, and Jesus of Nazareth had some degree of divine vision, but not the fully divine nature. They did not come into incarnation, as he did, with the fully divine powers intact. They did not perform miracles at the age of six. They had to learn. Sai Baba says: "I engage in no asceticism. I do not meditate on anything at all. I do not study. I am no aspirant, seeker, student or sage."

He has said that no previous *avatar* has been recognised during his lifetime. For the first time divinity, in Sai Baba, has been recognised all over the world whilst actually incarnate. This was not even so with Krishna. It is true that Sai Baba has the twin advantages of the printing press and of modern communications. It is also true that Jesus of Nazareth raised the dead, materialised food, and controlled the elements. But Sai Baba has raised the dead at least twice (Walter Cowan and Radhakrishna), has cured virtually every disease known to man, has raised steel girders by the power of sound, has appeared in embodied form as three different persons at the same time (when masquerading as friends of the civil servant who was suicidal, just at the moment when he was about to shoot himself), and has projected himself, also physically, and lived with a devotee and his family for two days, eating, talking, and sleeping, while his real presence was 600 miles away attending to his mission.

This latter has been described in India as the longest 'projection' in world scripture.

For Dr Hislop he materialised a wooden cross with a silver image of Jesus on it from two stalks of jungle grass mentioning, as he handed it to Hislop for examination, that after two thousand years he had had some difficulty in "finding a sufficient quantity of the original wood". Hislop took it back to America and had the cross examined and tested by experts who concluded that the wood from which it was made was indeed two thousand years old!

Having studied Sai Baba through books for three years and, more important, having had the incomparable blessing of experiencing him, as at this moment, in five private interviews, it is my belief that he stands head and shoulders above any of the founders of the world religions. I believe that Jesus of Nazareth was a highly evolved soul, a master, who acquired miraculous powers through *yogic* development rather than from inherent *sankalpa*, and that he probably learned his 'Christianity' in India during the eighteen lost years between the ages of thirteen and thirty: his reverence for all life and disapproval of animal sacrifices from the Jains who revere all life, his teaching on reincarnation (excised from the Bible) from the Hindus, and his love and care for the poor and the sick from the Buddhists.

Is this, then, the final assessment of the question, "Who is Sai Baba?" That he is a *purna avatar*, of the calibre of Rama and Krishna? No. I believe he is more than this. At the risk of being accused of having an imagination that has run away with me I believe he is a cosmic rather than a solar being.

What does Sai Baba say about his nature, and such limitations as he may or may not have imposed upon himself in taking human form? It seems there are virtually no limitations. He claims to have both divine consciousness and human consciousness. He says: "The Lord has come in human form to move among men, so that he can be listened to, loved, revered, and obeyed. He has to speak the language of man and behave like human beings." Yet his omniscience, omnipresence and omnipotence have been proved a thousand times over. Anyone who takes the trouble to read Kasturi's four volumes of Baba's biography will recognise this.

"I have no characteristics; I am not bound by the law of cause and effect. I am neither man nor woman, old or young. I am all these . . . I am everywhere at all times. I need not go or come . . . I can go backward or forward in time, and know everything I wish. Time and space impose no limitations on me . . . The laws of your physics do not allow something to be created out of nothing, but this law does not hold good for me."

"I am with you always; your heart is my home . . . The world is my mansion; even those who deny me are mine; call me by any name, I shall respond; picture me in any form, I shall present myself before you. I am in the least of you as in the best. Do not slander or injure anyone, for you are slandering me who is in him."

Asked if he could transform a mountain, he replied, "Yes, but why should I interfere with nature?" Asked about his finger gesticulations at *darshan*, he said, "Sometimes I look as if I am writing in the air. I am communicating with people you do not see. I am engaged in tasks you cannot understand. I write replies to questions asked by someone far away. I help thousands of people every moment."

Of course his body has no *karmic* accretions — he has simply taken a body. Nor is he influenced by people and events. Dat Pathe makes this point rather graphically. He says: "When two individuals meet, what really meets are two psychological set-ups, each set confronting the other with a complex of experiences, stored memories, sentimental attachments, biased — favourable or unfavourable — dispositions towards various matters and situations, and countless idiosyncracies. These form the background and the source from which the words they use in conversation originate. But when Baba is talking one is struck by the discovery that on his side there is no such set-up at all." This is the All-knowing One who has not had to learn, and who is not impacted by experience.

In the spiritual sense, Sai Baba sees himself as all the names and forms of the One God. "Call me by any name — Krishna, Allah, Christ. Can you not recognise me in any form?" "Continue your worship of your chosen God along the lines already familiar to you, and you will find you are coming nearer and nearer to me, for all names and forms are mine."

"In this human form of Sai, every divine entity, every divine principle, that is to say all the names and forms ascribed to God by man, are manifest." This truly phenomenal announcement was made at the World Conference in Bombay in 1968 before 25,000 people, and it has been repeated many times. In the same year, during a tour of Kenya and Uganda, he materialised an image of Dattatreya (the symbolised embodiment of the Hindu trinity of Brahma, Vishnu and Shiva), but creating an image of his own head for all three. This, in Christian terms, is indicating that he is the Father, Son and Holy Spirit in one.

What do those around him think? As far back as 1960, Swami Abhedananda, a disciple of the great sage Ramana Maharshi, rebuked Professor Kasturi for referring to Baba as an *avatar* in the first volume of his biography. In his estimation, an *avatar* was just a facet of the Supreme *Brahman*. Sai Baba was the Supreme *Brahman*, or God. Swami Satchidananda refers to him as "the inner resident of all beings, omniscient, super-consciousness itself." Dr Gokak calls him a Cosmic Visitor. At the Bombay conference in 1968 he said, "In the beginning was the Word, that Word is Sai Baba." Kasturi, after being with Baba for thirty-four years, has 'unfolded' in his perception. After referring to him as an *avatar* in 1960, in volume 3 of his biography, he describes him as a "multi-faced *avatar*" — that is, Rama, Krishna, Christ, Buddha, Zoroaster and others, in one; and finally, in volume 4, as the *Purna Brahman*, the Universal Absolute, and as the *Sanathana Sarathi*, the Eternal Charioteer, who is the inner motivator in all ever since time was.

Of course, even those constantly with Baba cannot hold their vision always. Whilst in our mortal coil we cannot live permanently in the rarified atmosphere of the hilltops. Sometimes even Dr Gokak 'forgets', particularly when Swami walks into his room and asks to borrow his razor! He writes: "Baba is intensely human, yet he is so divine . . . It is mostly when I leave him, and come to America, and see how he manifests there, that I get a sense of awe. When I am with him I tend to forget that he is divine. When I travel and see *vibhuti* showering on photographs, images appearing from nowhere, and people going into ecstasies repeating his name, then it is that I say: 'Yes, this is the Cosmic Form'." Once Gokak asked Swami when he would show him his true Cosmic Form. Baba replied, "If I did, you would very soon wish me back as I am!"

Indulal Shah, Sai Baba's world convenor, had a similar experience of 'forgetting'. It was in Bombay, when rain threatened to wash

257

out a *darshan*. Shah begged Swami to cancel it. Baba simply walked over to the window, raised his palm and dispersed the clouds. Then, turning with a twinkle in his eyes, he said, "You forgot, didn't you?"

But of all the evidence and all the statements from the sages there is nothing that convinces me of Sai Baba's divinity more than his creation of *lingams* inside himself. Although he has now foregone the custom, at least in public, it used to be his practice to create a *lingam*, sometimes several, at the Mahashivaratri Festival (The Night of Great Shiva) each year. It was an experience like giving birth. His neck swelled, he coughed and choked. He was clearly in considerable pain. The crowds waited with tremulous expectation. Finally, the *lingam* was disgorged from his mouth, sometimes splitting his lip. It was an ovoid, about 2½ inches long, and made of gold, silver, or quartz crystal.

I believe I am correct in stating that this phenomenon is unique in the history of *avatars*. Only Sai Baba has performed it. The *lingam* is the symbol of the creative principle. It is symbolic of 'that into which all things merge and out of which all things emerge'. And the ONE becomes the MANY. Speaking to his college boys, Baba once said, "You are My forms, all. When I love you, I love Myself; when you love yourselves, you love Me. I have separated Myself from Myself so that I may love Myself." Surely, this is the breath of God creating multifarious form . . . Surely, it is only the Creator who could say this . . .

What, then, of the cosmic side of Sai Baba? Kasturi says that Baba is ever conscious that he is the Cosmic Divine Principle. He has said: "The Universe is held in My hand. I could in an instant make the entire Universe disappear." This is to say that it is Sai Baba's will that holds it in being. He has been known to sing verses about the Unseen Force that regulates the celestial bodies. When Dr Hislop asked him the blunt question: "Are you God?" Baba replied, "Let us say, I am the switch."

Once he posed the question which has perplexed the philosophers of all time. "Why does the sun rise and set every single day, with no delay or disruption? Why do the stars that light the sky to the delight of all eyes hide their splendrous faces when the day dawns and do not even slyly peer through the clouds to tell us where they are? Who has commanded the air to be around always, so that we can draw breath therefrom and live? Why do streams roar and murmur, gurgle and gossip over rock, pebble or sand as they meander along with never a halt towards the parent sea? How does it happen that the billions that constitute mankind are, though they are caskets treasuring the images of the same entity, distinct from each other in appearance, achievement, aspiration and attitude? This is the answer: Know that I am the One that ordained these be such and shall behave so."

And on creation: "There was no one to know who I was till I created the world, at my pleasure, with one Word. Immediately mountains rose up, rivers started flowing, earth and sky were formed, oceans, seas, lands and watersheds, sun, moon and desert sands sprang out of nowhere to prove My existence. Came all forms of beings, men, beasts and birds, flying, speaking, hearing. All powers were bestowed upon them under My orders. The first place was granted to mankind, and My knowledge was placed in man's mind."

"With one Word," I suppose, means *AUM,* the primal sound of the Universe. "My knowledge was placed in man's mind" surely means that we are potentially as gods. Clearly this account of Creation is made outside of Time.

What of the future? The time for sugar-coated language is past. Our planet is in danger of self-destruction. It has happened before in the Universe. Esotericists tell us that the asteroid belt was once the planet Maldek (which some call Vulcan) which destroyed itself and is now giant fragments of matter orbiting endlessly in space. But it will not happen here. Five thousand and six hundred years ago, the *Upanishads* prophesied a Machine Age and the materialism that has grown out of it, and that there would be a Triple Incarnation of Divinity to avert the calamity. That Incarnation is living among us today. Sai Baba has said: "The calamity which has come upon mankind will be averted; a new Golden Age will recur . . . The time will come when I will have to move across the sky and use the sky as an auditorium. Yes, that too will happen, believe Me."

I do believe that sometime in the 21st century Sai Baba will apport himself across the sky and, standing on a levitated rostrum, speak to perhaps ten million people on a campus of perhaps ten thousand acres. And that that, and that alone, will make our politicians and our media stand in fear and trembling.

To me, Sathya Sai Baba is the Law, the Word, the Creative Principle, the Fountainhead of Love, Wisdom and Power, the Almighty Spirit of Life, or the One we call God. As he says, "When there is a small local disturbance a police constable is enough to put it down, but when all mankind is threatened with moral ruin the Inspector General himself has to come, that is the Lord." Surely, it is up to every one of us to help him . . .

# POSTSCRIPT: MY DREAM

Dreamer of dreams, a man 'born out of my time', perhaps — although in my seventieth year I still hope for things which other men think impossible.

The world spends thirty million pounds a minute on armaments. If it would renounce this sum, one tiny minute's worth of expenditure in an entire year, I would build thirty churches across the face of the earth at a cost of a million pounds each. In Delhi, in Calcutta and Bombay. In New York. In London, Paris and Rome, and perhaps on vantage points on the world's major ley lines.

I would search for a modern Leonardo da Vinci and have a twelve-foot painting of Sathya Sai Baba done, and I would place it and replicas on the high altar of each church. Around the high altar would be a series of side chapels for the major faiths where devotees could worship in their own ways and as often as they wished.

But once a month they would gather together and turn to the high altar. Would it be too much to ask the theologians of the world's faiths to work out a common service, based simply and without dogma on the Brotherhood of Man and the Fatherhood of God? Surely, this would not be too difficult . . .

My hope would be that in a hundred years' time the side chapels would fall into disuse and *Sanathana Dharma*, the Sai world religion of Love, would become the planet's Universal Faith.

# BIBLIOGRAPHY

All books obtainable from
Sri Sathya Sai Centre, 35 Clifton Avenue,
Wembley, Middlesex HA9 6BN.

*Sai Baba, Man of Miracles*—Howard Murphet
*Sai Baba, Avatar*—Howard Murphet
*Sai Baba, Invitation to Glory*—Howard Murphet
*Sai Baba, the Holy Man and the Psychiatrist*—Dr Samuel Sandweiss
*Spirit and the Mind*—Dr Samuel Sandweiss
*Sai Baba, God Incarnate*—Victor Kanu
*Sai Baba, the Man and the Avatar*—Dr V. K. Gokak
*Sai Baba and His Message*—Eds Dr Robinson and Dr Ruhela
*Living Divinity*—Shakuntala Balu
*Divine Glory*—V. Balu and S. Balu
*My Baba and I*—Dr John Hislop
*Conversations with Sathya Sai Baba*—Dr John Hislop
*Sai Baba, the Ultimate Experience*—Phyllis Krystal
*Sai Messages for You and Me*—Lucas Ralli
*A Recapitulation of Sathya Sai Baba's Divine Teachings*—Grace MacMartin
*Sathyam Sivam Sundaram*—Prof N. Kasturi (The Life of Sathya Sai Baba in 4 paperback volumes)
*Vision of the Divine*—E. B. Fanibunda
*Loving God*—Prof N. Kasturi. (Memoirs of 45 years with Sathya Sai Baba.)
*Spirituality and Science*—Sathya Sai Trust, Bombay.
*Sathya Sai Speaks*—(Discourses in 11 paperback volumes.)
*Golden Age 1979*—a collection of 54 essays on Sai Baba by eminent writers from all countries
*Golden Age 1980*—a collection of 55 essays on Sai Baba by eminent writers from all countries
*Sai Chandana*—edited by Dr V. K. Gokak. 70 essays on all aspects of Sai Baba and his mission.
and many others.

261

The writings and discourses of Sai Baba edited by Prof. N. Kasturi

*Sathya Sai Speaks, vols. 1—10* (discourses)
*Voice of the Avatar, vols. 1 & 2* (extracts)
*The Teaching of Sai Baba* (simple extracts)
*Sadhana, the Inward Path* (spiritual endeavour)
*Spiritual Diary* (guidance for each day of the year)
*Prema Vahini* (love)
*Dhyana Vahini* (meditation)
*Prasanthi Vahini* (inner peace)
*Jnana Vahini* (wisdom)
*Dharma Vahini* (the right way of living)
*Gita Vahini* (on the *Bhagavad-Gita*)
*Bhagavatha Vahini* (on the *Srimad Bhagavata*)
*Upanishad Vahini* (on the Upanishads)
*Sandeha Nivarini* (the removal of doubt)
and many others.

The monthly magazine, Sanathana Sarathi, can be obtained from
Sri Sathya Sai Publications,
P.O. Prasanthi Nilayam,
District Anantapur,
Andhra Pradesh 515134,
India.

The quarterly magazine published by the Authors is obtainable from
The Kent & Sussex Sai Baba Study Centre,
The Lodge,
10 Broadwater Down,
Tunbridge Wells,
Kent TN2 5NG.